Engineering Vulnerability

Engineering

In Pursuit of Climate Adaptation

Vulnerability

SARAH E. VAUGHN

Duke University Press   *Durham and London*   2022

Printed in the United States of America on acid-free paper ∞
Designed by Courtney Leigh Richardson
Typeset in Warnock Pro by Westchester Publishing Services

Library of Congress Cataloging-in-Publication Data
Names: Vaughn, Sarah E., [date] author.
Title: Engineering vulnerability : in pursuit of climate adaptation
/ Sarah E. Vaughn.
Description: Durham : Duke University Press, 2022. | Includes
bibliographical references and index.
Identifiers: LCCN 2021025618 (print)
LCCN 2021025619 (ebook)
ISBN 9781478015482 (hardcover)
ISBN 9781478018100 (paperback)
ISBN 9781478022725 (ebook)
Subjects: LCSH: Climatic changes—Guyana. | Climate change
mitigation—Guyana. | Environmental education—Guyana. |
Floods—Guyana. | Guyana—Environmental conditions. |
BISAC: NATURE / Environmental Conservation & Protection |
HISTORY / Caribbean & West Indies / General
Classification: LCC QC903.2.G95 V384 2022 (print) |
LCC QC903.2.G95 (ebook) | DDC 363.738/745609881—dc23/
eng/20211008
LC record available at https://lccn.loc.gov/2021025618
LC ebook record available at https://lccn.loc.gov/2021025619

Cover art: Laborers folding geotextiles. Construction site of the
Hope Canal in Guyana, 2014. Courtesy of the author.

Publication of this book is supported by Duke University Press's
Scholars of Color First Book Fund.

CONTENTS

CAP	Conservation Adaptation Project
CARICOM	Caribbean Community
CDC	Civil Defence Commission
EDWC	East Demerara Water Conservancy
GD	Georgetown Datum
GDP	gross domestic product
GHRA	Guyana Human Rights Association
GUYSUCO	Guyana Sugar Corporation Inc.
GYD$	Guyanese dollars
LCDS	Low Carbon Development Strategy
MMA Scheme	Mahaica-Mahaicony-Abary Scheme
NDIA	National Drainage and Irrigation Authority
NGO	nongovernmental organization
PAHO	Pan American Health Organization
PNC	People's National Congress
PNC-R	People's National Congress-Reform
PPP	People's Progressive Party
TVA	Tennessee Valley Authority
UN	United Nations
UNFCCC	United Nations Framework Convention on Climate Change

UNICEF	United Nations Children's Fund
UN IPCC	United Nations Intergovernmental Panel on Climate Change
UN REDD+	United Nations Program on Reducing Emissions from Deforestation and Forest Degradation
VCA	vulnerability capacity assessment
WUA	Water Users Association

In Guyana, English is the national language, but Creole, or what is locally called *Creolese*, is widely spoken in both urban and rural areas. I became familiar with Creolese through daily conversation, reading newspapers, and attending seminars in the Department of Language and Cultural Studies at the University of Guyana, Turkeyen campus. To make the text easier to read, I have opted to translate interview quotations into Standard American English, adding Creolese terminology where relevant.

Race in Guyana also takes on fluid linguistic categorizations. The national census, for instance, has seven designated racial categories: African, Indian, Portuguese, Chinese, European, Amerindian, and Mixed Race. In daily conversation, however, many people use the terms *Afro-Guyanese* and *Black* when referring to African; *Indo-Guyanese* and *East Indian* when referring to Indian; *White* when referring to European; and *Indigenous peoples* when referring to Amerindian. To this end, it is important to note that the country name Guyana derives from the word Guiana, the original name for the region that formerly included the colonial territories of present-day Guyana, Suriname, French Guiana, and parts of Brazil and Venezuela. When noting the Dutch and British colonial eras, I refer to people of African and Indian descent by the historical denotation Afro-Guianese and Indo-Guianese, respectively.

Finally, I use a mix of pseudonyms and given names to identify people. I adhere to the requests of those who wanted me to refer to their given names and of those who wanted pseudonyms. All government agencies, nongovernmental organizations, development agencies, and engineering firms are identified by their most commonly used names. The engineering agency the Ministry of Public Works changed its name to the Ministry of Public Infrastructure circa 2014. For the sake of clarity, I identify the ministry by its current name in reference to ethnography I conducted between 2009 and 2019.

Engineering Vulnerability has been on my mind for quite some time, and I have many to thank for helping me put my ideas down on paper. I am grateful first and foremost to those I came to know, work with, and befriend in Guyana. My introduction to Guyana in 2007 would not have been possible without D. Alissa Trotz and the late Andaiye. Both lovingly made space for me on Bonasika Street and gave me the opportunity to contribute to the women's collective Red Thread. My time with Red Thread has shaped my perspective on the importance of uncompromising honesty in both research and life. The late Jocelyn Baccus, Karen De Souza, Halima Khan, Joy Marcus, and Wintress White all welcomed me with open arms. Andaiye's support for me and this project was infinite. I cannot thank her enough for simply being a friend and interlocutor.

Residents of Sophia, especially Colin Marks and Louie, as well as residents of Hope/Dochfour, particularly David and Roy Doodnauth, were gracious enough to share with me their knowledge of community-level flood response. They invited me to meetings, introduced me to people, and were simply interested enough in the project to spend time and talk with me. Through them I came to understand that critical dialogues about flooding often led one to seek out not only the advice but the encyclopedic knowledge of engineers. The late Philip Allsopp, Bert Carter, Agnes Dalrymple, the late Terence Fletcher, Charles Sohan, and Maurice Veecock, in particular, were my interlocutors throughout this project. Their generosity and lack of pretention inspired me to create an intellectual space for the engineering sciences in this book. And as I wrote, this book took on a form that became a partial response to engineers affiliated with the Ministry of Agriculture, Ministry of Public Infrastructure, Caribbean Engineering and Management Consulting Inc. (CEMCO), and SKRN Engineering who asked if I had a "social solution" for flooding. Jermaine Braithwaite, Fredrick Flatts, Krishna Naraine, Carmichael Thorne, and Sheik Yussuff provided introductions and helped me complete fieldwork with these agencies. Likewise, staff at the Guyana Civil Defence Commission were overwhelmingly generous with their time and resources.

Denise Fraser, Rufus Lewis, Rupert Roopnarine, the late George Simon, and Patrick Williams were also tremendous interlocutors as I figured out how to form an idea about flooding. The Institute for Development Studies at the University of Guyana provided me an academic home during my yearlong 2009–10 fieldwork. Finally, the joy, humor, and spirit of Christopher Carrico, Christopher Chin, Rene Edwards, Zoisa Edwards, Vidyaratha Kissoon, Omar Ramcharran, Anand Roopsind, Alistair Sonaram, and Charlene Wilkinson made Guyana feel familiar to me. They imparted wisdom like no other.

David Scott from the Department of Anthropology at Columbia University provided unwavering support for the potential of this project. In my writing, I tried to figure out, as he often puts it, "Why Guyana, why now?" Conversations with David always leave me recharged to write, and his critical eye never fails me. Most of all, he has showed me how to use texts in ways that draw connections to the unfamiliar. I was also fortunate to benefit from the mentorship of Brian Larkin, Elizabeth Povinelli, Hugh Raffles, and Paige West. Brian and Hugh offered close readings that helped me see why my arguments matter. Elizabeth's insights always tested my intellectual comfort zone. She showed me how to pursue expansive lines of inquiry while staying grounded in my own interests. Paige instills perspective and inspires intellectual confidence. She showed me how to commit to generous critical engagements. In addition to these mentors, I owe a special debt to Dominic Boyer, Hirokazu Miyazaki, Viranjini Munasinghe, Hortense Spillers, James Turner, and the late Terence Turner.

While a Provost's Postdoctoral Fellow in the Department of Anthropology at the University of Chicago, I appreciated engagements with Hussain Agrama, Shannon Dawdy, Michael Fisch, Andy Graan, Elina Hartikainan, Joseph Masco, Constantine V. Nakassis, the late Marshall Sahlins, Bettina Stoetzer, Karl Swinehart, and Eli Thorkelson as I developed this book. They transformed talks, lunches, and workshops into warm gatherings. As a James and Mary Pinchot Sustainability Fellow at the Yale School of the Environment (YSE), I had time off from the University of California, Berkeley, to write the first draft of this book. Michael Dove created an inviting space for me to share my ideas, especially through the Environmental Anthropology Research Lab. Michael Mendez was a daily interlocutor on all matters and made YSE feel like home. I am also grateful for K. Sivaramakrishnan's intellectual engagement and for inviting me to participate in the Agrarian Studies Program's talk series.

At the University of California, Berkeley, my colleagues have provided invaluable mentorship, especially Stephen Collier, Mariane Ferme, and Aihwa

Ong. Likewise, the feedback received from colleagues at talks has shaped this book in some form or fashion. An earlier version of chapter 4 was presented at Rice University's Department of Anthropology Brown Bag Series and at the Department of Anthropology Colloquium at the University of California, Santa Cruz. Parts of chapter 3 were presented at Harvard University's Center for the Environment Colloquium. An earlier version of chapter 5 was presented at the 2018 American Anthropological Association Panel "Touch" (organized by Zoë Wool and Tyler Zoanni) and read as a keynote lecture at the Montreal Centre for International Studies Summer School at the University of Montreal. An earlier version of chapter 7 was presented at Vanderbilt University's Department of Anthropology Colloquium and at Yale University's Department of Anthropology Colloquium.

I received ample support from colleagues and friends over the years. My gratitude runs deep to all, including Vincanne Adams, Sophie Bjork-James, Alex Blanchette, Janette Bulkan, Jessica Catellino, Lawrence Cohen, John Collins, Seema Golestaneh, Bridget Guarasci, Stefan Helmreich, Kaet Heupel, James Holsten, Daniel Kammen, Naveeda Khan, Fatima Mojaddedi, Amelia Moore, Ryo Morimoto, Laura Nader, Karen Nakamura, Alondra Nelson, Natacha Nsabimana, Benjamin Orlove, Anand Pandian, the late Paul Rabinow, Anand Taneja, D. Alissa Trotz, Matt West, Nigel Westmass, William White, Laurie Wilkie, Darryl Wilkinson, and Ariela Zycherman. I am indebted to Paulla Ebron, Tim McLellan, Donald Moore, Ram Natarajan, Anna Tsing, and Natalie Vena for reading drafts of book chapters. During the final stages of editing, I also benefited from the feedback of Wiebe Bijker, Christopher Carrico, and Richard and Sally Price.

I am grateful for Ken Wissoker's long-standing interest in this project. He has been a wonderful editor and source of critical insight. I also thank Lisl Hampton and Joshua Tranen at Duke University Press and illustrator Christine Riggio as well as three anonymous reviewers for their sharp and deep engagements with my book. The research, writing, and editing for this book were funded by the Social Science Research Council; the Woodrow Wilson Foundation; the American Council of Learned Societies; the University of California, Berkeley, Institute of International Studies; and the Institute for Advanced Study at Princeton.

Above all, my parents, Carolyn and Larry Vaughn, and sisters, Jessica A. Vaughn and Leah J. Zepeda-Vaughn, have been more than loving. They taught me how to observe and make time for the things that matter. Finally, I write in memory of Shawn Prakash, the runs we had, and the ones we have yet to finish.

INTRODUCTION. "Where Would I Go?
There Was No Place with No Water"

In the years immediately following a disastrous flood in 2005, the Guyanese state embarked on the multimillion-dollar enhancement of irrigation and drainage infrastructures. In August 2009 when I visited, earthmoving equipment dotted the coastline. These machines clawed through peatlands, locally known by the Creolese term *pegasse*, in an effort to reinforce a dam. Excavations were gaining momentum because of the state's plans for ventures in carbon markets and the World Bank's Global Environment Facility grants. The enhancements were not the first in Guyana's history but were building on over two centuries of engineers transforming the country's Atlantic coastal region into a place suitable for sugar plantations. The state insisted that these enhancements were different because they would offer a first step toward adapting the nation to climate change. They are expected to help the country better withstand torrential rainstorms and make it easier to store and drain water during a flood. The extreme nature of today's climatic events has compelled the state's rethinking of coastal life in Guyana. This has led me to treat climate adaptation as requiring analysis on its own terms, as a large-scale project that alters understandings of settlement or the multilayered processes that contribute to dwelling and the habitation of a place.

Climate adaptation and its connections to settlement provide this book's unifying theme. I draw on ethnography, oral histories, colonial records, photographs, and engineering reports to make these connections visible. I ask: How can Guyanese who felt abandoned by the state during the 2005 disaster come to believe in or at least consider climate adaptation? What can their vulnerability tell us about the persistent forms of technological optimism that frame climate adaptation as a project that has the potential to advance and sustain the settlement of nation-states? What would it mean for the state or the citizen not to partake in climate adaptation? And what would such a refusal do to one's sense of belonging? The climate adaptation of irrigation and drainage infrastructures has occurred along Guyana's low-lying coastal plain, where roughly 90 percent of the country's population resides. In addition to enhancing irrigation and drainage infrastructures, climate adaptation has enabled many to mobilize support from state officials and NGOs for water, disaster preparedness, food security, housing, and environmental conservation. Even still, many Guyanese face difficult dilemmas as they attempt to square the 2005 disaster and their past experiences of state abandonment with climate change.

My aim in this book is twofold. First, *Engineering Vulnerability* tells the story of how climate adaptation's importance lies not only in its technological feats but also in constituting political imaginations. Each chapter focuses on the ways knowledge of flooding becomes situated in Guyanese state-sponsored climate adaptation projects. This focus gives ethnographic specificity to popular and academic understandings of climate change as a lived reality of settlement rather than as an abstract risk. Climate adaptation reshapes the links between forms of state welfare and reform. By making these links visible through ethnography, this book complements scholarship on climate adaptation policy making and postdevelopmentalism.

Second, I analyze climate adaptation by tracking the demands people make on one another as they recognize that race is a source of vulnerability to climate change. The book contributes to theories of vulnerability to climate change by foregrounding the enactment of race beyond human bodies to include flood-prone environments. Throughout, I explore the coproduction of vulnerability and race as exemplified through questions about scale, measurement, and temporality that climate-related flooding in Guyana incites. My aim is to develop an analytical framework that takes seriously the uneven and speculative ways race comes to shape climate adaptation. Put another

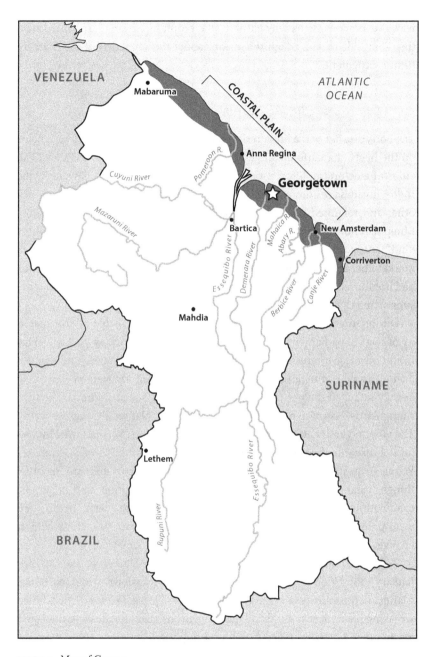

MAP I.1. Map of Guyana

way, this book explains why climate adaptation in Guyana has gained traction alongside racialized apprehensions about the suitability of the coast for future settlement.

From Disaster to Climate Adaptation

The 2005 disaster was a life-altering event for most Guyanese I know. It came on the heels of a national surge in crime and violence tied to the racial calculus of electoral politics, especially among the coast's Afro-Guyanese and Indo-Guyanese residents. The surge in crime pitted generations against each other and reignited the racial sentiment that Guyanese call *apaan jaat*, a Bhojpuri-Hindi phrase loosely translated into Creolese as "vote for your own kind." The state was nearly twenty years into a transition from socialism to market liberalization during the height of the crime surge. But the transition had not loosened the state's grip on the economy, and elected political elites supporting the interests of an international business class emerged.

During this time, the People's Progressive Party (PPP) held both the majority of seats in parliament and the presidential office. Known as a party serving Indo-Guyanese interests, the PPP took steps to concentrate executive power over all aspects of national decision-making. Such efforts were nothing new, as they reflected the political opportunism during socialism under the then ruling Afro-Guyanese political party, the People's National Congress (PNC). The 1997 and 2001 national elections, nonetheless, were overshadowed by feelings of discontent among Afro-Guyanese and sympathetic Indo-Guyanese.[1] People protested in the streets for constitutional reforms and, among other things, a national agenda to eradicate poverty, corruption, and racial discrimination in public sector hiring. But when the storms came in 2005, few were prepared to expand the dialogue about apaan jaat to include climate change.

Torrential rains pounded Guyana's coast from late December 2004 to early January 2005. Houses once protected on stilts were transformed into marooned islands. Leptospirosis, a zoonotic waterborne disease, knew no boundaries, wreaking havoc across rural and urban environs alike. Roads were damaged, leaving many with no place to sell and buy food, supplies, and water. The flooding was prolonged by a major dam system, the East Demerara Water Conservancy (EDWC), overfilling with water. In response, the Civil Defence Commission (CDC), a state-sponsored disaster relief agency, and NGOs repurposed school buildings into shelters and pickup points for relief hampers (emergency rations). Even when the rain stopped, the talk of floodwaters persisted as engineers and state officials affiliated with the Ministry of Agriculture worked to reinforce the EDWC. By the spring of that year, the country was fortunate enough to count only thirty-four people dead.

One of the places hardest hit was Sophia, a former squatter town located on the fringe of Guyana's capital city, Georgetown. I became familiar with Sophia through the work of residents involved in climate change awareness and disaster preparedness activities sponsored by the Guyana Red Cross. By the early 2000s Sophia was known as an Afro-Guyanese working- and lower-middle-class neighborhood, with many residents in transition working to secure land titles. Sophia's unfinished network of canals and sloped terrain shaped the state's timid disaster response. Residents recount using refrigerators as boats to meet state officials at public roads to retrieve relief hampers. Margaret, one of the residents who participated in the Red Cross activities, knew these roads well. I frequented her vendor stall where she sold sweets and refreshments (see figure I.1). As a street vendor she could map the spaces

FIGURE I.1. Boys sitting at Margaret's vendor stall

where floodwaters were most prone to accumulate, the makeshift bridges residents maintained for emergency evacuation, and areas not to visit when the sky turns gray.

This know-how, she insisted, informed all the "mess" she saw during the disaster. I asked what she meant by "mess": "At some point you knew no one was coming. Back then, I was a security guard at the Georgetown Botanical Gardens and Zoo. People [zoo staff] called in to tell me animals—the manatees—were going to swim into the streets. We saw caiman in the canals here too. Everyone just had to do their thing . . . until it ended." I asked if all the mess made her want to go somewhere else to wait out the storms. "No. Where would I go? There was no place with no water." The rainfall was unprecedented, and the flooding was inescapable. And by the time the storms came, Margaret realized that she and state officials were too late to change course or, simply, to retreat to higher ground.

In the months following the initial storms, the national government partnered with the United Nations (UN) Economic Commission for Latin America and the Caribbean to report disaster statistics. The estimated damages were in excess of GYD$93 billion (US$465 million), and the floods reversed that year's gross domestic product growth from 0.4 percent to -2.6 percent (World Bank 2009). Economic damage was severe in the country's agricultural, manufacturing, and retail sectors. Subsistence farmers, small-business owners, and street vendors suffered the most because of a paralyzed supply chain and liquidity constraints. The state attempted to revitalize the economy by providing relief checks to workers as well as to those categorized as living in low-income households.

There are no reported statistics that break down the distribution of relief checks by race. Yet the checks can still provide helpful insight about the influence of apaan jaat on the disaster. According to the 2002 census, Guyana's 750,000 citizens were distributed across seven racial groups: 43.5 percent Indian, 30 percent African, 16.7 percent Mixed Race, 9.2 percent Amerindian, and less than 1 percent Portuguese, Chinese, or European (Beaie 2007, 27). Roughly two-thirds of the population lived in poverty, with the majority counted as Indo-Guyanese and concentrated in rural coastal areas (Gampat 2002).[2] At the same time, the distribution of wealth tells another story: there was a small—but growing—upper class of Indo-Guyanese with access to capital for small-business development and a large proportion of Afro-Guyanese concentrated in the ranks of the lower middle and working classes (Gampat 2002, 16–17). Everyone—including an elite business class—was in need of disaster assistance. The 2005 disaster momentarily blurred the life chances of Guyana's racial majority and minorities while underscoring the ecological and material contingencies of apaan jaat to statecraft.

Engineers responded with a promise to adapt Guyana's coast to torrential rainfall, sea-level rise, and erratic storms related to climate change. By May 2005, they were already pouring millions into damming and building canals in ways that anticipated the attempts to revive the levee system and hurricane-ravaged coast of post-Katrina Louisiana just a few months later (Bijker 2007). And while these coastal disasters had very different causes, infrastructural origins, needs, and environments, race emerged in both locales as a condition of vulnerability.

A state-mandated evacuation during Hurricane Katrina, for instance, has contributed to a New Orleans diaspora of African Americans that is reconstituting the racial demographics of the city and surrounding Mississippi delta region (Adams 2013; Johnson 2006, 147). Engineering priorities for building levees and reclaiming wetlands have followed suit by focusing on areas deemed worthy of real estate and business reinvestment. Unsurprisingly, these areas are majority White with capital to rebuild (Bullard and Wright 2009). On the other hand, Guyana's 2005 disaster did not involve a state-mandated evacuation nor inspire the long-term mass exodus of residents to other parts of the country.[3] So whereas in New Orleans engineers have attempted to separate areas of the coast into adaptable and inadaptable zones, in Guyana—at the time of writing, no such distinctions have been made.[4] All racial groups have become associated with state-sponsored climate adaptation, albeit in different, uneven, and tenuous ways.

Engineers have focused their climate adaptation efforts on the EDWC. The 355-square-mile (571-square-kilometer) structure comprises what is locally called a *water conservancy* (reservoir), a forty-two-mile (67-kilometer) embankment dam, and an intricate system of primary and secondary channels that connect to canals that drain water into the Atlantic Ocean (Bovolo 2014). The embankment dam's walls are composed of compacted soil, sand, clay, and rock. In 2005, when water overtopped the EDWC, many blamed engineers for not closely monitoring where erosion along the embankment dam was occurring. Trenches and canals were also clogged with trash, particularly in Georgetown, which made engineers' decisions about when to release water from the EDWC inconsistent. Engineers releasing water between high tides was crucial for avoiding further flooding in residential and farming areas adjacent to the EDWC. While they were eventually able to release water between high tides, the danger of water overtopping the EDWC has become the primary motivation shaping engineers' commitments to climate adaptation.

The possibility of repeated disastrous flooding, however, cannot in itself explain why climate adaptation has taken hold in Guyana. The contested role of global governance in climate adaptation is, in many ways, central to the EDWC's enhancements. The term *climate adaptation* has its roots in ecological theories of resilience that assume a sociobiological system can absorb shock, transform, and ultimately maintain itself in the face of external stresses. Integrated into UN-related climate-policy agendas in the late 1990s, climate adaptation is treated as an alternative to the steps nation-states have already taken to reduce carbon emissions (Pelling 2010).[5]

In the most basic policy terms, climate adaptation involves nation-states governing in response to actual or expected climate change effects. The UN climate governance institution, the Intergovernmental Panel on Climate Change (IPCC), has called on political leaders across the Global North and Global South to advance climate adaptation projects. The UN IPCC has designated funding sources for those countries that cannot afford to do climate adaptation on their own. The diplomatic value of the UN IPCC, then, is in its claim to inclusivity and commitment to the differential needs, expertise, and ambitions of nation-states responding to climate change. To date, UN IPCC funding for adaptive interventions has ranged from the enhancement of infrastructure systems, ecosystem services, and information networks to health care across urban and rural sites (Adger et al. 2005; Orlove 2009).

Guyana has not only benefited from but also helped define the trajectory of such UN IPCC initiatives. In 2009, President Bharrat Jagdeo held a press conference in Guyana with a handful of foreign dignitaries to release the Low Carbon Development Strategy (LCDS), a report detailing the country's plans for climate adaptation (Government of Guyana 2010, 11). Ambitious in scope, LCDS looks to the country's forests as a resource for carbon trading schemes with Norway. The funds raised from these schemes are intended to partially sponsor the long-term adaptation of, among other things, irrigation and drainage infrastructures.[6]

The LCDS also contributes to the government's Second National Communication to the United Nations Framework Convention on Climate Change (UNFCCC). The communication highlights the improved management of engineering data and technologies as an invaluable component of climate adaptation. Climate change in Guyana is expected to materialize as a 4.2-degree increase in average temperature, 10-millimeter decrease in rainfall, and 40-centimeter sea-level rise by the end of this century (Solomon et al. 2007). Laying out these national data around the various blind spots of the UNFCCC, the LCDS creates a critical nexus between transnational climate negotiations and research networks needed to sustain them.

Jagdeo made a plea for the LCDS through diplomatic partnerships with Conservation International, lecture tours at foreign universities, and interviews with celebrity environmentalists, including American actor Harrison Ford. He also attended the fifteenth session of the UNFCCC in 2009 in Copenhagen. Selling the LCDS to a sympathetic audience, he explained that all Global South nation-states are not alike and that those that are not high emitters of carbon dioxide emissions have a stake in climate negotiations. Guyana was not alone in taking such a stance, as chronicled in the documentary *Island President* (2011). At Copenhagen, Guyanese envoys aligned themselves with those from the Caribbean and the Maldives, a country that had taken the lead in previous UNFCCC meetings representing small island states. They argued that, although it is not a literal island, Guyana is a *small island state*—a country with a population so at risk it will either get wiped off the map by climate change or never be able to afford to adapt on its own (see also Sealey-Huggins 2017).[7] Their use of the phrase *small island state* offered a way to put climate change at the center of Guyana's modern understanding of itself as a nation. It signaled that the composition of the nation's future population—its size and demographics—is in question.

More than a simple description of geography, the phrase *small island state* is symbolic of Guyana's concern that climate change has the potential to drive a further wedge between its racial majority and minority groups. Arjun Appadurai (2006) has articulated similar insights in his analysis of the sovereign preoccupation with scale and population or what he calls "the fear of small numbers." Globalization in the post–Cold War era, Appadurai notes, has rested on the assumption that with the expansion of free markets, finance capital, human rights, and democracy, racial inequalities would recede worldwide. But in many instances the opposite has unfolded, with racial inequalities deepening and violence becoming a mainstay of national political life. This anxiety about well-being, about the lack of consensus between racial populations, and about the enumeration of racial populations via census data creates the conditions for "the fear of small numbers." Moreover, the sense of social injustice that characterizes the fear of small numbers is not bound to any single identity or geopolitical territory. As the Copenhagen meeting demonstrates, the fear is often rationalized through efforts at comparing levels of socioecological degradation across as well as within nation-state contexts.

The fear of small numbers, in other words, is not limited to the question of the human: the binary preoccupation with racial majority and minority has, over time, ravaged environments or the terrain nation-states call home.

Against this backdrop of fear and diplomacy, climate adaptation may not only hinge on efforts to design so-called resilient infrastructure systems. It also seeks to influence public attitudes about the importance of lessening racial inequalities while bringing attention to the fact that all people—no matter their race—are vulnerable to climate change. By *race*, I mean "a set of sociopolitical processes that discipline humanity into full humans, not-quite-humans, and nonhumans" worthy of survival (Weheliye 2014, 4). Climate adaptation puts pressure on this conventional framing of race as a hierarchy of difference predicated on the "administration of life" or a biopolitics of the population (Foucault 1990). This is because climate adaptation creates space for people to develop a racialized awareness about the contingencies, risks, and instabilities that characterize the environments in which they live.

Scholars, for instance, have begun to ask if combining the insights of the climate sciences with paleoanthropology provides a new vantage point on race as a social construct (Gunaratnam and Clark 2012). This proposed shift in perspective warns against treating climate adaptation as an inherently progressive project that advances humanity along a predetermined path.[8] In turn, those typically counted as on the margins of society stand in as key figures for reconstructing the nation-state's histories of interracial strife as well as its solidarities (see also Abu El-Haj 2002; Collins 2015; Thomas 2011).

Improving race relations in climate adaptation often coalesces around compensation for resettlement and community-level climate change awareness programs that emphasize inclusivity. By not dismissing long patterns of suffering, such forms of redress demonstrate the difficulty involved in simultaneously attributing responsibility for racial inequalities and envisioning antiracist futures. Climate adaptation, in other words, demands a precise historical accounting of the ways in which people speculate about the end of race.

Engineering Vulnerability offers such an account by analyzing climate adaptation's unfolding in the daily lives of ordinary citizens and a variety of experts. Climate adaptation's impacts on Guyana cannot be evaluated with censuses and statistics alone. Enhancements of the EDWC and related irrigation and drainage infrastructures enable Guyanese to reconsider how they want to live and to what extent they care or even interpret racial sentiments, such as apaan jaat, as shaping their futures. I understand these reflections as essential to climate adaptation, whereby people evaluate how past events contribute to vulnerability in the present, in order to consider what actions are needed to live with climate change moving forward. Climate adaptation is eerie: the lessons of the past are known only indirectly, and the future is associated with a world filled with risk instead of aversion to it. Why and how people decide which pasts matter for enacting climate adaptation is the question that animates the rest of this book.

Vulnerability

The EDWC is the thing that connects all Guyanese to the coast. It is the object of intervention in climate adaptation whereby national life is situated in an emergent, sometimes ill-maintained system of irrigation and drainage infrastructures. Many think about the EDWC only when they have flashbacks about the 2005 disaster, see too much water in their yards, or hear meteorologists warn of a rain-drenched forecast. This is why community-oriented interventions such as the Red Cross project in Sophia have become ubiquitous throughout the country since 2005. Many people have come to see such interventions as complementing engineers' efforts to enhance the EDWC. But in no way do the actions of ordinary citizens and engineers rely on similar timelines, histories, or technologies. Their actions are discontinuous, with multiple origins and sites of knowledge production about flooding. No single person can make climate adaptation happen, nor does anyone appear to have the desire to claim such authority. All individuals come equipped with their own perspective on what counts as vulnerability, and in the process of climate adaptation they seek to become aware of what the EDWC is doing.

In the Atlantic coastal subregion called the East Demerara Coast, the main source of irrigation and potable water is the EDWC.[9] Torrential rainfall similar to the weather in 2005 has informed engineers' efforts to create models to monitor the EDWC's water levels. They use these models to determine when to release water to stop the EDWC from overtopping and its pegasse-laden walls from eroding. Whereas engineers once emphasized the storage of floodwaters in the EDWC, climate adaptation unfolds with the sole purpose of building large canals that can drain floodwaters quickly and coordinate with nearby rivers.[10]

Engineers' decision not to abandon but redesign the EDWC brings into focus neocolonial associations of irrigation and drainage infrastructures with sugar plantations, the political geography of terrain qua the nation, and day-to-day experiences of apaan jaat. Specifically, climate adaptation complicates ideas of coastal Guyana as a place where vulnerability is structured by a dependency on the engineering inventions and sciences of its colonial past. I often heard people lament that they did not altogether trust the work of engineers but nevertheless hoped that they could figure out how to maintain the EDWC. This skepticism toward state-sponsored climate adaptation mobilized many to take climate adaptation into their own hands. From building embankments on their property to creating flood evacuation routes, they envisioned vulnerability as manageable in discrete and pragmatic ways.

Anthropologists analyzing climate change have increasingly theorized vulnerability less as a condition of exposure than as an effort in becoming aware of disturbance (Vaughn 2019).[11] Anna Tsing (2015, 35) argues that the "art of noticing" involves people telling stories about the flourishing of biological and social life in the ruins of capitalist landscapes. Adriana Petryna (2015) offers the concept of the horizon to detail the practices that push people to take action even when climate change appears daunting or out of control. They and other scholars have shown that vulnerability is reproduced in everyday encounters with environmental transformations that are often unintentional or without precedent (Barnes and Dove 2015; Cons 2018; Crate 2011; Günel 2019; Moore 2019; O'Reilly 2017; Whitington 2016).[12] Vulnerability constitutes a complex set of ethical relations that draw people into caring about environments in ways they never would if they felt more secure (Khan 2014; Mathews 2017). Questions of how vulnerability maintains specific social arrangements of care become especially acute in climate adaptation. What happens when people decide not to draw direct attention to the things that make them vulnerable? Are there some forms of vulnerability that are more essential than others?

These questions are not neutral for Guyanese who aim to pursue climate adaptation in ways that do not get stalled by apaan jaat or undermined by it. Apaan jaat has functioned as a means for upholding a *racial political order* wherein an individual's racial identity or affiliation with a racial group determines access to resources, information, and protection from the state.[13] In theory, apaan jaat ought to benefit an individual whose race is well represented or is the majority in state bureaucracy. Likewise, for those who are not, they may find it advantageous to maintain relationships with the majority. Even so, a single experience of racialized resentment or indifference can breed contempt for apaan jaat, to the point where one would rather turn to nonstate institutions—from NGOs to gangs—for care. Within this tenuous field of address and response, apaan jaat can easily exceed boundaries of the state and creep into daily life, shaping how an individual pursues work, intimacy, worship, commerce, and the like. Race, as David T. Goldberg (2001) argues, is integral to standardizing state arrangements, reminding us that forms of political influence are marked symbolically and affectively as well as physically. And yet apaan jaat does not unfold in ways that simply replicate existing state institutional norms and values. Apaan jaat takes on a new sense of import, and perhaps urgency, every time Guyanese engage state bureaucracy. Climate adaptation is one such instance.

Past political events, alliances, and forces inform assumptions about the role apaan jaat will play in climate adaptation. But the various ways in which Guyanese articulate these pasts, while subject to emphasizing flooding as a common threat, reveal that apaan jaat's powers of incitement and intensity of variation are not equally distributed. A gap opens between their efforts to let go of apaan jaat and their struggles to identify how it might linger and accumulate over time as a source of vulnerability. This dynamic of embodiment, apaan jaat, and distribution reinforces a subtle process in climate adaptation activities. People make decisions about when to pay attention to or even ignore race in their assessments about how they want to live moving forward. To be sure, race does not determine the scope of climate adaptation, but it does serve as an important, and at times fleeting, point of reference.

Taking into account this dynamic, I draw on the philosopher of science Karen Barad (2007), especially her work on measurement. She argues that measurement is not an individual act but a process of cutting together/ apart the agentic qualities of a phenomenon. In particular, measuring apparatuses such as a kitchen scale, which people use to identify and make sense of, say, a piece of fruit, illustrate how agency emerges from being in *intra-action* rather than an individual property. To quote Barad, measuring apparatuses are not "static arrangements"; they produce boundaries or "agential cuts," which allow people to observe certain things in the world and not others (816).[14] Measuring apparatuses have a dual nature: the act of observation makes cuts in what is included or excluded while creating new understandings about the way responsibility, or ethical relations, might be maintained.

By far, the most repeated comment about ethics posed to me by my informants, especially engineers, when I described my research was that I ought to find a social solution for flooding. For some, this suggestion was a judgment about my status as an anthropologist without a background in hydraulic or geotechnical engineering. Others gestured to frustrations with apaan jaat as a strategy of flood management and life on the coast more generally. In both cases, they assumed that flooding was reducible not to racial conflict but to struggles over who or which entities had authority to provide resources and skills to make climate adaptation happen. In making such distinctions, my informants often parsed out the different capacities of state ministries, NGOs, and civic groups to offer them assistance. These distinctions were based on their experiences leveraging and organizing the interests of local communities, or villages as they are called outside of Georgetown.

How they recall episodes of flooding is a strategy for keeping together or disentangling flood knowledges from apaan jaat and is central to what they mean by having a social solution for flooding. And as these flood knowledges circulate in climate adaptation activities, they shape and are reshaped by the actions of irrigation and drainage infrastructures, pegasse, and other more-than-human flood hazards. Thus, it is important to know whether particular ideas about apaan jaat existed before or are a creation of national efforts at climate adaptation and the environments within which ways of knowing disturbance, or vulnerability, materialize.

Engineers have not been the only experts in search of a social solution for flooding. Through coordination with disaster management consultants and military personnel affiliated with the CDC, engineers have developed a flood early warning system. Inspired by the media, technology, and data related to this system, nonstate or community-based drainage monitoring programs were established in the villages I engaged during my fieldwork. These interventions gave ordinary citizens space to debate the usefulness of the flood early warning system or do away with it altogether, as they invented their own methods for living with what they called big flood and intense flooding, or floodwater levels that came near, met, or exceeded those of the flooding in 2005.[15] In making such distinctions, experts and ordinary citizens alike were not treating climate adaptation as an extension of developmentalism (see Chandler 2019; Grove 2014). Instead, they were approaching climate adaptation as an intervention that exposes gaps in the state's investments in development agendas.

And as they became comfortable speaking about climate adaptation from an authoritative angle, they grew more aware of the various material forms apaan jaat can take—from pegasse, irrigation, and drainage infrastructures to water filtration kits. They sought to invert hierarchical and exclusionary relations of expertise across sites of governance (see also Boyer 2008; Carr 2006). They depended on not only the flood early warning system but other measuring apparatuses, including hydraulic models, accounting and bookkeeping ledgers, and vulnerability assessments, to quell and, in a few cases, reimagine apaan jaat's meaning.

Ethnographic attention to measuring apparatuses and their redistribution across climate adaptation activities reveals that all racial groups—whether Afro-Guyanese, Indo-Guyanese, Amerindian, Mixed Race, Portuguese, Chinese, or European—are affected by the EDWC and its enhancements.[16] Following Barad's (2012, 15) phrasing, the use of measuring apparatuses by experts and ordinary citizens reveals that "each 'individual' is made up of all possible histories of virtual intra-actions with all Others." Measuring apparatuses, in other words, highlights the latent arrangements of settlement, race, and vulnerability at stake in climate adaptation. In this respect, climate adaptation remains symbolic of a larger unresolved environmental problem in Guyana—that of a nation-state whose fear of small numbers is entangled in a particular history of race.

Situating Apaan Jaat

Named after the Amerindian term(s) *land of many waters/water people*, Guyana is located on the northeast coast of South America (Marco 2013). The country comprises 83,000 square miles and is divided into three geographic zones—forest, savannah, and coast. Varying in width and with areas up to six feet below sea level, its 248-mile coastline is subject to inundation from the Atlantic Ocean. Mudbanks and patches of mangrove forest have dotted the coastline for millennia, offering a natural form of protection. As it is located south of the eastern Caribbean hurricane belt, a biannual wet season and the swelling of large rivers also contribute to flooding. The upper reaches of these rivers originate in the country's interior forests, producing massive tons of silt that add to the coast's nutrient-rich swamps and peaty soils. Essential to the ecoregion known as the Guiana Shield, these rivers, peatlands, and forests encompass varied ecosystems that store globally significant amounts of water and carbon. Historically, this biodiversity, along with flooding, has made the coast a costly and time-consuming place to settle.

The reclamation of coastlands by the Dutch for permanent settlement began in the eighteenth century (see chapter 2). After securing outposts upriver through violent force and trade treaties with Amerindian groups, the Dutch established sugar and tobacco plantations along the direct coastline. The digging and construction of irrigation and drainage infrastructures for plantations were completed by enslaved Africans. When the colony transitioned to British rule in 1814, not only canals but large-scale damming became integral to coastal settlement. With slave emancipation in 1838, indentured laborers from India, China, Portuguese Madeira, and the West Indian islands were imported to work plantations and facilitate damming (Rodney 1981). By 1880, freedmen (formerly enslaved persons) and indentured laborers completed the EDWC and radically transformed the coastal geography by connecting all working plantation estates to a single dam source for water and flood management. Despite their major contribution to the colony, however, planters perpetuated forms of wage and employment discrimination, particularly between Afro-Guianese and Indo-Guianese. By the mid-twentieth century, this exploitation became the groundings for anticolonial mobilization and the formation of a nationalist political movement led by the PPP.

The various personalities, interests, and trade union activities that informed the PPP's founding in 1950 are well documented (Chase 1964; Jagan 1997; Seecharan 2005). For my purposes of tracing a history of race alongside the fear of small numbers, it is important to note that the party began as a multiracial coalition that called for progressive social reforms. The PPP was led by Cheddi Jagan, the son of an Indo-Guianese sugar estate laborer who found professional success as a dentist and union organizer and Forbes Burnham, an Afro-Guianese lawyer from Georgetown. Building on the recommendation of the Waddington Commission, the PPP proposed a new constitution that mandated, among other things, universal adult suffrage and a general election. In 1953 an election was held, and the PPP won the majority of votes. The PPP's elected ministers sought to challenge the enormous economic influence the sugar empire, Booker Brothers, had on the colony. But the PPP's interracial class mobilization proved a threat to the British colonial bureaucracy. Within 133 days, the colonial governor declared a state of emergency, the constitution was suspended, and many PPP ministers were removed from office and imprisoned (Palmer 2010).

During the constitutional crisis, disagreements arose within the PPP leadership about the ideological direction of the party (Fraser 2004). In particular, arguments centered on whether British Guiana should join the West Indian Federation, an organization comprising colonies in the region that intended to become independent from Britain as a single state. Jagan spoke openly at the time against federation, citing other Caribbean nationalist leaders as unsupportive of his Marxist-Leninist approach to national liberation (Birbalsingh 2007, 32–33; Jagan 1997). A number of Afro-Guianese PPP members criticized Jagan, viewing his reluctance as "in part driven by a desire not to be marginalized within a federal structure in which African-Caribbean people would be the dominant grouping" (Fraser 2007, 14). Shattering a sense of civility within party ranks, the question of federation put pressure on PPP members to appease requests from the British for a slower and incremental transition to independence (Hintzen 2019).

By the 1957 general election, the PPP had split into two factions. The Jaganite faction embraced a communist platform, while the Burnhamite faction embraced a Fabian socialist platform. During the campaign cycle, both factions mobilized racially charged campaigns that invoked the sentiment apaan jaat for the first time (Birbalsingh 2007; Jagan 1997; Palmer 2010). Some political commentators argue, however, that apaan jaat was predated by Afro-Guianese candidates who used the phrase "Black fuh Black" during the 1940s legislative elections (Rickford 2019). While this may have been the case, the wide circulation of the phrase "apaan jaat" serves as a testament to Hindi and Indian political media shaping attitudes about decolonization in British Guiana (Persram 2004). Either way, the Jaganite faction won the election by gaining substantial support from across the working class, especially from Indo-Guianese residing in rural areas.[17]

Following the 1957 election, Burnham left the party to establish the PNC. His intent was to build a base of middle- and working-class Afro-Guianese and Mixed Race voters residing in urban areas. But he might have been overly ambitious in his plans. According to historian Colin Palmer (2010), much of the voting electorate, regardless of race, still envisioned a rosy future for the budding nation under PPP leadership. As Palmer notes, colonial officials were amazed that "although the politicians slung racial mud among themselves, this did not mean that the society as a whole consisted of racially hostile camps with no social interaction" (200). The PPP's subsequent win over the PNC in the 1961 general election is a testament to their observation.

But under pressure from the American government to contain communist influence in the Caribbean, the British again interfered in British Guiana's transition to independence. This time the British and Americans provoked labor disputes that contributed to the eruption of antigovernment protests and race riots (Rabe 2005; Waters and Daniels 2005). In response, the British implemented a constitutional reform for proportional representation, an electoral system under which parties gain seats in parliament based on the number of votes cast for them. British and American operatives also provided financial support and intelligence to the PNC campaign. Seeking to exploit the new electoral system, the PNC built a coalition with the probusiness party the United Force, which targeted Portuguese, Amerindian, and Mixed Race voters. The coalition proved successful, with the PNC winning the 1966 general election and Burnham taking office as Guyana's first head of state and prime minister.

Despite grand proclamations for interracial unity and modernization, Burnham failed to see through needed reforms in land, voting, and education during his tenure (1966–85). His critics attributed the failure to many factors, especially his rigging of elections, declaring Guyana a socialist republic in 1970, and creating diplomatic relations with Cuba (Premdas 1982). These decisions contributed to the withholding of aid by Western lenders, the country's mushrooming debt, and the underresourcing of public services. Meanwhile, political violence escalated, and critics of the PNC deemed the country's future crippled by race. As the economy worsened, middle-class professionals migrated. Burnham only aggravated the migration by awarding government jobs and contracts to people who demonstrated their loyalty to the party. He also implemented constitutional referenda in 1980 that replaced the premiership with the office of the presidency and extended executive power over all branches of government (Chandisingh 1982). Many critics, and even PNC members, interpreted these actions as evidence of a budding authoritarian state (Birbalsingh 2007; Thomas 1984).

Within this context, Guyanese learned to invoke apaan jaat in daily life as a method to protect their racial group interests but not at the expense (or the detriment) of other racial groups. This was a delicate act whereby many participated in governmental activities (e.g., civic and cooperative groups) to help build the nation while staying vigilant of the moments when apaan jaat had the potential of transforming into racism.[18] This dynamic has made apaan jaat distinct from Guyana's national motto, "One People, One Nation, One Destiny," in that apaan jaat indexes individual agency and not only a social ontology of community.[19] And given that rigged elections and the abuse of power characterized Burnham's administration, apaan jaat began to shape relations of not only political opportunism but also trust. As Brackette Williams (1991) argues of the socialist era, people drew on good and bad racial stereotypes in order to make sense of what an individual had to contribute to the nation. Her point, of course, is that people could never know for certain if their friends, neighbors, family members, or foes were voting for their own kind. Individuals simply did what they needed to do in order to rationalize their deepening sense of social alienation.[20]

Socialism ended with Burnham's death in 1985. A transition government headed by the PNC worked with the World Bank and the International Monetary Fund to introduce structural adjustment policies to the country. Still, market and democratic liberalization in the late 1980s through the early 1990s provided little incentive to do away with or nuance apaan jaat (Hintzen 1989). After the PNC-led transition government implemented World Bank structural adjustment policies, foreign observers provided support to monitor the national elections in 1992. In what was deemed Guyana's "first free and fair election," the PPP won the majority of seats in parliament, and Cheddi Jagan reentered the national political scene as president.

Pejoratively described by its critics as ushering in a Hindu revival, the Jagan administration distinguished itself not only in terms of its racial leadership. Structural adjustment policies supported projects that developed mining and logging, while agriculture was cautiously diversified to further accommodate sugar, rice, and cash crops. This diversification may have advanced employment in agriculture, but it did not directly address funding for neglected public services. Over the next decade the austerity measures that accompanied structural adjustment contributed to escalating poverty. So, although the national economy grew by 7 percent between 1998 and 2014 under PPP leadership, Guyana was ranked by international funding agencies as a below-medium development country (Vezzoli 2014). Many critics attribute the ranking to the lack of agreement between the parties over the kinds of constitutional reforms needed to curtail state corruption (Bulkan and Trotz 2019).

The country's shifting racial demographics have only further reinforced this political gridlock. On the one hand, Guyanese out-migration has decreased since the early 1990s; on the other, the national population has stayed stable at just under 800,000 people, according to the 2012 census. Moreover, while Indians remain the largest racial population (39.8 percent) followed by Africans (29.2 percent), their overall numbers decreased compared to an increase among those who self-identify as Mixed Race (19.9 percent) and Amerindian (10.5 percent). This is not to say, however, that the census captures everyone. (Un)documented immigrants from Brazil, Haiti, Cuba, China, and Venezuela have made homes in Guyana at record numbers in the last decade and a half (*Stabroek News* 2019). As either merchants or trafficked refugees, many earn Guyanese resident status on their way to other destinations. At the same time, the ongoing humanitarian crisis in Venezuela is having the reverse effect. Not only has it increased the population in Guyana's interior (specifically Region 1), but it has inspired the remigration of Amerindian Guyanese and their descendants (Valencia 2020). Dreading that the humanitarian crisis will change the racial demographics of the voting electorate, (il)legal immigration has become a platform for campaigning (Chabrol 2020).

This dread sheds light on the varied forms of state corruption and violence that have become the Achilles' heel of both parties since the end of state socialism. In particular, Guyana is now a Caribbean–South American hub for drug trafficking (Hill and Morris 2018). Murders of state officials and ordinary citizens have been associated with the trade (Thakur 2019). This violence has tested citizens' beliefs that apaan jaat can mobilize national development in industries such as agriculture, logging, and mining and especially new ventures in carbon markets and offshore oil, with the latter less reliant on local expertise. Even with the electoral victory of the People's National Congress Reform (formerly the PNC) in 2015, the pleas Jagdeo made at the 2009 Copenhagen meeting for the LCDS were only slightly repackaged with the slogan and report "The Green State Development Strategy."

In short, apaan jaat persists because it makes coastal settlement appear familiar even as racial demographics transfigure, markets transition, resources deplete, and political regimes collapse. Apaan jaat offers an image of a people either on the road to ruin or striving to make a home elsewhere. As Achille Mbembe (2019) notes of the twenty-first century, the planet Earth has been "repeopled." He explains: "Repeopling is about shake-ups, large and small dislocations and transfers, in short, new figures of exodus. The new circulatory dynamics and creations of diasporas pass in large part via trade and commerce, wars, ecological disasters and environmental catastrophes, including cultural transfers of all sorts" (12). Such dynamics suggest that apaan jaat offers a dwindling sense of normalcy for Guyanese and, perhaps more broadly, a model for political representation. With the Cold War a fading memory, apaan jaat has not only challenged their commitments to the nation but asked them to reconsider what it might take to make a good life that is not determined by the fear of small numbers. Climate adaptation is one such effort. During the 2005 disaster, witnessing the erosion of the EDWC, caimans in trenches, and refrigerators repurposed as boats was enough to convince many that climate adaptation provides an opportunity to renounce apaan jaat.

Race as a critical focus of analysis has gelled in recent years in the environmental humanities and social science studies of climate change. The case of Western states' security policies that manage climate refugees as racial others with no "political status" has stood as a prime example (Baldwin 2013, 1474). In other instances, scholars point to how climate change materializes in tension with ongoing processes of environmental racism (Nixon 2013). This insight is also implicit in scholarship on the Anthropocene, a term that characterizes the current geological epoch in which human activities contribute to geological change. Here, race is referred to as liberal humanism's failure to think beyond the social category of Man, or the White/Euro-American, carbon-dependent subject (Wynter 2015; Yusoff 2018).

The problem with these conclusions is not that they are inadequately sup-ported by evidence; they are, and they have provided fruitful terrain for ex-amining the intersections of race and climate change. The difficulty is that the evidence for them is sustained by multiscalar relations of knowledge ex-change and agency and not only racialized subjugation. In other words, the causality attributed to race, vulnerability, and climate adaptation is nonlinear. A tension unfolds between race as lived experience and *how* race emerges as a framework that shapes people's commitment to climate adaptation as an environmental, technopolitical, and ethical project.

In short, climate adaptation is without guarantees. This reminds us of Paul Gilroy's (2000, 126) insight that the attempt to "free ourselves from the bonds of all raciology" is a world-making act (see also Gilroy 2002). Climate adaptation allows for a surplus of praxis that emphasizes pursuit alongside acts of reform, force, and resistance. In this way, climate adapta-tion troubles the historical division of White, Black, Asian, and Indigenous while making visible so-called minor or peripheral histories of race.

Engineering Vulnerability considers the world-making potential of cli-mate adaptation alongside the material underpinning of concepts, subjec-tivities, and imaginings indebted to race. Each chapter approaches climate adaptation as a practice fundamentally shaped by two interrelated historical processes: knowledge exchange and claims of belonging. In this respect, climate adaptation is not only informed by the racial political orders of liberal gov-ernance (e.g., parliamentary democracy). Climate adaptation also reflects people's ongoing efforts to square race with the active force of "the past" lingering as memory, legacy, deferral, nostalgia, and burden.

With these efforts in mind, it is important to note that climate adapta-tion does not enact a clean break with high modernism, which many have long noted, (re)produces intellectual investments in race as a bio-physical property and web of sociocultural meaning (Du Bois 2007). Climate adap-tation, in other words, is entangled in humanist and technoscientific con-versations about race. Taking this entanglement seriously requires freeing race from a singular leftist model of future revolution to focus on models of local transformation that negotiate the uneven rhythm and flow of climate change.[21]

A critical approach to climate adaptation, then, involves mapping the very sites people are invested in calling home for the foreseeable future. Take, for instance, that anyone browsing Guyana's geological reports would find a plethora of references to the coastal plain's topography and, more specifi-cally, its layers of pegasse (see figure 1.2). It settles on the coast's back lands,

FIGURE I.2. A mound of pegasse soils mixed with clay soils

in contrast to the clays, white sands, and swamp-bed soils that settle on the direct coastline.

Dark brown-black in color, porous, squishy, and wet to the touch, pegasse is a shape-shifter that has accumulated overtime as peatlands crossing human and more-than-human worlds. Following Stuart McLean (2011, 610), peatlands and other water-logged lands, possess "an active principle, one that, much as [they] participate in a variety of ways in human history making, nonetheless subsist independently of their implication in any possible version of the story of modernity." Peatlands "shift in modality"—from solid to liquid to goo—making visible the discontinuities in culturally and politically specified boundaries (592). Indeed, peatlands are not only life generating but life taking. Recent ecology and biogeography studies have dubbed peatlands "an enormous missing contribution to global warming" (Mooney 2021). Identified as main players in the story of the planet's climate crisis, "the mass conversion of carbon-rich peatlands for agricultural use since the industrial era has added over 250 billion tons of carbon dioxide to the atmosphere" (Mooney 2021). And the peatlands of Guyana are no exception.

Guyana's pegasse-laden coast continues to endure glacial retreats, uprooted forests, migrating mudbanks, and engineering projects. Pegasse's deep history, along with its industrial manipulation, reminds us that human understanding of the past is always incomplete. And since no one in Guyana is immune from its conduct or erosive effects, pegasse offers a counterpoint of reference—to apaan jaat—as Guyanese figure out what they want of climate adaptation and how to put it into action.

What's more, encounters with pegasse may matter not only for empirical reasons. They shed light on the colonial assumption that still begs to be questioned today: Was and is the ongoing settlement of the nation-state necessary at any and all costs? In posing this question I do not intend to provide a definitive answer by the end of this book. Rather, I point in the direction of treating climate adaptation as a practice that creates space for *counter-racial thinking*. By this I mean an ethico-political stance whereby people simultaneously acknowledge race while creating distance from it in order to imagine a new, or at least different, kind of engagement with the planet.

Developing counter-racial thinking as both a description of climate adaptation and an analytic, this book attempts to come to terms with race haunting both extremes of climate change's social reality—mass extinction and utopia. Counter-racial thinking not only offers a way to trace the racial political orders that lurk in the shadows of scientizing debates about climate change but also brings to the fore practices that insist on action across a variety of scales. More specifically, counter-racial thinking makes visible the forms of denial in liberal humanist institutions that block action on climate change and racism.

Tracing the dynamics of counter-racial thinking falls in line with the concerns of Candis Callison (2014) when she muses about how climate change comes to matter—an idea that positions anthropology toward mobilizing facts as much as sentiments. From the vantage point of Guyana, when ethnographic descriptions of people's life chances to survive climate change become conflated with race, anthropology is *engineering vulnerability*. Ethnography of climate adaptation requires attention to the everyday realities that make race relevant to people, while at other times it may limit their political imaginations of climate change. Such a focus might help anthropology learn something more about the way our own understandings of race have been (re)constituted by not only the materiality of science, culture, and economy but the warming planet Earth.[22]

Problematizing the relationship between race and materiality is a persistent theme in the discipline, especially for scholars examining the promissory claims of evolution, the life sciences, and biotechnologies (Baker 1998; Fullwiley 2011; Hartigan 2017; Helmreich 2009). But climate change also lays bare that radical critiques of race create potential openings as well as closures for analyzing the vulnerability of a given place. I return to this point in the conclusion. For now, I raise it to suggest that race—as a concept—has varied pasts that scholars need to reckon with in order to imagine more livable futures.

Organization and Scope

Engineering Vulnerability is based on yearlong fieldwork I conducted in coastal Guyana in 2009–10 and during shorter visits in 2012, 2014, and 2019. When researching this book, I assumed that I would tell a story about a place on the margins of American anthropologies of the Caribbean. But within a few months of being in the field I realized that the disciplinary distinctions of regionality are as much a spatial as a temporal demand. The state's post-2005 disaster LCDS agenda, which tied the coast's future to that of the interior's, incited my own discomfort with categorizing Guyana as on the margins of something. It seemed to me that the state was trying desperately to challenge the idea that Guyana's coastal flooding is unmanageable. Colonial explorers were the first to write about the coast as a wild place. The moniker was an effort to rationalize their travels in the colony's interior region, which they called Amazonia and where they encountered abundant biodiversity in nature and Indigenous peoples (Whitehead 2009). I was interested in how a state newly conscious of climate change attempts to undo the wild coast moniker while rebranding Guyana's nested experience of regionality. I tracked these attempts by spending time in the coastal administrative districts Region 4, Demerara-Mahaica, and Region 5, Mahaica-Berbice.

A Guyana Red Cross official who had recently completed a project in Sophia and handed its stewardship off to residents was the first to introduce me to ordinary citizens doing things that were parallel to engineers' work on the EDWC. I volunteered time organizing meetings and writing reports with Sophia Red Cross participants and attended festivals and other informal social events. I lived in Campbellville, a mixed-income and racially heterogeneous neighborhood in Georgetown, located roughly half a mile from Sophia. With access to major transportation routes along the coast and into Georgetown, my residence in Campbellville made engagements in Sophia, research at government archives, and travel across the country feasible. Through these engagements I made contact with engineers and other state officials implementing climate adaptation projects across Region 4 and Region 5. I observed planning, excavation, and construction for the EDWC and the creation of its flood early warning system. At these sites I also observed residents of rural villages located near the EDWC design their own flood protection. I attended meetings sponsored by state ministries and social events residents organized, including harvests, selling at markets, and *jhandis* (Hindu celebrations). My time accompanying engineers and state officials provided perspective on the sheer scale of Guyana's irrigation and drainage grid and its relation to people's desires for coastal settlement.

All of these sites are critical to the book advancing a historical and ethnographic analysis of climate adaptation. In doing this I draw on oral histories along with the Guyana National Archives, HathiTrust's digital collection for the natural history journal *Timehri*, the National Archives, Kew (digital collections) for colonial records from the mid-nineteenth century through today, drainage and irrigation legislation, and engineering reports related to the EDWC. I have relied on the historiography of slavery, emancipation, and empire to help situate these materials, given the relative scarcity of archival records on the EDWC. The discovery of facts about the EDWC entailed working across disciplinary boundaries of Caribbean-Amazonian studies and the history of science. This book is not, however, a theoretical elaboration on archival forms; nor is it a standard ethnography of one object, social group, or place.[23] Instead, it demonstrates the dynamic intrusion of the past onto the present and the forms of expertise as well as translation that make such observations possible and, at other times, unthinkable (Buck-Morss 2020). Climate adaptation unfolds as particular arrangements of people and measuring apparatuses interested in making the past legible.

Engineering Vulnerability reflects on these arrangements as they gain uneven traction across sites. For this reason, the book's argument is meant to be interpreted on two levels. The book's theoretical claim about counterracial thinking stresses that the commonality between Global South and Global North responses to climate change is the question of race. On another level, the book undoes the commonly held belief that climate change is all about the future and letting go of the past. Each chapter challenges this idea by drawing on varied historical and ethnographic data. In this respect, the book is meant to be read as a whole, with the initial chapters offering a roadmap for tracing the historical narratives, metaphors, arguments, and models climate adaptation seeks to confront in the present.

Chapter 1 details the 2005 disaster to demonstrate how disaster evidence creates the conditions of possibility for climate adaptation. It elaborates the theoretical perspective on climate adaptation that guides my research by emphasizing the forms of reflexivity that become available to people as they reconsider their expectations of state welfare and reform. Distinguishing climate adaptation from disaster management teases out how climate change has reconstituted the temporality of settlement. This distinction allows us to consider what is and is not a moment of political transformation and which citizen—or who of the body politic—has the potential of being addressed in different ways through state-sponsored climate adaptation.

Chapter 2 argues that the 2005 disaster was only one event among many that has shifted the relationship between claims of belonging and flood knowledge in Guyana. To make this point, the chapter traces how flood knowledges of the colonial past shape political desires for climate adaptation in the present. Specifically, I consider the historical emergence of flood management practices, first with Dutch settler colonialism and the introduction of empoldering and later with British settler colonialism and its dependence on large-scale damming. These engineering practices brought about a form of settler identity based as much in a racialized regime of flood knowledges as in land rights. Thus, settler colonialism is an ongoing process that has contemporary ramifications for how people envision climate adaptation as a project invested in counter-racial thinking. Chapter 3 links climate adaptation to engineers' professional ethos for keeping archival records of dam designs. How do such records help cultivate engineers' professional status as unbiased experts? These records serve the purpose of mobilizing a sense of epistemic community and belonging among engineers despite transitions in racial political orders, from slavery through apaan jaat. Engineers' archival practices and commitments matter not only for making visible the technopolitical assemblages that historically constitute climate adaptation. They also help slow down an academic analysis that would rush to treat climate adaptation as merely perpetuating forms of White-colonial domination. Instead, the chapter gives focus to Guyanese engineers' formulation of race (and its historical fragmentation) across state engineering bureaucracies.

Chapter 4 explores the racializing tropes of compensation that undergird climate adaptation and its relationship to liberal multicultural governance. It focuses on farmers' skepticism toward compensation packages the state offered to resettle them for the construction of a storm relief channel called the Hope Canal (also known as the East Demerara Water Conservancy Northern Relief Channel). Their skepticism centered on the fear that compensation was replicating apaan jaat instead of creating a space for the integration of their flood knowledges into the project. They believed that the state treated them as "Indian small men" as opposed to citizens with expertise that contributes to the EDWC's adaptation. Compensation for the Hope Canal brings to the fore the relationship between race and materiality, especially as it shapes questions of belonging. Chapter 5 continues the discussion of race and materiality but by asking whether climate adaptation depends on particular discourses about settlement in order to gain traction. Moving across an ethnography of engineers' day-to-day work of damming and their collaborations with CDC staff to create a flood early warning system, the chapter details what I call love stories about the EDWC. Love stories open up the narrative relation between encounter, desire, and expertise to show how predictive measures, such as hydraulic modeling, often fail to mobilize engineers' interest in settlement. Love stories reinforce engineers' credibility, despite moments when they recognize apaan jaat as having an effect on power differentials within engineering-CDC collaborations.

Chapter 6 explores what love stories and these new collaborations mean for the CDC staff's sense of accountability to engineers and Guyanese publics. The ethnography focuses on the efforts of CDC staff and engineers to develop a national flood plan that does not reinforce the racialized logics of witnessing endemic to the other branches of the military in Guyana. When viewed from within the state, accountability is anchored as much in apaan jaat and flood knowledges as in CDC staff and engineers learning to manage a sliding scale of expert status, force, and persuasion. In chapter 7, I return to Sophia to examine how participatory climate adaptation projects are shaped by an emerging logic of governance that is centered less on the management of biological life than on knowledge of the ordinary. The target of intervention and analysis of such projects are testimonials about how conditions of crisis reconfigure people's day-to-day interactions with climate-related flooding.

The rain kept pouring, but I was told it was nothing compared to what happened before. "It will pass," people advised. Georgetown resembles a ghost town when there's a storm. Everyone on the street scrambles to the nearest building to take shelter. They peer at the rain from windows and the open passageways of storefronts. Lightning and thunder often accompany rain in Georgetown. The rain's constant patter is deafening and can transform every other sound into mere background noise. It can blanket streets and coat buildings in a subtle sheen that makes worn Dutch colonial shutters and balconies appear new. As it falls, canals lined with mud, weeds, and garbage become submerged and disappear into a surrounding pool of murk.

Few admit that they can estimate how much rain falls when this happens. In their defense, it is a lot. They suspect that it is much more than what Hydromet, the state-sponsored weather service, forecasts. Their expectation is that the rain can get as high as it did during the 2005 disaster. But since then, many do not speak of watermarks. There's no need. Instead, many just assume that their long boots (rain boots), rice bags full of sand, and chlorine are not enough to protect them when the storms come. For those who lived through the 2005 disaster and are familiar with state efforts to enhance the EDWC, climate adaptation is seemingly never-ending. With every flood, engineers are quick to point out that the event will be instructive for climate adaptation, while ordinary citizens wonder at what and whose cost.

The sense of lingering disruption that characterizes post-2005 Guyana would not surprise most social theorists of risk and modernization.[1] Concerns about repeated disaster are deeply rooted in questions about *what* the nation-state is recognizing as loss and its efforts to document it (Blanchot 1995). In Guyana, many were adamant about what was at stake in the 2005 disaster: decades of apaan jaat contributed to a lack of vigilance by the EDWC. Simply saying the phrase "apaan jaat" evokes repetition. It encourages a process whereby citizens who look like each other vote for those who look like them. And apaan jaat may be interpreted as a haunting that dictates not only past racial political patterns of behavior but present and future ones as well. Yet the 2005 disaster also produced doubt about the EDWC's operations, which suggests that the event unfolded across a range of multiscalar temporalities (e.g., the time it takes to drain water during a wet season, hour, day, high tide, etc.) through which Guyanese accounted for loss. Furthermore, in the background of the blaming and activities to rebuild, Guyanese acknowledge that they will need to expect and learn how to anticipate intense flooding.

The 2005 disaster is an event that offers a point of reference for assessing the kind of floods that Guyanese deem reasonable and acceptable. Under these circumstances, how does disaster transform into evidence for climate adaptation? And why must Guyanese provide—or at least become invested in—such evidence in order to gain public sympathy and access to resources for climate adaptation? Evidence—whether testimonials, engineering reports, memories, meteorological forecasts, images, or statistics—has become a powerful tool through which the 2005 disaster has received the status of historical fact by publics, climate governing institutions, and humanitarian organizations outside of Guyana. If scholars are to come to analytical grips with climate adaptation, we need to recognize how disaster evidence produces political imaginaries of belonging and inclusion. Disaster evidence provides insights into how the state failed to enact lifesaving measures for its citizenry, thereby raising awareness about the (in)capacities of state institutions and infrastructures. In the absence of disaster evidence, however, images of loss persist that are productive of (more) state abandonment and othering (Scott 2014).

The American popular media, for instance, have depicted climate-related disasters, including Hurricanes Katrina and Maria, as events that exposed US citizens living in conditions that mimic those in the Global South (Bump 2017; Schwartz 2017). The comparison carries significance relative to other nation-states, such as Guyana, that are considered by many Americans not to be part of the Global North. The history and force of this comparison are emblematic of a moral attitude that seeks to challenge images of what counts as a national disaster and to assert the coevalness of seemingly disparate locales. But the comparison lacks a critical reflection on the structural-technological variables that make the circulation of disaster evidence (im)possible across Global North and Global South locales. Gestures to mutual vulnerability fall short if they do not challenge assumptions about what counts as disaster evidence, its significance in demands for social welfare, and the different moments in history when such demands are first articulated. Disaster evidence is world making; it circulates with the potential of offering nation-states signposts for climate adaptation.[2]

On the Brink of Collapse

"I woke up the next day, after Christmas, and there was just water everywhere. It wouldn't stop." This was an observation many of my informants made about the 2005 disaster. They were struck by the idea that in only a few hours there could be so much water on the ground. It was not just the amount of rain but the multiple storms within the span of just over four weeks that made the 2005 disaster so unbelievable.

In December 2004 the coast experienced fifteen inches of rain. Over 87 percent of it fell in the last nine days of the month across the administrative regions of West Demerara/Essequibo Islands (Region 3), Demerara/Mahaica (Region 4), and Mahaica/Berbice (Region 5) (Blommestein et al. 2005) (see map 1.1). The rain continued into early January, followed by a dry period from January 9 to January 13. The initial storms were an effect of low atmospheric pressure, also known as a trough—a condition that produces clouds, heavy rains, and wind shifts.

From January 14 to January 22, however, storms suddenly intensified, and coastal Guyana experienced over fifty-two inches of rain. The rain was unprecedented, compared to engineers' records dating back to 1888 that estimated nine inches as the average monthly rainfall. Many attributed the late January storms to climate change because wind and cloud fluctuations

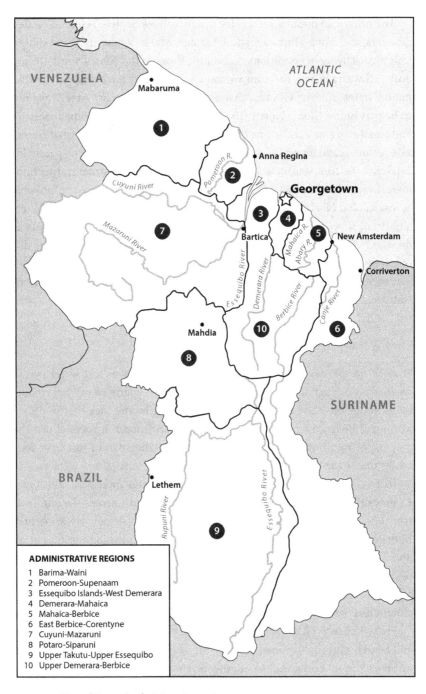

MAP 1.1. Map of Guyana's administrative regions

ADMINISTRATIVE REGIONS

1 Barima-Waini
2 Pomeroon-Supenaam
3 Essequibo Islands-West Demerara
4 Demerara-Mahaica
5 Mahaica-Berbice
6 East Berbice-Corentyne
7 Cuyuni-Mazaruni
8 Potaro-Siparuni
9 Upper Takutu-Upper Essequibo
10 Upper Demerara-Berbice

were influenced by weather systems associated with the Southern Hemisphere (Blommestein et al. 2005). These storms were characterized by heavy winds from the west that swept in clouds from the Amazon and formed zones of instability off the Atlantic shoreline. On January 18, President Jagdeo declared a state of emergency across the three administrative regions and reported that nearly 200,000 people were directly affected by flooding.

Satellite infrared images provided by meteorologists at Guyana's Hydromet Services reveal the staggering pace at which the January storms unfolded. The images make evident the multiple origins of the storms and the considerable distances they traveled. The rain fell in what appeared like an endless swell, and as storm clouds swirled, water saturated the ground. Apart from observing storm clouds, engineers and meteorologists knew that the flooding would not cease because the EDWC was overflowing with water.

The EDWC covers an area of 571 square kilometers, and its water storage capacity is approximately 250 million cubic meters (Bovolo 2014, 2). The discharge of water from the EDWC is controlled by sluices, also known by the Dutch word *koker*, which are large gates at the heads of canals that are opened manually at strategic points along the coast. Sluices are opened according to a complex schedule for supplying potable water to Georgetown and water allocation on state-operated sugar estates, privately held rice estates, and small-scale cash crop farms. Given the EDWC's large size, a series of secondary canals, sluices, and pumping stations also supports the discharge of water (see map 1.2).

This system proved to be fallible in 2005 not only because of the amount of rainwater that filled the EDWC. Engineers measure the EDWC's water levels in terms of meters above the Georgetown datum (*m* GD), a local reference point set to 17.07 meters below mean sea level. But because the EDWC is situated on a downward slope, its system has pockets of uneven water flow. Engineers recognized that these pockets, combined with the floodwaters, put enormous pressure on the EDWC's embankment dam (Bovolo 2014).

Given the extended weeks of flooding, spring tides also complicated engineers' efforts to release water from the EDWC. If water were released at high tide, the coast would be inundated by the sea. Whereas if they waited for the high tides to pass, they ran the risk of water putting even more pressure on the EDWC's embankment dam and causing its collapse. To avoid both scenarios, engineers devised a schedule for water release. After the majority of the water was released into the Demerara River sluice, the excess water was drained at two points along the Mahaica River. The schedule provided immediate relief for the EDWC but not for many rural communities. They were

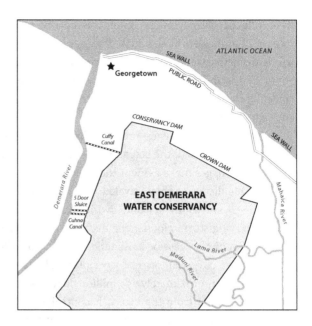

MAP 1.2. Map of the EDWC depicting its dams and main river channels

ATLANTIC OCEAN

SEA WALL

★ Georgetown

PUBLIC ROAD

CONSERVANCY DAM

Cuffy Canal

CROWN DAM

SEA WALL

Demerara River

5 Door Sluice

Cuhna Canal

EAST DEMERARA WATER CONSERVANCY

Mahaica River

Lama River

Maduni River

flooded out by the Mahaica River, which was quite silted and whose capacity was already diminished because of the EDWC's eroding internal drainage channels.[3]

As engineers turned their attention to the Mahaica River, flooding took on new dimensions across the East Coast Demerara region. Georgetown's water levels were the first to recede, in some areas within a few days of the January storms. Many attributed this to the fact that engineers routed the EDWC's water through the Mahaica River and not the Lamaha Canal, the only canal that provides a direct water channel from the EDWC to Georgetown. Throughout Georgetown, engineers placed sandbags along streets, used diesel pumps to drain water into the ocean, and attempted to secure the city's electrical grid and water filtration plant. At the same time, they repaired parts of the EDWC's embankment dam and set up posts to monitor rainfall in its system and along the Mahaica and Demerara Rivers. As engineers worked, rural communities experienced floods for three to five weeks, while those closest to the Mahaica River were reported to have been flooded for months. Through these discrete efforts, the EDWC transformed into what Stephen Collier and Andrew Lakoff (2014) call a "vital infrastructure system" or an object for reflecting on and assessing the various activities, repairs, and accommodations for collective life on the coast.

When Jagdeo declared a state of emergency on January 18, he called a meeting with his cabinet ministers, the Georgetown City Council, and the Joint Services, a branch of the military. They organized a disaster committee that was splintered into five groups to manage operations for water, food, shelter, health, and infrastructure. The committee met at the police headquarters in Georgetown while flood relief supplies were housed and distributed at the president's residence, known as the State House. Many affiliated with the local media and oppositional political parties speculated that the decision to store flood relief supplies at the State House would prove a logistical nightmare. On the one hand, they went to great lengths to publicize that, like the rest of the country, the State House was severely flooded. On the other, they viewed the State House stockpiling as a symbolic gesture that sent a signal of strongman leadership to the citizenry. Their speculations were only further exacerbated by Jagdeo's decision not to involve private sector, foreign humanitarian, or NGO support in initial logistical planning.

Within two days, Jagdeo allocated GYD$4.2 million (US$20,128) from the national budget to purchase flood relief supplies. No public records available offer a clear breakdown of how or where the monies were spent. They appear to have been used to purchase several mobile drainage pumps and what are locally called relief hampers or containers filled with basic necessities, including dry rations, linens, bottled water, chlorine, and other disinfectants. The water and infrastructure committees used the drainage pumps at different locations to channel water into the Atlantic Ocean and to clear sewage and silt from water sources. The food, shelter, and health committees worked jointly to fill relief hampers. Meanwhile, the army and members of the Joint Services created plans to open shelters in public schools and other government-operated buildings. By January 19, the CDC took over this responsibility and went into communities to launch shelters, distribute relief hampers, and encourage people to evacuate their homes. At the peak of the 2005 disaster, the CDC ran fifty shelters that housed over five thousand people, nearly 50 percent of whom were children. This suggests that the CDC was working beyond its prescribed mandate of providing flood relief supplies and morphed into an agency that organized social services as well (Blommestein et al. 2005, 17).

A week after opening the shelters, Jagdeo acknowledged that the disaster committee and CDC were overwhelmed. He announced that Guyana would solicit help from other nation-states and the private sector as well as from local and foreign NGOs. Brazil provided the first donation, with a gift of 10,050 pounds of chlorine cylinders. This donation ensured that the disaster committee's water group could work with the food and shelter committees to deliver bottled water to areas with no access to roads. At the same time, the Ministry of Health requested assistance from the US Centers for Disease Control and Prevention to improve surveillance for waterborne diseases (Dechet et al. 2012). The Guyana offices of the Red Cross and the Pan American Health Organization (PAHO) also gave support to health facilities affected by the flooding. Their health workers found that twenty-five out of forty-eight health facilities in administrative Region 3 and Region 4, where the flooding was most extensive, suffered damaged water pumps and refrigerators and lost supplies (e.g., needles, cotton, and bandages).

In turn, the Red Cross–PAHO partnership focused on disease prevention by providing immediate health services to people in shelters. The organizations sponsored mobile units of doctors to train personnel affiliated with the Ministry of Health in blood sample collection, water purification, and the restoration of damaged equipment. The most widespread threat was leptospirosis, a bacterial disease caused by exposure to water, food, or soils contaminated by animal urine. Prior to the 2005 disaster, leptospirosis had been detected in humans and livestock, but no outbreaks were ever reported in Guyana (Dechet et al. 2012). But on January 29, health officials became concerned about an outbreak when a twenty-eight-year-old male visited the Georgetown Public Hospital with symptoms of the disease—diarrhea, nausea, chills, and fatigue—and died a few days later. Over two hundred suspected cases of leptospirosis were eventually reported at the Georgetown Public Hospital, with around twenty resulting in death.

After the first reported case, the Ministry of Health and Red Cross–PAHO health workers set up an emergency center at the Georgetown Public Hospital. They traveled by truck to deliver treatments—doses of docycline—to shelters outside of Georgetown. Meanwhile, a government-owned pharmacy converted all its production efforts to docycline (Dechet et al. 2012). The Ministry of Health and Red Cross–PAHO mobile unit included volunteers who provided twenty-four-hour radio, loudspeaker, and television announcements about the threat of leptospirosis and places to find treatment. By the end of the antileptospirosis campaign in March, over three hundred thousand people were provided treatment (a week of medication). Health workers believe that the antileptospirosis campaign helped diminish the outbreak of related waterborne diseases, including dengue fever and filariasis. Even so, leptospirosis was the leading cause of death, followed by accidental drownings (Dechet et al. 2012).[4]

The antileptospirosis campaign made intense flooding appear as a threat that could be managed in a targeted or insular way. People were safe from floods, so health workers thought, as long as water was not contaminated. But the problem with the focus on disease was the assumption that the impacts of intense flooding could best be understood from the vantage point of human injury alone. As the multiple January storms indicated, flood situations at the village or even household scale did not offer much insight about the physical status and operations of the EDWC. In many respects, the health workers' spatial and temporal understanding of intense flooding was in tension with those of the other key experts managing the disaster—namely, engineers.

During the 2005 disaster, engineers faced difficulties gauging where and when to do emergency work on the EDWC. By late January, the government solicited support from World Bank engineering consultants to assist Guyanese engineers' real-time repairs. The consultants arrived in time to witness a crew of 150 Guyanese engineers and rangers sandbag the crest of the EDWC and use pegasse to raise the height of its dam. The reinforcement of the EDWC with more pegasse, however, could not offer a long-term solution. As the World Bank's consultants summarized in a February 2005 report, "The current floods have also brought to light the extreme urgency for rehabilitating protective drainage structures and strengthening the [EDWC]. . . . Without intervention, the weakened dam structure continues to place some 450,000 regional inhabitants at risk from catastrophic flooding. . . . The objective of this report is to provide a preliminary assessment . . . with a special focus on reconstruction needs likely to emerge once the phase [disaster] is over . . . and the possible intervention within six months to a year following the emergency created by the floods" (Blommestein et al. 2005, 1, 3).

The consultants intimate that Guyanese engineers would have to consider a comprehensive redesign of the EDWC after the disaster and, specifically, that pegasse erosion signaled the need for a more robust dam construction. The report gestures to what eventually became the multiyear project sponsored by the World Bank's Global Environment Fund for the climate adaptation of the EDWC. The project would require engineers to complete a study to map drainage flows, create new hydraulic models that incorporate climate-induced sea-level rise and weather-change patterns, rehabilitate old canals by dredging and reinforcing their embankments, create an automated network for reading the EDWC's water levels, and rehabilitate parts of the EDWC's embankment dam.

The differences between the emergency repairs and the proposed climate adaptation project were subtle but consequential. The climate adaptation activities would allow engineers to use pegasse not only to physically secure the EDWC's embankment dam but also to direct and guide their methods for replanning its internal drainage. Engineers knew they would face challenges moving forward: the EDWC's terrain is overrun with pegasse, a medium they had found difficult to build with in the past. As the World Bank's head engineer noted, "A well targeted and *creative intervention* would help prolong the life of the dam structure allowing breathing space to realize the necessary major repairs" (Blommestein et al. 2005, 12, emphasis added). In the moment of the disaster, the material substance and erosive qualities of pegasse were made visible to engineers. From their perspective, there is something quite jaw-dropping about eroding pegasse on a dam embankment in that it demonstrates the contingencies of human concepts, planning, and humanly assigned value granted to practices of settlement.

Extending a Disaster's Knowledge Networks

Very few people I know who lived through the disaster were aware of what was happening to the EDWC at the time. "We heard word from the television and radio that the EDWC had a lot of water, nothing else; we were left in the dark," one informant struggled to explain to me. While Hydromet provided consistent updates about the storms, the Ministry of Agriculture provided the public very few updates about what engineers were doing. In response and as a last resort for safety, many people opted to go to shelters.

The most severe flooding occurred on back lands, or land that is several miles from the Atlantic coast's main thruway, the East Demerara Road. Those who lived on back lands had fewer shelter options compared to those living in Georgetown or in rural communities located closer to the thruway. Staff from the CDC and volunteers from the Guyana office of the United Nations Children's Fund (UNICEF) took on the role of organizing the day-to-day needs of the shelters. They focused their efforts on transporting supplies to shelters in the back lands. Many of these shelters were sparse one-room schools with little infrastructure and furniture, which required shelter workers to create makeshift living spaces and command centers by draping sheets over desks and bookshelves.

While the CDC completed a number of search-and-rescue boat operations to take people to shelters, most arrived on their own. Once registered with the CDC, they were given access to a mattress and food. Cooked in Georgetown by CDC staff, meals and rations were transported daily by truck to the shelters. Volunteers from UNICEF distributed meals to the heads of households based on the number of people registered in a family. But people moved in and out of shelters on a daily basis, which meant it was unclear to shelter workers if every person registered was actually receiving aid. As one shelter worker recounted, "I mean it was like migration; a rapid migration. When we were dealing with this kind of flood, it was difficult to get a lot of data, to know what was going on and where supplies were going."

Some shelter workers reported having up to sixty people one week and the next week less than half that number at the same shelter. In many instances, people tried to stay in their homes, but when the floodwaters became unbearable, they went to neighbors or family who had homes on stilts or had concocted makeshift drainage in response to the storms. When these methods became untenable, people decided to relocate to shelters.

At the shelters, family units were reorganized. Many children were left with one parent while the other or a family friend went to their homes to find food. Some families separated and moved between shelters to source additional supplies. On a handful of occasions, UNICEF reported fathers as having registered the names of their children at multiple shelters to receive more rations than allowed. Given that family registration ensured that people were fed, the shelters were reported to have been split almost evenly between women and men. Women overwhelmingly partnered with shelter workers to care for children and clean living spaces, while men attempted to hitch rides into Georgetown with the hopes of finding day work amid the ongoing floods. Those who stayed at shelters in many ways relied on what could be called a nested knowledge network. They followed the rules of the shelters (e.g., family registration and sanitation procedures) but learned to cooperate and cohabitate with strangers to keep their nuclear familial units intact. Thus, despite the rapid movement of people, the disaster and intense flooding reinforced gendered relations of knowledge, dependency, and labor (Trotz 2010).

Life at the shelters, however, did not always offer sanctuary. The bathroom facilities at many were initially set up outside, which required that people wade through floodwaters to bathe and defecate. Eventually a system was implemented where water was fetched and they could bathe on the upper floors or walkways of shelters. With the leadership of Guyana Water Inc. and Oxfam International, CDC staff supplied and transported potable water and water vats from Georgetown. The daily wait for water led to long lines for baths, while some simply opted not to bathe. There were food shortages; in the worst instances, people ate only biscuits, and some parents rationed one meal per day between their children. With few spare boats, shelter workers could not easily relocate people to other shelters when supplies were depleted. In these instances, the shelters became cramped and tensions ran high. There were fights and verbal assaults between men and women. Some shelter workers were blocked from entering buildings until they could guarantee (or at least convince) those living in shelters that adequate food would be delivered. Amid the flooding, many shelter workers quit, reportedly fearing for their safety; became exhausted by the lack of support they received from CDC staff; or became infected with leptospirosis.

Although many of the shelter workers admitted that the lack of organized flood relief supplies was a result of poor planning on the part of the CDC staff, they still described a feeling of shock during the peak of the January storms. As one shelter worker explained to me:

> People were surprised. The period of time before the disaster, there was a lot of breakdown with the canals and there were the changes in the weather. The kokers weren't working the way they were supposed to. The dam levels were already high. But the average person doesn't take the time to think about all that and put it all together. I mean, we are below sea level. We do expect to flood. But we did not expect it at this scale. The level of flooding and how long it lasted and the amount of damage caught everyone off guard. And you have to understand, when you have next to nothing and you lose it all, you don't know what the hell you are going to do. I guess if you checked our statistics on the number of suicides after the flood, you'd have probably seen some jump there.

Despite being taken by surprise, people's expectations about flood relief supplies registered well beyond the national government's neglect of irrigation and drainage infrastructures or logistical mismanagement of shelters. As floodwaters persisted, those who did not migrate to shelters devised their own methods for survival.

Many of those living in Georgetown who had money and transportation stayed in the city's two hotels. Churches, Hindu temples, and mosques set up relief centers and opened shelters within the initial days of the floods.

Likewise, a well-known gang leader and criminal on the run organized a fleet of trucks to distribute flood relief supplies to people throughout the city and many of its suburbs. But perhaps the most extensive nongovernmental aid came from Guyanese living in the diaspora. Those marooned in their homes reported to relatives abroad via phone and social media about the lack of support they were receiving from the state. Those in the diaspora set up donation drives, mostly in the New York City area. There were a number of disputes between the donors and the Guyanese state over what, if any, import tax should apply to the donations, which ultimately delayed their distribution in Guyana. Nevertheless, Guyanese from the New York area donated over GYD$10 million (US$48,000) in flood relief supplies, a sum that nearly matched the individual humanitarian aid of the American and French governments, the largest grants from any foreign government (Blommestein et al. 2005, 19).

As information about the disaster trickled in from social media, a number of private citizens in Guyana with backgrounds in engineering, military operations, humanitarian aid, and environmental conservation took action. They formed the Guyana Citizens' Initiative after a retired army general took a reconnaissance flight over the EDWC to assess its condition and the water overtopping. These aerial surveys, along with on-the-ground images of marooned communities taken by a Guyanese photographer, were important resources for the state. The data from the aerial surveys were used by Jagdeo's disaster committee to create a real-time archive of rainfall counts and changes in the EDWC's water level. In the meantime, the Guyana Citizens' Initiative used the aerial surveys to gather information and map the impacts of flooding on sanitation and potable water at the community level.

These impromptu partnerships revealed that public trust in the EDWC's operations was dwindling at the same time that the citizenry expected the state to reinvest in irrigation and drainage infrastructures in more efficient ways. The state was confronted with a new reality: its appeals to modernization were not enough to provide its citizenry with a sense of comfort and to elicit sympathy, aid, and resources from a foreign, global audience.[5] Instead, the state made appeals to the loss of linear and progressive time. The state accepted that even if it committed to "improving" the EDWC's operations, what is feared—in this case, flooding—can reemerge in the future in different, varied, and intensified forms. There was a distinction, in other words, between the state's commitment to disaster preparedness/management and its commitment to climate adaptation. The former involves the state organizing resources and responsibilities during a disaster with an eye toward lessening the impacts of the event and ending it. The latter is centered on the state learning to observe disturbance while reinvesting in social services to address an unknown future.[6]

Transitions

Although during the disaster Guyanese engineers were preoccupied with collaborating with other state officials and technocrats, they were just as committed to improving communication within their existing professional networks. By 2005, Guyana had a few hundred engineers affiliated with several private firms alongside the Ministry of Agriculture and the Ministry of Public Infrastructure. Responsible for the construction of not only irrigation and drainage infrastructures but also roads and sea defenses, as well as surveying for extractive industries (e.g., oil, wells, and minerals), Guyanese engineers have been trained in and are masters of geotechnical, civil, and hydraulic engineering's many subfields. But most identify themselves as civil engineers with little interest in taking on a specialized title when practicing. As one engineer explained to me, "When you are in a small country, everyone does everything. If something breaks, who is going to fix it?"

Nearly all of Guyana's engineers are male, the profession is racially diverse and integrated, and engineers hail from across the country's rural and urban districts. They enter the profession for a variety of reasons. Some described to me their love of the outdoors and making mathematics real; others hope to apply their agricultural knowledge to a more lucrative career than farming, while a few aspire to follow in the footsteps of their fathers, who found political and cultural prominence as technocrats in colonial and postcolonial Guyana. Despite their differences, most complete college at the University of Guyana with an engineering degree. Upon completion they take low-level field positions with one of the ministries, and some take a government scholarship to pursue postgraduate education abroad, usually in the United Kingdom but also increasingly in India, Australia, the Netherlands, the United States, Canada, or Cuba. After completing their postgraduate degrees, they return to serve several years with the ministries to pay back the scholarship. Many grudgingly describe the return as an apprenticeship and use the time to decide their professional focus on either drainage and irrigation or sea defense and roads. The competitive market of local private engineering firms for state contracts, however, complicates this decision.

Most contracts for irrigation and drainage infrastructures are coordinated by the Ministry of Agriculture when development organizations, such as the World Bank, propose a project. The state posts a bid or what is called an advertisement in the local newspapers (and increasingly on the internet) requesting services. Local firms apply by sending offers, detailing their expertise and price to complete the project. Given that the ministries are understaffed and underresourced, bidding has both filled a technological gap and buttressed a fraternity for the competitive career advancement of engineers across private firms. Engineers assume that as long as this contract bid approach focuses on projects that involve the consistent maintenance of the grid—such as desilting clogged canals and repairing broken sluice gates—they can manage EDWC's water levels and drainage effectively.

The World Bank consultants in February 2005 reinforced this point: their report identified areas of the EDWC's embankment dam that *should not* be repaired until drainage studies could be completed by engineers (World Bank Mission 2005). The planning activities for these repairs needed more in-depth analysis than was required for a maintenance inspection. This insight led to stalled decision-making during the disaster. Some engineers, for instance, circumvented Jagdeo's disaster committee and sought out guidance from retired engineers and those in the Guyanese diaspora who once worked on the EDWC. Many recall that these retired engineers helped them decide which channels and structures of the EDWC were crucial to inspect during the disaster and which could wait until the Conservation Adaptation Project (CAP) started.

Engineers' efforts and their sense of fraternity reflect a key insight offered by Ulrich Beck (2015, 75) about climate change. He argues that climate change has a "hidden emancipatory side," which goes beyond the negative side effects and risks of modernity to "produce normative horizons of common goods." Pushing against a nation-centered notion of risk, Beck notes that the "scale of change" climate change has brought about is "beyond [human] imagination" and undercuts "traditional boundaries between nation-states and social classes" (76). He invites us to reimagine a global landscape of risk, wherein support for social welfare is organized not by nation-states as such but by the distinction between experts responsible for making decisions to manage climate change and the ordinary citizens affected by these decisions.

Guyana's 2005 disaster presses us to take up Beck's invitation, but in a slightly different way. The appeals for climate adaptation break down the division between experts and ordinary citizens. As the event demonstrated, different publics in and outside of Guyana privileged certain forms of disaster evidence over others to push the state to do something new, or at least different, first to save people and then to keep the EDWC operational. This disaster evidence was sourced from across various situated perspectives: engineering reports about pegasse, the Guyanese diaspora's tax receipts, flood survivors' social media feeds, the health awareness antileptospirosis campaigns, the military's aerial surveys of the EDWC, shelter workers' reports, and so on.

In short, disaster evidence has a dual purpose: it is a political tool of survival but also of civic representation. What counts as the political is not only about defining power as a rationally calculable resource negotiated between people. It also involves, in the words of Sheila Jasanoff (2003, 224), "how to live democratically and at peace with the knowledge our societies are inevitably 'at risk.'" Guyana's 2005 disaster is instructive for grappling with this insight. The slow effort on the part of the PPP administration was not only evidence of poor judgment or, perhaps, lack of experience. It was a symptom of a state that had become too complacent with conceiving of governmental action as a bipartisan or racially motivated affair. The PPP administration had an empty toolkit for responding to intense flooding that affects every citizen and district simultaneously and with the same intensity. The PPP administration had no clear political foe to blame for the 2005 disaster. However, what played out during the event, and in the years after, was an attempt by the PPP administration to use climate adaptation projects to redistribute responsibility for intense flooding.

In this endeavor, state officials found a political foe in climate change and shifted the terms of political-electoral engagement. In turn, both experts and ordinary citizens began to perceive apaan jaat, and racial political orders more broadly, as indebted to a narrative of developmentalist progress that no longer served the nation-state. One possible alternative to apaan jaat is counter-racial thinking. During the 2005 disaster and as the PPP administration sought the initial grants for climate adaptation projects, no one was quite sure about the quality and amount of disaster evidence the government and ordinary citizens possessed. Indeed, much had yet to be collected and recorded (see chapters 5, 6, and 7). In much the same way, counter-racial thinking often plays out as a fleeting hope or a partially realized ambition as people make decisions and commit themselves to climate adaptation.

The rub, however, is whether Guyanese interpret disaster evidence as individually or collectively motivated, a distinction that stirred feelings of distrust, for example, in the management of shelters in 2005. Questions about where and how the sources for disaster evidence originated during the event also reveal that Beck's appeal for emancipatory catastrophism is never evenly distributed across racial populations. In this vein, the spectral aspects of apaan jaat—or the mark of its certain return embodied in intense flooding, infrastructural breakdown, and related political stalemates—ground a point of reference for all Guyanese about a justice yet to come (Derrida 2006).

The Guyanese state's commitment to climate adaptation has transformed the temporal horizon of coastal settlement and related projects of nation-state building. With climate adaptation in mind, intense flooding and meteorological events become prominent dimensions of national technological fantasy and political lifestyle in Guyana. This is not to say that prior to the 2005 disaster engineers and other state officials did not attempt or succeed at keeping the EDWC at the forefront of nation-building agendas. They did, on countless occasions. But when they did, climate change was not referred to per se; instead, they treated the EDWC's operations as if they were determined by racialized understandings of who counts as a settler of the coast. This framework of coastal settlement did not dissipate with the emergence of climate change as a known problem of a world at risk, but rather parallels its unfolding.

THE RACIAL POLITICS OF SETTLERS

I encourage everyone I know when they are in Guyana to drive from George-town along the East Coast Demerara Road toward the EDWC. On both sides of the road you will see villages separated by water-filled earthen canals. Dark and stagnant, the water creates the illusion that millennia ago the canals emerged from some geologic rupture—as if they burst through the earth to expose streams of water from the underworld on a journey to the shores of the Atlantic. Thriving communities of weeds and globs of mud in the canals can make this journey difficult, sending a message to the water that it is not the only life-generating force on the coast. As you drive closer to the EDWC, you move farther away from the sea. The air gets hotter and drier. The villages drop out of sight and are replaced by coconut trees that peel off into the EDWC's abyss.

The dynamism of the EDWC's water world is mesmerizing. It will make you briefly forget how cruel and unforgiving water can be during the wet season. It can convince you that the coast was settled by people who believed that a life aquatic entails persistence. The first day I was out on the EDWC with engineers, I tried to think about what facilitates persistence and visualized a light breeze, a passing cloud, and a drizzle of rain cooling my body. The British colonial explorer Richard Schomburgk ([1922] 2015) wrote that the Dutch called Guiana the wild coast, in homage to the Orinoco tributaries that wreaked havoc on their trade routes and plantations. That description misses the point or, at the very least, is shortsighted. On that day the coast felt like its own being, more than anything else.

Despite wearing boat shoes, I stumbled across the EDWC's embankment. Each time I lifted my leg I carried soil that encrusted the bottom of my shoes. My feet felt heavy, like boulders. My legs began to weaken, and I could no longer tell the difference between the sweat on my clothes and my body. The sunlight radiated off the EDWC's water, creating a glare that made it nearly impossible to discern anything past the brim of my baseball cap. All I could focus on was the partially completed concrete sluice that towered in front of me. The sluice was intended for the Hope Canal. It overwhelmed the landscape. The EDWC now looked like it was being recolonized by some alien structure ready to turn the tide of its waters and the scope of its purpose. But engineers feared that completing the Hope Canal's construction would pose more trouble than it was worth because, like the EDWC, the excavation site was overrun with pegasse.

Walking the excavation site, they kicked rocks, dug at the ground with their feet, and crumbled pieces of soil in their hands to find areas to start a soil analysis (see figure 2.1). Engineers instructed the project's foreman to collect samples so that they could take them to the University of Guyana's soil laboratory. Private local engineering firms, such as the one leading the Hope Canal project, often ask faculty to run soil tests for their projects. Soil laboratories are too expensive for many firms to invest in, and those at the Ministry of Public Infrastructure are often understaffed. In return, students receive hands-on experience analyzing soils and the university gains some professional recognition in its pursuit of nurturing the country's engineering talent.

The soil exchange is quick, dispassionate, and methodic. Engineers shuffle large plastic bags full of soil from the backs of pickup trucks to the arms of unassuming students. Parting with the bags provides relief to the engineers but also launches an unfortunate period of waiting for days, coupled with flashes of anticipation about what the tests will reveal. Engineers are often too busy to stay and watch where the bags go in the university's applied sciences building. For the moment, the bags become someone else's responsibility. A few engineers complain that with the increasing number of private-sector construction projects in the country, this arrangement may become unsustainable. Others lament the state's inability to secure international aid and

FIGURE 2.1. An engineer inspecting soils

grants to maintain the ministry's laboratory. Whether from the perspective of the present or the future, engineers assume they will continue to be reliant on the university and other outside contract work to analyze soils.

As people who move soil for a living, engineers also acknowledge that it is unfortunate that soil laboratories are hard to come by in Guyana. Indeed, the analysis of soil foundations is essential to civil, hydraulic, and geotechnical engineering anywhere on the planet, but it is especially so in a place like Guyana, where pegasse overwhelms its coast. Clear plastic bags filled with five or ten pounds of soil can tell engineers a lot. Their samples can contain heaps of pegasse's dark brown-black particles along with pale oatmeal–, burnt tan–, and rusty copper–colored particles—an indication that pegasse mingles well with clay and other types of soil. Pegasse's ability to pass is a mixed blessing because it means that when engineers build, they have to take extra safety precautions.

The value of pegasse to engineers cannot be understood in isolation. It always carries meaning in relation to engineers' design measures. Accordingly, pegasse allows engineers to envision a temporality to coastal settlement that is radically different from that of any vision of linear progress, one in which pegasse remains both a potential danger and a creative resource in the engineering sciences. But even their acknowledgment of pegasse's materiality does not completely capture the complexity or crude effort that entails climate adaptation.

The variables, processes, and agents that inform climate adaptation defy simple institutional description because the EDWC was not initially designed to serve the coastal population in equal ways. Specifically, the engineering sciences in Guyana, as elsewhere, were conceived out of settler colonial modes of racialized slavery and indentured labor that enabled strategies for flood management. In essence, one cannot understand the climate adaptation of the EDWC unless one considers that engineers are in a position of playing a game of catch-up. They recognize that climate change has contributed to the occurrence of intensified and torrential storms. At the same time, they are at the mercy of a centuries-old irrigation and drainage grid that never made the settlement of the coast easy or desirable for all people.

Addressing this engineering game of catch-up begs reconsideration of how and why settler colonialism has come to structure race in contemporary Guyana. Given the official and popular connotations of colonialism, *White* would appear to be the most colonial of the settler racial categories. Settler colonialism in the Americas has been widely assessed as a dual strategy that facilitates the spatial displacement of capital and the liberal representation of the New World as terra incognita (Wolfe 2006; Wynter 1995).[1] Peel back the layers, however, and settler colonialism appears to take multiple paths—as it unfolds through competing ideas of race, expertise, and rights.

The reproduction of a settler identity persists today in Guyana.[2] The original irrigation and drainage infrastructures dug by enslaved Africans and Asian and Portuguese indentured laborers during colonial rule are still in operation. Coastal Amerindians—once removed for the digging of these infrastructures—resettled either in the interior region or along the coast by integrating into Afro- and Indo-Guyanese villages, while some have been granted communal land rights on Amerindian reserves (*Kaieteur News* 2016; Sanders 1976; Wishart 2014). In Guyana, settler identity stems from the recognition that labor for land tenure has and always will be yoked to water-logged terrain, some of which simply requires too much of an investment to maintain.[3] From this point of view, coastal settlement perpetuates the never-ending discovery of new flood knowledges for land tenure.

Climate adaptation is connected to this longer history of settler colonialism and knowledge exchange. Accounting for this history involves shifting from a focus on the problem of evidence for climate adaptation to how flood knowledges shape the ways in which the past is perceived and confronted by people. Flood knowledges open ways of thinking about human hubris while challenging the divide between natural and social histories. What if, I wonder, we were to value flood knowledges for more than their practical purposes but for their theoretical capacities as well? What are flood knowledges, and why do people know them as social practices in Guyana? Why do flood knowledges sometimes collapse into hierarchical understandings of the human—such as race—and not at other times? And relatedly, when do people decide to treat flood knowledges as a resource for broadening their historical metaphors and models of belonging? Dutch permanent settlement of the coast, slave emancipation, and decolonization are helpful reference points for answering these questions.

Migrations

Beginning six thousand years ago, the coastal terrain possessed tidal clay flats that extended inward into the mouths of the Orinoco and Essequibo Rivers. This shoreline formed elongated peninsulas and islands along freshwater tributaries that integrated the biotic systems of upland rainforests with savannahs and swamps. At the same time, the postglacial sea began to rise, and it continued to deposit marine clays along the shore. The marine clays contributed to the development of mangrove forests, which became the primary food source for the Waraos, also known as boat people, believed to be the first humans to inhabit the coast (Williams 2003, 57). Comprising bands of no more than two or three extended families, Waraos survived on the snails and shellfish they collected in relatively inaccessible swamps along the Orinoco Delta (Edwards and Gibson 1979).

At the beginning of the wet season in the spring, the bands set up camps at the heads of freshwater creeks, where fish migrated to spawn. From there, they traveled long trade routes to mine rock materials for fishing tools. This seasonal migration helped them creatively circumvent centuries of environmental transformations and the perils of coastal flooding (Williams 2003). The relative inaccessibility of the swamps and housing built on stilts high above riverbanks helped protect Waraos from the raids of other Amerindians and isolated them from contact with Spanish traders when they arrived at the Orinoco Basin in 1531.

Conversely, the neighboring coastal Arawaks became "conquers and enslavers" of "lesser tribes in the region" by creating trading partnerships with the Spanish (Edwards and Gibson 1979, 164; Whitehead 2009). Known by archaeologists as establishing "shell mound cultures," Arawaks lived on earthen mounds bounded by ditches and adapted burial practices to the advance and retreat of the shoreline (Williams 2003, 111). The historic overlaps in settlement of individual mounds resulted in a "mosaic of habitable niches" demarcated by the different shellfish species Arawaks collected and consumed (100). Mounds were composed on "land high enough to escape flooding in the rainy season," while river tributaries with few patches of savannah and high lands were avoided (Evans and Meggers 1960, 179; Verill 1918; Wishart 2014). But unlike an earlier generation of Amazonian archaeologies that characterized mounds as lacking in technological sophistication and as representative of Amazonia's supposed environmental and cultural scarcity, recent analyses suggest otherwise (Whitehead, Heckenberger, and Simon 2010). Mounds were integrated into long-distance trade routes, supported intensified agriculture, and were utilized as a defense system, particularly against Carib raids. Likewise, Arawaks used their knowledge of riverbanks (which was based on a broader cosmology of divinities) to help European explorers and missionaries map settlements (Whitehead 1998).

The complete characterization of Arawakan material responses to flooding awaits comprehensive excavation and analysis (Whitehead, Heckenberger, and Simon 2010). For the time being, it is important to note that, because of flooding, the permanent settlement of the entire coastline was not an obvious advantage; only some areas proved worth inhabiting. In turn, flooding produced spatial relations that challenged human-centered narratives of natural history, settlement, and conquest (Raffles 2002, 36–37).

The subsequent arrival of the British and Dutch to the upper rivers of Guiana further reconstituted the sociohydro meaning of settlement. *In Discoveries of Guiana*, British explorer Sir Walter Raleigh invokes the notion of "borders" to describe the different Amerindian groups he encountered (Whitehead 2009, 4). His notion of borders aligned with the ways in which Dutch settlers sought to enact ethnically based military trade alliances with Amerindians. Such alliances supported the Dutch enslaving Amerindians to further the trade of annatto, a seed used for decorative dyes and medicine. The alliances served political stereotypes that pitted Amerindian groups against each other (Whitaker 2016). Caribs, for instance, were believed to be fierce warriors who were reliable slave raiders and allies against the Spanish. Likewise, the Dutch gave Arawaks the legal authority to make selective military trade alliances because they had proven to be politically astute (Whitehead 2009, 7). But with the introduction of enslaved Africans in the mid-seventeenth century for sugar, coffee, and cotton plantations, the annatto trade declined, and Dutch-Amerindian alliances against the Spanish deteriorated (Whitaker 2016). By 1744, the Dutch had rushed to secure Fort Zeelandia on a fluvial island in the Essequibo Delta. With Fort Zeelandia, the Dutch West Indies Company gave planters permission to establish plantation estates downriver and to import more enslaved Africans (Benjamin 1992).

With their relocation to the Atlantic coast, the Dutch enacted in 1793 a prohibition against Amerindian slavery in the hopes of recruiting Amerindians to track down runaway enslaved Africans and thwart slave rebellions. Enslaved Africans' work on coastal plantations was particularly difficult. Planters and engineers instructed them in a method of empoldering that involves the maintenance of polders or low-lying land that has been drained and protected from erosion and flooding by a system of dikes and canals. As was the case in the thirteenth-century Netherlands, when water boards were first created to schedule empoldering, planters in Guiana intended to use polders to regulate water allocation on individual plantation estates (Hoeksema 2007).[4]

But in the context of settler colonialism, where Amerindians' river-based flood knowledge provided the Dutch a method to simultaneously explore the colony's interior and develop the coast, empoldering took on a dual significance. It was an engineering technique that provided a model for what Cedric Robinson (2000) calls racial capitalism or the valuation and division of labor based on race. By deriving economic value from the racial identity of enslaved Africans, planters were able to propel forward a system of empoldering that relied on the militarization of the colony alongside the marginalization of Amerindian kinship and political practices.

Empoldering shaped the violent conditions through which colonized peoples could act as creative human beings who had a stake in permanently settling the coast. Indeed, the majority of those who first empoldered—enslaved Africans—were not natives of the coast, but forced migrants. As Shona Jackson (2012, 4) argues, historically in Guyana, the term *native* has indexed "an objective identification of Indigenous Peoples that positions them with regard to European time and Renaissance through Enlightenment modes of determining humanity, and second as a term appropriated by Creoles [of any race] to signal fixity with regard to belonging." In the case of flooding, the term *native* takes on renewed material significance because what counts as fixity is indebted to the act of empoldering and the literal integrity of the terrain, particularly soil's porosity. What's more, empoldering brings about a sense of artificial permanence to coastal spaces and a new historical time for Waraos, Arawaks, and Caribs who lived on semipermanent coastal settlements well before Dutch contact.

As historians W. Edwards and K. Gibson (1979, 168) note, the Carib way of life was displaced by plantations to the point that "by the end of Black slavery

[they] began to move further inland partly out of fear for the ex-slaves and partly to search for a new Amerindian slave trade, a market which they found in Brazil." So even as some Amerindians, such as the Carib, created new arrangements for slavery and trade in the interior region, European coastal settlement flourished. The Arawakan and Carib migration transformed empoldering into a formal practice of settler colonialism because planters "presumed [the] absence of," or at least Amerindians' withdrawal from, coastal life (Jackson 2012, 42).

Planters in Dutch Guiana were not the only Europeans during this period to equate a colony's environmental disadvantages with settlement and Black slavery. In the British North American colonies, colonial state officials launched resettlement campaigns that encouraged White settlers to cut down forests in order to transform the region's climate from cold to temperate (Zilberstein 2016). They also recruited Jamaican Maroons or fugitive enslaved Africans to aid in these pursuits in the effort of increasing White presence over Indigenous presence in the colonies. These migration and labor policies for Maroon recruitment into temperate regions were buttressed by race science arguments about climatic determinism and practices of acclimatization or seasoning (Asaka 2017; Delbourgo 2012). Settler colonialism, in this respect, undergirded political justifications for Black slavery as a method for expanding the scope of forestry and the conservation sciences of the period.

In turn, weather events such as flooding slipped easily into engineering problems that created a hierarchy of who or which racialized bodies had the skill sets or expertise to manage them. Dutch planters' commitments to coastal settlement in Guiana were linked to the idea that settlement could be achieved only as long as there were enslaved Africans and Black Creoles to empolder and Amerindians to discipline rebellious ones. Just as important were planters' beliefs that as a people (or *volk*), the Dutch possessed some level of engineering know-how that could be replicated anywhere on the planet. But this belief was not foolproof.

During their early period of colonization across the Atlantic world (1620–70s), the Dutch invested very few resources in establishing plantation estates (Klooster 2016). Instead, they were notorious merchants, staking a claim in the mines of the African Gold Coast and providing loans for manufacturing to other European empires and ammunition to their Indigenous foes. For instance, with the loss of Brazil and New Netherland (New York Hudson Valley) circa 1664, "the directors of the [West Indies Company] acknowledged that the Dutch were not cut out to be colonial farmers, unlike the English who were excellent colonists, as the recent transformations in Barbados had shown" (5).[5]

Some historians have doubled down on this view of the Dutch inadequacies, or at least their self-consciousness about exporting empoldering methods, suggesting that they took inspiration from British engineering in Barbados and Antigua (Lakhan 1994, 172). Empoldering, in other words, was not a fait accompli for Dutch settlers and planters. It was an engineering technique that required orchestrated efforts on the part of the Dutch to categorize colonized peoples along racial lines while utilizing Black slavery to accelerate its teaching and implementation the world over.

Regulating Flood Knowledges

Empoldering, along with its irrigation and drainage infrastructures, intended to yoke the life chances of the enslaved African to that of the White planter. In the case of Guiana, flood management also helped integrate the colony into the broader historical-cultural imagination of Caribbean plantation societies (Mandle 1972; Wagley 1960). This meant that flood knowledge was a matter not only of the violent exploitation of labor and knowledge but of control over colonized populations' movements within a given space.

By the 1660s the enslaved African population numbered about 2,500 and Amerindians were estimated at 50,000. Sister Mary Noel Menezes (2011) argues that as Dutch coastal sugar plantations became lucrative, planters had growing concerns about their relationships with Amerindians. In response, Dutch colonial administrators began to spend more on what was called the present policy. They gave money (guilders) and gifts—looking glasses, razors, silver collars, cutlasses, fishing hooks, and rum—to Amerindian militias for their services hunting down runaway and enslaved Africans. In particular, on bush exhibitions Amerindians' knowledge of rivers' flow and geography proved invaluable (72–82). The continued support of Amerindian militias might explain why this territory of the Guianas had few active Maroon communities relative to Surinam and French Guiana. In particular, Dutch control incorporated three administrative colonies: Demerara, Essequibo, and Berbice. Demerara was the largest and stretched across the coast; it had numerous plantations and was the central commercial site for slave trading (Smith 1962).

Plantations in Demerara were laid out twelve feet apart, with a limit of one thousand acres established for sugar and five thousand acres for coffee (Da Costa 1997, 44). This pattern of settlement led to a high concentration of enslaved Africans in rural villages and made contact among them easy, particularly since plantations were connected by canals and a main road (44).

To control their movements, the Rule on the Treatment of Servants and Slaves was established in 1772. The regulations focused on how enslaved Africans used technology and irrigation and drainage infrastructures. The fear of infrastructural sabotage, for instance, led to the decree that enslaved Africans were prohibited from carrying guns or sharp weapons on a dam unless they were huntsmen. They were also not allowed to walk on small dams or canals at night without a pass from their masters.

If enslaved Africans were caught in violation, masters were permitted twenty-five lashes or could send them to confinement in a fortress on the outskirts of the estate (45). While masters were allowed to enforce physical discipline, they were also obligated to provide enslaved Africans some gift, such as provision grounds (their own land to farm subsistence crops), Sunday rest, a supply of clothes, and a weekly allowance for their labor. In this way, the regulations were similar to others imposed in slave societies throughout the New World except for one difference: in Demerara, an official known as a fiscal was responsible for ensuring that masters obeyed the regulations, and if they did not, enslaved Africans could appeal to him for compensation.[6]

Enslaved Africans were quick to learn that the regulations provided them cover from being overworked. This was especially the case by 1814, when the colony changed hands to the British. By this time, the British Empire had ended the slave trade in its colonies, which made slave-owning planters hyperinvested in warding off moral indictments from American abolitionists and export levies from other sugar-producing locales, such as India (Smith 1962). The colonial status of Demerara was particularly precarious. Demerara did not have a diversified internal cash-crop market; as a result, its economy was geared toward international sugar markets (Farley 1955). During the transition from Dutch to British rule, the value of planters' property fell, production costs increased, and planters could not compete with those in locales such as Cuba and Brazil, where the slave trade had yet to be abolished (Da Costa 1997, 48).

In turn, the work regimes of enslaved Africans become more regimented and specialized in Demerara. Male enslaved Africans, for instance, were preferred over their female counterparts for work in the fields. Plantation managers divided them into two or three gangs according to age and sex. Women were responsible for weeding sugar fields and carrying bags of *megasse* (leftover pulp) removed from sugar-refinery furnaces (58). Strenuous work for men was reserved for task gangs or subcontracts on estates for a specific job, usually for harvesting land or constructing, digging, and cleaning canals (Smith 1962).

The majority of complaints to fiscals were made by these task gangs, followed by women who worked the fields (Da Costa 1997; Smith 1962). They complained about not having proper tools for their work, excessive flogging, and being forced to work past sundown. Masters often threatened fiscals with violence if they tried to investigate or report violations. However, after the colony's 1823 slave rebellion, colonial state officials intervened on behalf of fiscals more directly. Fiscals were given the power to keep records of complaints, schedule public hearings, investigate plantation managers' allegations against enslaved Africans, and, in a few cases, recommend redress for enslaved Africans.

The regulations created a situation in which enslaved Africans were involved in a grievance procedure or were dealt with as people rather than as property or things (Da Costa 1997, 72). Saidiya Hartman (1997) has argued that such grievance procedures were part of a broader process through which White authorities tested the parameters of what postemancipation Black citizenship would entail. She has shown that grievance procedures—particularly those related to the rapes of enslaved African women in the antebellum American South—proved that liberal principles of racial equality were based in patriarchy. Through the court's objectification of physical injuries, gendered flesh became the site for adjudicating questions of Black citizenship.

In Demerara, the model for what constituted grievance for enslaved Africans was also shaped by patriarchy because most fiscal hearings related to irrigation and drainage infrastructures were filed by workers of the male-dominated task gangs. Enslaved Africans testified to not only their hardships but also the functioning of canals and small dams that planters overlooked in daily inspections. The fiscal hearings reaffirmed that the formation of flood knowledges was entangled in settler processes that created gendered and racialized hierarchies of expertise. Thus, while enslaved Africans viewed grievance procedures as an important tool for enacting reciprocal obligations—and albeit some semblance of compensation—plantation managers and planters simply viewed them as crucial to controlling the day-to-day operations of estates.

With slave emancipation ushered in throughout the British Empire in 1838, race continued to play a critical role in reaffirming how Guianese envisioned coastal settlement and knowledge exchange about flooding. British Guiana saw the introduction of indentured laborers from India, China, Portuguese Madeira, and the West Indian islands to work on plantations. Freedmen collectively purchased abandoned estates, contributing to the establishment of a chain of coastal settlements known as the village movement.[7] As O. Nigel Bolland (1981, 599) describes, "By 1842, some 15,000 former slaves had settled on 4,506 acres, 40,000 ex-slaves owned 17,000 acres in 9,797 freeholds in 1848, and by 1851 there were 11,152 smallholdings and 46,368 people lived in villages."[8] The village movement was significant because it allowed freedmen not only to purchase land but to establish a lending system among themselves to circumvent White institutions of banking and finance (Kwayana 1999). In response to this wave of Black resettlement, by the late nineteenth century, colonial state officials had decreased the price per acre of land to diversify the cash crop market and quell competition from freedmen in sugar cultivation. Meanwhile, the majority of indentured laborers worked and lived in freedmen's old estate barracks called *logies*.[9]

As Walter Rodney (1981) notes, freedmen and indentured laborers were different racial groups with competing labor commitments to the British Crown. Rodney's magnum opus, *A History of the Guyanese Working People, 1881–1905*, tracks in detail the disagreements between planters, freedmen, and indentured laborers over how irrigation and drainage infrastructures could be maintained. Every racial group dealt with flooding while struggling to make the colony profitable. Rodney recognizes the racial nuance in flood knowledge that supported empoldering and continued settlement of the coast. With each wet season, Rodney describes freedmen's and indentured laborers' loss of profits, thereby emphasizing that the flood knowledge they used to survive was decidedly horticultural in nature. Rice cultivation and the flooding of its grounds, for instance, took on distinct racial-ethnic hues among the freedmen who lived in the upper catchments of rivers, away from plantations, compared to those Indians and Chinese who lived in logies, a point later mined in scholarship on ethnobotany and slavery (Carney 2002). Flood knowledge, in Rodney's view, played a key role in shaping a multiracial agrarian sense of collective agency and purpose in coastal settlement.

Rodney's analysis of freedmen's and indentured laborers' overlapping experiences of discrimination and denied access to flood management resources is what makes his analysis of flooding so deeply concerned with an antiracist humanism. Yet his emphasis on settlement as tied to agricultural market activities underplays the racialized forms of knowledge exchange *across* professions that brought about a settler experience for non-Whites in the first place.[10] The dynamics among engineers, planters, and working people were never completely antagonistic; rather, they were often mediated by flood knowledges about such hazards as erosion and cracked dams (see chapters 3 and 5). If instead we also consider how the engineering sciences were racialized and supported by different social interests and perspectives on flooding, the problem of settler identity becomes animated by a variety of key historical debates beyond agricultural market development. In particular, infrastructural design and its relationship to shifts in weather and atmospheric conditions are important aspects to consider in analyses about race and coastal settlement in British Guiana.

Planters, for instance, were in a precarious position during the village movement, not only because freedmen were appropriating abandoned estates but because it was a period of severe drought. In the years leading up to slave emancipation, planters were already known in Georgetown for siphoning water from one another at a destructive rate (Rodway 2010). In response, engineers were recruited and hired to design the EDWC to link flood management with the potable-water needs of the city and the irrigation needs of planters (Kirke 1893). The situation was like no other, with engineers recording that these drought conditions persisted on and off for decades, culminating with a major El Niño in 1877–78.

Described by Mike Davis (2002) as a "late Victorian holocaust," the drought wreaked havoc across the world. In Algeria, vast tracks of grain harvest were lost and much of Morocco depopulated, while in India and China fifteen to twenty million people died of famine. The impacts were devastating in the Brazilian Nordeste, where the threat of famine contributed to the displacement and migration of two million people, the onset of smallpox epidemics, and death rates of more than four hundred thousand (Aceituno et al. 2009). In neighboring British Guiana, there were reports that colonial state officials successfully managed cholera and yellow fever epidemics while planning and constructing the EDWC (Rodway 2010).

Yet colonial state officials' commitments to the EDWC and related ordinances did not, in and of themselves, make postemancipation coastal settlements imaginable. Well into the late 1870s, planters were reluctant to entertain the idea of permanently settling time-expired indentured laborers, fearing that their small-landholdings like the freedmen villages would take away labor from established sugar estates. At the same time, many indentured laborers grew disenchanted with the prospect of staying in the colony because of low wages and the high cost of land development. By 1880, the number of Indians entitled to a free return passage grew to sixty thousand, which galvanized colonial state officials to ease immigration policy and implement land ordinances that facilitated settlement on productive and well-drained lands (Mangru 2012, 205). In lieu of paying for their return to India and losing a cheap labor pool, in 1882 colonial state officials passed Ordinance 9, which supported transport deeds to time-expired indentured laborers (207).

While the settlements of freedmen and indentured laborers were supported by colonial state officials, little to no plans were ever devised to resettle those Amerindians who remained on the coast (Sanders 1976). By the time of slave emancipation (circa 1834–38), the Dutch-inherited policy of giving presents to Amerindian militias had ceased. The colonial courts had deemed the policy as taking away needed resources from sugar estates. Without the incentive of gifts, planters became increasingly concerned about whether Amerindians would rebel. The Court of Policy and Combined Court responded in 1835 by replacing the presents policy with Ordinance 6, which on a regular basis provided both interior and coastal Amerindian populations with rations (e.g., salt fish and plantains) and allowances of 1,500 guilders (Menezes 2011, 87). Planters also put forth a proposal in 1844 to recruit Amerindians to work as laborers on estates in Demerara. But ultimately the Court of Policy deemed it a "chimera," asking, "What truth of science, what mystery of art has been carefully unfolded to him [Amerindians]?" (92). With the proposal for formal coastal settlements rejected, Amerindians took steps to further resettle inland, away from plantations. Similar to the other British settler colonies of the time—Nyasaland, South Zambezia, and Cape Colony—colonial state officials "adjudicated their responsibility for the natives to huge philanthropic corporations and institutions" and missionary settlements (92).

The tension between engineers' planning for the EDWC and the resettlement efforts of planters, freedmen, indentured laborers, and Amerindians suggests two things. First, Amerindian flood knowledges became marginal to coastal settlement with the end of the present policy and were replaced by other forms of flood knowledge about rivers, specifically large-scale damming. Second, engineers' employment patterns did not necessarily coincide with structural changes in property, labor, and immigration legislation ushered in with the village movement, indentured labor, or Amerindian resettlement in the interior. Thus, engineers increasingly treated flood management as a response not only to racial demographic changes but also to freedmen and indentured laborers recognizing themselves as settlers or as a class of citizens with rights to land not originally their own. They now had land that, either by choice or force, had different water and flood management needs in order to be productive. This nested dynamic of non-White settler identity further justified the professionalization of engineering as a scientific field in water supply rather than as what it had been—a subtrade dominated solely by White political interests.

In other words, freedmen, planters, and indentured laborers alike used slave emancipation to justify the continued settlement of the coast. The communal lots in freedmen villages and the indentured settlements near sugar estates became the metric for gauging the colony's future. But given that slave emancipation did not usher in equal access to irrigation and drainage infrastructures across all racial groups, freedmen and indentured laborers were compelled, more than ever, to monitor discriminatory water allocation and flood management practices. Freedmen working between rural villages and Georgetown were often employed in low-level positions as estate managers, although few were given the authority to develop water, sanitation, or land policies (De Barros 2003). Likewise, slave emancipation justified the idea that the engineering sciences were shaped by a paternalistic ethic for the improvement of non-Whites (Drayton 2000). Throughout the circum-Caribbean, this ethic emerged in the aftermath of not only flooding and drought but other environmental phenomena, especially hurricanes.

As Stuart Schwartz (2016, 134) notes, the 1831 hurricane in Barbados that killed one thousand enslaved Africans and cost over $1.6 million (Barbados dollars) in property damage contributed to planters' fears that emancipation would ruin their livelihoods. Newspapers reported that enslaved Africans were caught looting shops and that some of them were unwilling to help in the recovery effort. Others detailed the lectures planters gave in town squares in order to convince enslaved Africans to contribute to the disaster's recovery. As one witness explained, "'He [a planter] endeavored to impress on their minds that the uproar of the elements could not sever the tie that existed between them and their owners . . . and that on every occasion it is the interest of all to make one general effort for the preservation of property'" (136).

Slave emancipation had enormous consequences for how planters envisioned their abilities to protect property and the kind of racial political subjectivities freedmen needed in order to rebuild the colony. Christopher Church (2017) notes that, in Martinique, planters' concerns about freedmen's loyalty to France inspired public debates about a hurricane recovery effort in 1891. He summarizes the commentary of the populist French newspaper *Les Colonies*: "The ancestors of the Martiniquais were not Gauls but hardworking slaves who had rebuilt the island following major hurricanes in 1723, 1724, 1756,

1758, 1766, 1779, 1789 and 1788 by force. These slaves had become republicans themselves, despite lacking a Gallic ancestry, and would rebuild the island again, but not under duress. Now that slavery has been abolished . . . Martinique's laborers would work hard to recover, but like everyone else in France, they would do so for pay" (112). Martiniquais acknowledged that hurricane recovery would be faster after emancipation because Black people were no longer under duress. Thus, planters and freedmen viewed their capacities for settlement and rebuilding as a skill set all citizens could learn, no matter their race, simply because of their familiarity and cultural experiences with inclement weather.

Some planters went so far as to note that hyperintensive and fossil fuel–based agriculture practices contributed to the uneven development of the circum-Caribbean. For instance, planters in British Guiana in the early twentieth century shared the confidence that biofuels, including megasse, were the cheapest and least destructive way to run sugar mills. They believed that engineers would eventually patent furnaces for their commercial use that would rival the American steam engine (Abell 1897; Glennie 1966). If engineers were keen to use megasse to improve sugar yields, then they could also prove that they were good capitalists who undercut carbon economies in industrial America while enhancing the coastal settlement of the colony.

Irrigation and drainage infrastructures and these related innovations in engineering positioned settler colonialism as a tool of not only imperialism but global environmental change (Ghosh 2016). The effect of all of this is that Black freedoms were never historically only a political, moral, or legal claim but an environmental one as well. Dramatic droughts, El Niños, and shifts in weather patterns encouraged planters, colonial state officials, and engineers to invest in the EDWC and, in turn, support improvements in flood management and water supply. Yet such ecological events also demonstrated the historical contradictions between discourses of belonging and practices of settlement in the colony. Therefore, being a non-White settler played out as an ambiguous identity that was difficult to resolve, if not embody. On the one hand, as settlers, Afro-Guianese and Indo-Guianese became citizens with land whose productivity depended on the colonial state investing in centralized flood management. On the other, they became citizens who had to learn how to self-identify with the forms of expertise, land regulations, and infrastructure systems that once subjugated them and displaced Amerindians. This tension would become only more self-evident and difficult to overcome with colonial independence.

A Blueprint for Decolonization

In British Guiana, flood management did not emerge from a binary opposition between subaltern/local knowledge and hegemonic/Western technoscience. It required, instead, settler ambitions that overlapped with the desire to enact first empoldering and later large-scale damming. By the early twentieth century, large-scale damming and agricultural development that could extend from the coast and into the interior became an aspiration that solidified the objectives of British royal commissions and measured efforts to transition the colony into independence (Jagan 1997). It was a desire that traversed geographies of imperialism, as when, for instance, the British Crown in 1938 suggested that the colony open its hinterland on the Essequibo River to European war refugees as well as to Jews in Mandatory Palestine (Jewish Telegraph Agency 1938). Dubbed the *first* effort in history that attempted to resettle "large numbers of whites in the tropics," the plan was put to rest after health studies concluded, among other things, that the interior region's climate would be too harsh for White bodies (Holdridge 1939, 623–24; Sherman 1994).

The persistent belief among the British that settlement and race were but two sides of the same coin ushered in a mindset toward flood management preoccupied with nationalistic ends. The preindependence social reform agendas of the colony's major political parties offer a case in point. By the late 1940s, anticolonial nationalist movements had come onto the scene in the blood of labor riots and constitutional referenda for universal suffrage. In the early PPP campaign agenda (circa 1953), party leaders Jagan and Burnham threw their weight behind an ambitious two-pronged policy (Smith 1962). On the one hand, they sought international aid partnerships to construct more dams to support the EDWC and small-scale agriculture. On the other, they wanted to develop a program to finance jobs for Guianese in civil service and, in particular, across other agriculture-related government agencies that would service the colony's further settlement. But with the eventual PPP and PNC split, political leaders anticipated that the agenda to recruit a local civil service would become complicated or even stalled by apaan jaat.

By the time independence came in 1966, the national government had invested immense amounts of resources into producing reports that were solely focused on describing strategies to maintain a racially balanced field of labor and expertise that served the aims of national development. Take, for example, the way that Burnham conceived of race as an integral component for establishing a well-trained civil service. In April 1965 he wrote a letter to the International Commission of Jurists in Geneva, espousing what he believed was the importance of "racial balance" to the welfare of the country and its public sector labor force. He noted:

> My Government has recently been considering the question of racial imbalance in various fields of activity in British Guiana. Our concern has been to determine whether such imbalance as may exist in any particular field can be corrected and, if so, what is the shortest practicable period for such correction. In these deliberations, my Government has been deeply concerned with the need to remove from our society sources of racial disharmony and to promote the right of each individual, whatever his ethnic origin, to have an equal opportunity to play a meaningful part in the life of the community. (International Commission of Jurists 1965, 9)

Burnham's letter eventually became the introductory note to the report *Racial Problems in the Public Service*. He would learn, however, that while the Ministry of Agriculture had a majority Indo-Guyanese staff, the Ministry of Works and Hydraulics—the agency cited in the report as responsible for sea defense and roads—was more integrated, with a near-even split of Afro- and Indo-Guyanese represented, along with a few staff members who were of Mixed Race, Portuguese, Chinese, or Amerindian ancestry (83). A multiracial and national cohort of engineers was seemingly possible and already at the state's disposal.

But Burnham had either failed to articulate a coherent agenda or had very little to say about how flood knowledges were central to the nation's development. Throughout his tenure, he espoused a style of Afrocentric socialism and self-help agricultural programs that failed to coordinate with the work of these engineers (see chapter 3).[11] And as state resources and dreams of large-scale damming ran dry, so too did the aspirations of engineers and other public servants. As A. J. Strachan (1983) argues, most Guyanese who migrated during this period, across race and class lines, did so to earn job credentials, and few had the desire to renew their visas; but on their return to Guyana, they found no jobs and resources to sustain them.

With Burnham's death in 1985, large-scale damming and irrigation and drainage infrastructures were still not immediate priorities of the state. The PNC chose Desmond Hoyte as Burnham's successor to lead political and economic reforms. The Hoyte administration renegotiated the country's debt and ushered in structural adjustment programs that catered to the privatization of nonagricultural sectors in the forested interior region (Colchester

1997). The state invested millions of US dollars, partnering with Asian and Brazilian firms to open up the interior for a type of late twentieth-century frontier capitalism already unfolding in the neighboring Brazilian Amazon and Southeast Asia (Hogg 1993). The Hoyte administration even established the Iwokrama research and tourism center in an attempt to enact sustainable development through biodiversity conservation.

Meanwhile on the coast, Hoyte's structural adjustment programs involved an economic recovery program that created a vacuum in state spending on irrigation and drainage, particularly with regard to the maintenance of drainage canals in Georgetown (Pelling 1999). The drop in spending was also precipitated by global events during the 1980s, such as the low wheat and rice prices associated with the technologies of the green revolution (Carruthers, Rosegrant, and Seckler 1997; Marks and Ellis 2013). Despite these economic downturns, the Guyanese government was able to piece together a few research studies, particularly with the US Army Corps of Engineers, which sponsored a soil laboratory.

The financial downturn only reinforced the fact that since Burnham's time in office the government had failed to offer a clear plan for providing secure employment and a professional workplace that was not politically charged or overdetermined by apaan jaat. With ministries financially strapped and unable to provide lucrative salaries, many experienced engineers left their posts to work for established local private firms. For the most part, these private firms were successful at recruitment; the state provided tax incentives for business start-ups and engineers in the diaspora who wished to contribute to the country's transition (France 2005). Much of the nonstate sector of engineering came under the control of Indo-Guyanese elites, who further reaped the benefits of their historic dominance in the country's small-scale rice sector, which was never nationalized under the socialist government (Hintzen 1989).

By 1992, the Jagan-led PPP administration attempted to bridge the state's interests in both interior and coastal efforts at settlement. Jagan continued Hoyte's vision of sustainable development in the interior while cautiously reinvesting in sugar and rice. He did this by pledging a policy titled the National Environmental Action Plan. An attempt to map the forms of economic poverty that stood in the way of sustainable development, the plan was like many of the period: self-conscious but forward-looking. As Jagan noted, "Sometime ago it was mooted that development creates destruction of the environment but now it is recognized clearly that it is poverty which is endangering the environment" (quoted in Chandarpal n.d., 17). This was a striking statement, given that Jagan ascribed his presidential victory to ushering in the true aims of the PPP: to do away with apaan jaat and to bring about equality within a racially plural nation-state. Environmental consciousness and sustainable development, Jagan argued, were two ways to make this happen. But his administration offered few details about who would be responsible for his anti–apaan jaat environmentalism or how it could be put in sync with the lived realities of the majority of Guyanese who resided on the coast.

"Yuh Gettin' Tru?"

With the EDWC's neglect, flood management along the coast took a dramatic turn with liberalization. The Jagan administration looked to jump-start urban housing renewal programs to service the well over two hundred thousand people who lived in Georgetown and its surrounding suburbs. But the structural adjustment loans that financed these programs required ministries to streamline budgets by cutting staff, which in turn diminished ministry resources to monitor related infrastructure systems, such as roads and canals (Pelling 1998).[12] Moreover, given that Guyana had not experienced a disastrous flood since 1934, engineers remained content to invest in less capital-intensive resources such as marketing and seeds. The constraints of structural adjustment forced engineers to focus on irrigation and drainage maintenance in rural areas, thereby servicing a majority Indo-Guyanese population.

What was seemingly also at stake, in this moment of neoliberal structural adjustment, was that the state embarked on a mode of participatory governance. As in other contexts of liberalization and environmental management, participatory governance was the battleground for making technical information for state-sponsored projects more accessible to the public (Agrawal 2005). In Guyana, participation was bitterly contested around the formation of civic groups that worked with locally elected council members (as opposed to the national government) to develop reports about their flood management needs. What's more, the most populated area, Georgetown, was majority Afro-Guyanese, and the mayor's office was overwhelmingly represented by PNC officials. Thus, urban civic groups were perceived as enacting their own style of apaan jaat meant to counter that of the PPP's presidential rule through the Cheddi and Janet Jagan administration(s) (1992–99), the Jagdeo administrations (1999–2011), and the Donald Ramotar administration (2011–15). However, such resistance proved to have uneven results, given that the city council had relatively little control over how the national government sought international donors, such as the International Development Bank, to fund urban renewal programs (Pelling 1998).

In turn, rather than experiencing accessibility, civic groups have often been ignored by the national government, unless they cater to, or at least try to negotiate their needs around, the interests of whichever political party holds the presidential office. The Creolese phrase "Yuh gettin' tru?" is illustrative of this racialized participation-information-patronage dynamic. During my fieldwork, I heard state officials constantly pose the question to people waiting in the hallways of offices to attend state-sponsored workshops. State officials wanted to know if the person waiting knew the hosts of the workshops personally. "Yuh gettin' tru?" was followed by a smile and a short phone call to the host of the event—or an indefinite wait if you gave the wrong answer.

In an era of liberalization, when participation often materializes as a discourse about countering the racially discriminatory circulation of information, infrastructure systems have become important symbols of citizens' skepticism toward race-based or ethnic nationalisms. For instance, in urban India (Anand 2017) and South Africa (Von Schnitzler 2016), when public water and electricity networks fail to provide service, citizens fear that engineers and technocrats may be not only corrupt but arbitrarily biased in their planning activities. In turn, mismanaged infrastructure systems have become sites for public debate about the ways responsibility can be made quantifiable or more objective. As Wendy Brown (2003, 7) notes, "Even as liberal democracy converges with capitalist values . . . the formal distinction it establishes between moral and political principles on the one hand and the economic order on the other has also served as insulation against the ghastliness of life exhaustively ordered by the market and measured by market values." The "ghastliness of life" Brown describes is expressed through the austerity of neoliberal economic policies and the electorate or national body politic itself. In Guyana's case, by the early 2000s, third parties had a competitive influence on apaan jaat by having an approach based less in strategies of power sharing than in promoting intraracial party platforms that cater to the advancement of public services.

Many Guyanese I know, including engineers, resent that the state's investments in irrigation and drainage infrastructures have devolved to and become associated with apaan jaat. More often than not, they blame apaan jaat for the Ministry of Agriculture's poor allocation of economic and human resources for flood management. The effect has been a charged racial and political discourse about flooding that produces ethnic distinctions in drainage, which pivot on a flooding reality of urban Afro-Guyanese and a flooding reality of rural Indo-Guyanese. In turn, flooding has been treated by most Guyanese I know as a lingering settler colonial process that continues to yoke individual rights—particularly land—to contested claims of belonging.

Tracing the entangled histories of race and settler identities, we run up against what Alondra Nelson (2002) has recognized as the persistent forms of racism that mark images, tropes, and discourses of technological progress. On the digital divide between Black and White Americans, Nelson observes: "In these politics of the future, supposedly novel paradigms for understanding technology smack of old racial ideologies. In each scenario, racial identity, and blackness in particular, is the anti-avatar of digital life . . . Blackness gets connected as always oppositional to technologically driven chronicles of progress" (2). I take seriously Nelson's diagnosis that anti-Black racism can feed desires for technological progress. But I would also add that, in light of climate change, "the politics of the future" takes on an added significance across racial divides. Unprecedented storms, such as those that contributed to the 2005 disaster, have brought to the surface that settler colonialism not only proves to be unsustainable, because of its massive technological interventions and investment; it also has had climatic effects across national territories and borders.

Climate adaptation, then, circulates as a metaphor about how the state can transform society toward new logics of belonging and governance less invested in race. In Guyana, this is not to say that simply drawing inspiration from the Arawakan original mound grid is the solution to the country's flood woes. The mound grid was not designed with the intention to engage or respond to race as an organizing principle of settlement. As empoldering and large-scale damming colonized the coast and produced a racialized regime of flood knowledges, so too did the contours of rivers and soils shift into something new. The outcome of this environmental transformation has been the dominance of apaan jaat in influencing contemporary flood management. But it is also worth asking how all of this happened and why. And in answering this question, it is important to remember that apaan jaat is the product of both racial political power and the engineering sciences. Engineers, in other words, are not only settlers but also casualties of apaan jaat. They have been Guyana's primary players responsible for correcting and breaking with the flooding woes of the past.

3

ENGINEERING, ARCHIVES, AND EXPERTS

In 2005, engineering consultants sponsored by the World Bank and the UN created a diagram that charted the route of the EDWC's floodwaters (see figure 3.1). As water drained from the EDWC it traveled past the conservancy dam, the crown dam (also known as a supporting dam), an outer embankment, adjacent drainage channels, roads, residential areas, the seawall, and eventually into the Atlantic Ocean. However, because of the extreme rainfall, some of the floodwaters never traveled this route and instead spilled onto surrounding land. As engineers observed, the overtopping can contribute not only to flooding but also to sections of the Conservancy Dam eroding and weakening over time, or "pipping" (Mott McDonald 2005).

The relationship between overtopping and erosion is not self-evident; a number of postdisaster field observations were required to determine it. As the diagram author notes, "[There are] no soil investigations or recent data available to support a detailed assessment of the EDWC" (Joint UNEP/OCHA 2005, 7). The EDWC's care, in other words, is dependent on an archive of documents that describe soils and rainfall, among other things. In the broadest

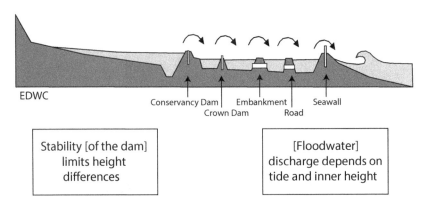

FIGURE 3.1. Cross section of the EDWC and the path of its floodwaters in 2005. Courtesy of the Government of Guyana and the Economic Commission for Latin America and the Caribbean (ECLAC).

sense, engineers' professional ethics of archiving is built on the expectation that the state will provide resources, technologies, and equipment that will aid their data collection (see also Mullenite 2020). This expectation introduces a number of difficulties about the way engineers come to know the EDWC as an infrastructure of both coastal settlement and shifting racial political orders, beginning with slavery through contemporary formations of apaan jaat. I saw how these difficulties unfolded among state-sponsored and private sector engineers while they were in the field. They faced the demands of coordinating construction and a monitoring program for the EDWC, on the one hand, and of creating designs and hydraulic models to enhance its internal drainage system, on the other. The difficulties of their fieldwork in these instances were matched only by the struggle to advance flood knowledge through a state apparatus intent on making itself more conscious of climate change.

Reading back into the archival records of the EDWC is one way to address how and if such awareness can materialize. Engineers intend to use archival records of the EDWC in ways that position them as unbiased experts dedicated to maintaining the irrigation and drainage grid. Thus, the crucial question animating the content of the records is how engineers identify key moments in history that shape their expertise in dam design. Many of these moments center on race and its shifting importance to the state's mobilization of institutions, data sets, people, natures, and infrastructures for flood management.

Their efforts remind us that a concept of race in climate adaptation is not synonymous with a static configuration of White domination/Black subjugation/

Asian exploitation/Indigenous removal. Rather, it involves a complex process of racialized encounter and (dis)engagement. Engineers' commitment to archiving is a critical dimension of this process and, by extension, so are settler colonial discourses about race. Archives, in other words, are social artifacts of professional life and technoscience (Bowker 2005; Stoler 2010; Trouillot 2004). They provide a perspective on who counts as expert in climate adaptation while bringing to light historic patterns of racialization in the engineering profession. In this way, the expectation to archive carries with it particular assumptions about humanism, secular time, and fraternity. Understanding engineers' uneven but nonetheless enduring engagements with archives helps clarify why climate adaptation can have transformative meaning across racial divides and geographies.

Enumeration

In 1882, members of the Royal Agricultural and Commercial Society of British Guiana gathered in Georgetown to choose a name for their journal. Initially, several members objected to calling the journal by the society's name, because it was an "inconvenient mouthful" that did not express the true intentions of its members (Thurn 1882, 1). While many were of the colony's agricultural elite, few members interpreted the society's mission as focused solely on agriculture and commerce. They recognized themselves as a body of men gifted with diverse technical specialties and a love for literature and the arts. They conceived of the journal as a way to "store up, as fast as time and opportunity allow, so much of the half or wholly forgotten collected facts as may yet be rescued" about the colony (2). After much debate, they decided to call the journal *Timehri*, a Carib word meaning *rock inscriptions* or *petroglyphs*.

The journal's editor, E. F. Im Thurn, a well-known botanist, colonial administrator, and curator of the colony's natural history museum, viewed the journal's naming as an opportunity. He explained that because *timehri* is not a Latin or Greek word, authors would have the latitude to "trace the history of scientific origins" in their articles (Thurn 1882, 5). Thurn noted in the journal's inaugural "Editorial Prologue" that articles would complement the colony's tradition of scientific enterprises paved by the Schomburgk brothers, Carl Appun, and Darwin's colleague Alfred Russel Wallace earlier in the century. By all accounts an experiment in science, *Timehri* proved to be a vital medium for technical men who wished to ponder the past while shaping the direction of the colony's future.

One of these technical men was Henry Kirke, a former sheriff of Demerara. In his 1893 article "The Early Years of the Lamaha Canal," Kirke was convinced that the colony had the potential to rise from utter obscurity and transform into a crown jewel. Life in the colony at the time was brutal. Plagued by a series of water famines (droughts) and competition from beet sugar on the world market, there was little food and land to go around in Demerara (Bellairs 1892). The situation was so dire that even planters, including the legendary Quintin Hogg, chairman of the North British and Mercantile Insurance Company, were unable to secure loans from the colonial legislature for irrigation water. In response, many took "private action which proved prejudicial to small cultivations and house owners" (Rodney 1981, 18). The ad hoc and discriminatory management of water led to a situation that Kirke called unscientific. "No doubt for years," he contended, "we [planters] were working on false data or rather false premises" about the colony's water supply (Kirke 1893, 285).

Kirke noted, however, that this "false data" did not just appear out of thin air; it had been apparent to planters decades before the food shortages, droughts, and the colony's economic decline. He details how in the late 1820s the colony's water supply went through a rapid transformation. The colonial governor, after the death of a prominent plantation owner named Lacey, sold off an unprecedented 244 lots to shopkeepers (Rodway 1997). But with the expansion of Georgetown, wells dried up and planters started a black market for the purchase of trenches. Municipal authorities held numerous meetings with planters to settle disputes over trenches and to implement a plan to bring water to town. Ten of the colony's largest estate owners convened with the city's board of police to discuss the digging of a canal. The technical dimensions of the canal were designed according to what Kirke (1893, 288) called an "idea of fairness," providing planters a market arrangement for irrigation water while also expecting them to work collectively to sponsor and manage the canal. It would be roughly five miles (8,000 meters) long, fifteen feet (4.5 meters) deep, and six feet wide (1.8 meters) and would be cut in such a way that it could flow uninterrupted into the Lamaha Creek.

These dimensions were suitable for the number of enslaved Africans each planter owned and the expected compensation the planter would receive from the governor and Court of Policy for the labor of enslaved Africans. Digging the canal was an arduous task that involved enslaved Africans clearing forests, leveling embankments, and calculating the distance between rivers. They had to complete this work in the months between the biannual wet seasons. In addition to the threat of flooding, the head of the Lamaha Creek had the tendency to silt up when it rained. Nonetheless, by 1833 they prevailed, and the Lamaha Canal was completed. Planters responded by establishing the Lamaha committee to manage water between the ten estates and Georgetown. In turn, the colonial governor placed a "poll tax of f3 [three guilders] a head on the negro slaves of the estates" (Kirke 1893, 292).

But hindsight is not always 20/20. The poll tax proved futile in deterring exploitative planters and regulating the city's water supply. Perhaps the changing racial demographics of the colony had an influence as well. Slave emancipation and the importation of indentured laborers brought about wage hikes in agricultural labor (Adamson 1973). Given these wage hikes, planters seemingly had few financial resources or incentives to reinvest in water, irrigation, and drainage with their individual or personal funds (Rodney 1981). Yellow fever outbreaks and tenement fires in rapidly expanding Georgetown also put an unanticipated strain on the Lamaha Canal (De Barros 2003). Similar to other water improvement projects in the British Empire at the time, the Lamaha Canal had multiple purposes and uneven effects. Water improvement projects justified Britain's economic expansion while reterritorializing dependencies between colonizer and colonized, between design and planning, and between nature and technology, all in the name of progress (Scott 1999). Nonetheless, as Kirke notes, the canal was dug with false premises in mind.

"So much mortality," Kirke (1893, 294) said, referring to a letter written to the Lamaha committee by one of the colony's medical examiners, Dr. Blair. Throughout the colony, canal diggers, particularly those who migrated from Portuguese Azores and Madeira, were falling ill of intermittent fever (malaria) in record numbers. Blair suggested that by "placing newly arrived Portuguese on the pegass land of the [Lamaha] Canal, [he could] experiment as to whether peat land is a preventive against intermittent fever" (294). He had high hopes. But the experiment never materialized after the Lamaha committee's chairman ridiculed him and discouraged him from attending future meetings. Other members accused him of conflating medical remedies with soil sampling and explained that they had more pressing issues to attend to, such as hiring a canal overseer.

But attention to why, rather than how, Dr. Blair wanted to collect data about malaria reveals that his proposal may not have been such a technical folly. Planters were concerned about droughts and their impacts on how long and where people could labor rather than solely the sheer statistics they had about water. With the pegasse experiment, Dr. Blair wanted to discern whether the number of Portuguese indentured laborers needed to dig a canal was dependent on the location of a project site and whether their average death rates were affected by the site. In an era when numbers—as much as economy—were commonly regarded as a technology for statecraft, minor sciences (those other than human medicine) became oriented toward statistics (Poovey 1998). Other doctors writing for *Timehri* also recognized the importance of statistics to the colony's ballooning population and shifting racial demographics:

> Classes of persons now discuss statistics and other dry topics, with a freedom which was quite unknown to the same class of persons half a century ago. Thus we find the question of population . . . its prospects, resources . . . are all familiar topics for enlarging upon by ordinary journals and such literature as seeks general popularity amongst the class which makes up the majority of the people; whilst the people no longer look upon the statist as a scientific creature, whose mania consists of the compilation of figures . . . and the deduction therefrom of theories tending to the consternation if not confusion of the uninitiated. (Macnamara 1894, 78)

For the Lamaha committee, the question of racial population was a central concern for monitoring outbreaks of malaria among indentured laborers and the canal's water levels. In particular, Dr. Blair was no different from planters who stepped outside of their designated slots of expertise—as entrepreneurs, seeking their fortunes in engineering (a minor science), for which they had very little training but plenty of tacit knowledge. Pegasse brought to light the potential design troubles and labor shortages planters would face developing the colony's water supply. It challenged their political imaginaries of which racial populations counted as productive laborers and what possible futures might become thinkable through a more sustained engagement with engineering design.

"Dream Land"

The Lamaha committee's decision not to go forward with the pegasse experiments makes evident the importance of data collection to the planning of irrigation and drainage infrastructures. Undeterred, the committee expanded its enterprise when it officially wrote to the governor and Crown in the 1870s to request permission to build a dam to store and manage water allocation at the head of the Lamaha Canal. The colonial governor hired William Russell, an emigrant from Glasgow who was a planter and accredited engineer, to advise the committee (Bache 1889).

In his *Timehri* writings, Kirke (1893, 286) offers a hagiographic treatment of Russell. "A man not daunted by challenges," Russell conquered swamps, sand reefs, and a "bottomless morass of pegasse" to complete a survey of the Lamaha Creek's basin. According to Kirke, Russell's survey was reliable. He traveled into the "back of the basin," unlike past engineers and colonial state officials who made it only to the basin's swampy edges because they were either injured walking or lost their equipment in its pegasse (286). During the expedition, Russell observed that the creek's water traveled northward and drained into the Mahaica River and not the Demerara River, as surveyors previously thought.

Similar to the traverse surveys undertaken by the Schomburgk brothers in search of El Dorado on the British Guiana–Venezuela frontier, Russell's surveying depended on landmarks (e.g., trees, roads, petroglyphs) to identify the spatial boundaries of rivers (Burnett 2000). Once he completed the survey, Russell wanted to figure out how to redirect the flow of water in the basin to create a dam at the head of the Lamaha Canal. He was obliged not only to represent clear, stable, and visible points of the Lamaha Creek but to physically constrain it as well. The best landmark had multiple associations: historical, aesthetic, ecological, hydrological, political, and geographical. In his 1882 *Timehri* article "Farming and Irrigation," Russell bemoaned that the colony had too few landmarks to reference. The early settlers, Dutchmen (circa 1595 to 1814), left no important engineering artifacts, at least on the riverscape, and so from his perspective did not contribute to the colony's collective engineering memory in a significant way. He declares that they created canals that functioned

> simply as highways for opening up sections of the colony, affording both navigation and drainage. But none of these works can be described as *conserving* fresh water. . . . Further, no one now living can give any account of this work or when it was done. . . . I am not astonished to find so few marks of *water conservation* in the Dutch time, because, as a nation, they have been more famed for keeping off water than for conserving it; and in the Holland of to-day no large works are to be found for impounding water for Guiana [Dutch Surinam], with its two wet and two dry seasons, said to have been more regular in the past than at the present day, it is not to be wondered that more was not done to provide against droughts. (Russell 1882, 88; emphasis added)

Russell perceived the coast as a place that was devoid of the living memory of human engineering or that it had an absence of ruins.[1] He feared that all his efforts "tapping upper rivers and digging canals the wrong way" would "relegate the [colony's] water supply to a dream land" (89). Demoralized, he found inspiration in a local newspaper article that described British engineers managing sudd (swamp) vegetation on the Nile River (see, for example, Barnes 2014). Across the Atlantic, engineers contended with "a curious little cabbage-like aquatic plant" that took root on fertile embankments (Russell 1882, 94). The plants clogged the Nile's arteries, in some areas creating small islands of forests. Instead of digging canals based on the Nile's current, engineers cut channels where these plants took root and where they could chop away enough vegetation to build up dams. The only risk with such work was that hippopotamuses feeding on embankments tended to get crushed by the mass of water that rushed down from the upper reaches of newly weeded channels. Russell noted that British Guiana had not hippopotami but anacondas to consider, and so he insisted that "in the same way a little attention in directing the vegetable aquatic growth . . . water may be guided at discretion" from the Lamaha Creek into a dam (95).

Russell called this technique "beavering dams" (97–98). Beavering required laborers to "[assort] saplings of bush and grass in a cradle or frame work of spars driven into the ground in the shape of an X, into the v part of which the saplings, etc., are placed until a mass about two feet thick is formed" (97). The laborers filled the fascine structures with fine grasses, debris, and pegasse and secured the fallen trees on embankments. Over time they let the embankment's area fill with water and then constructed an earthen wall within it to create a dam. Russell hired laborers to replicate this work at the head of the Lamaha Creek. He called the combined dam structure and body of water the East Demerara Water Conservancy (EDWC). When completed in 1880, it spanned one hundred square miles (160,934 square meters), from the Mahaica River to the east bank of the Demerara River (Mott McDonald 2005). According to Russell's surveys, the EDWC's elevation was slightly above that of the Lamaha Creek, and so water was drained by gravity into the channels of the Lamaha Canal. Given that the EDWC was constructed by "hand labour," there was "probably little selection of the best soil" and its soils had "minimal compaction" (5). Nonetheless, Russell hoped that the EDWC would provide not only a steady water supply for the colony but also flood management.

FIGURE 3.2. A bust of William Russell in Georgetown, Guyana. According to Russell's obituary, "The government of the colony has voted a large sum of money towards the erection of a statue in his memory, the first instance of record of such a testimonial to the worth of any public man in British Guiana" (Bache 1889, 339).

Dams in the Diaspora

Given that the EDWC's dam foundation was composed of an abundance of vegetation and pegasse but little clay, Russell's design efforts did not entirely reflect the British standards for what was called embankment damming. By the 1870s, British engineers developed a method for embankment dam construction that involved using puddle clay (wet mounds of clay) for lining structures dug on porous grounds. Construction procedures for embankment dams required retrieving clay from another location and bringing it to the embankment to "be placed in layers fifteen to twenty cm [centimeters] thick, watered and allowed to soak overnight, or for twenty-four hours, and then trodden, cross-cut and heeled in [compressed by the passage of cart or horse]" (Skempton 1989, 18). Puddle clay was intended to provide an added layer of protection for embankment dams against wear and erosion over time. By 1865, over sixty embankment dams with this design were in use and reported as successful across England, although some experienced leakage around their culverts and outlets. As this dam design became more popular, its height was increased and engineers began to rely on a mix of soils—for example, stones and shale—to strengthen embankments and walls. As one of the leading engineers of this design explained, "'The most clayey and earthy part of the stuff from the excavations is to be used for the heart of the embankment (adjacent to the core) and the core stony, gravelly or sandy portion is to be used in forming the slopes'" (21).

Using puddle clay proved a cost-effective method for embankment dams, compared to gravitation schemes (dams with concrete structures), which were being dug at a similar rate across Britain and in its Hong Kong and Colombo colonies in the late nineteenth century (Broich 2007). By all accounts British Guiana's pegassy terrain did not easily assimilate to embankment damming. Part of the work of damming was simply to make do with the environment at hand (Mukerji 2015). But Russell also confronted the complications that arise when hand labor is not supported or rewarded with equipment, time, and compensation. The long-term work of engineers such as Russell stationed in Crown colonies involved a tedious process of organizing staff, loans, and supplies for projects (Anderson 2011). R. A. Buchanan (1986) estimates that in 1850 there were roughly one thousand British engineers in the diaspora and that by 1914 their numbers increased to over forty thousand.

There was, in other words, no bureaucratic reason for Russell to question his design approach. And in the New World context of the Guianas, where embankment dams were the first large-scale infrastructures for permanent coastal settlement and flood management, it was not always clear to Russell how the floodplain would respond to the EDWC's presence. The EDWC's operations, in turn, were dependent as much on its design as on how water was being moved downstream into canals on landholdings.

With the aid of surveyors, freedmen developed communal villages with trenches that connected multiple plots. They divided landholdings into strips running north to south (Kwayana 1999). Each shareholder within a cooperative village held land that extended in strips between the sand reefs and the ocean and a southern boundary with the village. This layout caused confusion, however, because not every plot was directly linked to a trench, and irrigation water could be supplied only through drains that "cut over" other shareholders' plots (23–32). These arrangements made flooding a worry even outside of the wet season. To avoid flooding, the irrigation and drainage grid was under constant modification, which meant that the activities related to the EDWC planning, for all intents and purposes, were a constant annoyance in the everyday lives of freedmen, planters, and indentured laborers.

In short, embankment damming and village-level irrigation and drainage were entangled knowledge practices that over time became mutually dependent on one another. Even in professional engineering discourses of the period, engineers viewed embankment dam design as creating insecurities about competence or the exceptionalism of White people in the engineering sciences. Just as fast as colonial state officials could impose a hefty poll tax on Afro-Guianese and Indo-Guianese land, a mud bank, unruly tide, or unexpected downpour could make Russell's investments in the EDWC null. Some of Russell's harshest critics complained at length:

> On 2 March 1882, a public meeting on flood crisis was held at Geneva school in Canal No. 1. It was attended by a large number of residents, including Indian peasants who had begun to acquire lots in the district after their indentureship. . . . William Russell had told the legislature that the Canals Polder should be drained and the cost met by the peasants of the district, rather than being burden on the general taxpayers. Harman [a chairman and small landowning White planter] commented ironically, "How kind of Mr. Russell to protect the general taxpayers. How about the Best Groyne and the hundreds of thousands of dollars that had been fooled away behind the East Coast?" "But," Harman continued, "that had been done for the rich sugar estate proprietors and that made all the difference." (Rodney 1981, 17)

"The hundreds of thousands of dollars that had been fooled away" was in reference to the EDWC. Other engineers at the time, such as Herman, drew a sharp distinction between Russell's technical expertise in embankment damming and his ability to be a persuasive legislator (see also Rodway 2010). When not surveying the EDWC, much of Russell's time included organizing political campaigns bolstering propaganda for Indian indentured contract labor (Rodney 1981, 180). Russell's dual expert identities—as engineer and as anti-Creole (Black) labor lobbyist—did not always align, nor did they have to for him to move forward with the EDWC. He was well aware that because the Dutch did not build dams, the EDWC appeared to many as a risky investment.

In their *Timehri* articles on the EDWC planning, Russell and his colleagues voiced a not-yet-realized aspiration to transform a world of description and inscription into prediction. The racially discriminatory poll taxes colonial state officials imposed on Afro-Guianese and Indo-Guianese landowners facilitated engineers' thinking with naturalistic metaphors to justify embankment damming. British Guiana's settlers were like beavers: their landmarks and homes had to be managed in light of meteorological events—droughts and floods—over which they had very little control. Indeed, the metaphor of beavering as technology held sway well beyond the engineering sciences in British Guiana and British-occupied Egypt. Lewis Henry Morgan's (1886, viii) contemporaneous ethnozoological studies of beavers and railroad expansion in the American West argued that "the preserving labors of the beaver were suggestive of human industry." In this sense, the EDWC revealed the imperfect task of reconciling human memory of coastal settlement between the colonizer and the colonized with pegasse's deep history.

Russell was also comfortable admitting that the EDWC and the broader irrigation and drainage grid had complications, if not inherent problems, because it was dug from pegasse.[2] At the same time, his work on the ground surveying was shaped by problems of data collection, record keeping, and translation. Unconsciously, perhaps, Russell granted the possibility that not all forms of data about embankment damming could be similarly recorded and transmitted without the fear of finding a new problem with the EDWC. It is precisely to this conjuncture, where design techniques meet modes of prediction, that I now turn.

Data Architecture

The very definition of an embankment dam already assumes a complex relationship between space and time, bridging the dispersed waterways of an irrigation and drainage grid with an obsessive interest in predicting water supply. In further adjoining control with enumeration, embankment damming aspires to manage water across temporal scales, particularly during annual wet seasons, when dams replenish their water supplies. For engineers, these rather abstract ideas of enumeration consolidate around a very straightforward question: What constitutes a flood?

Early proponents of embankment damming believed that its slope was its most important factor (Skempton 1989). But in turn-of-the-twentieth-century British engineering journals, many began to argue that other factors had an influence on water supply. It was believed that rainfall was the "origin of all water supply" and that its amount could be recorded with simple technologies such as rain gauges (Robertson 1903, 186).[3] But would rainfall levels above the average of one year, or of a number of previous years, constitute a flood? How did rainfall affect rivers adjacent to embankment dams? And how long was it reasonable to attribute this average to an embankment dam's water supply? By relating water supply to rainfall count, engineers articulated a belief that both dams (technology) and rivers (nature) were equivalent forms of infrastructure in flood management.

For a design approach so preoccupied with problems of response time and the description of floods, it is of little surprise that issues of space and time would be central to engineers' ideas about embankment damming. What is somewhat more surprising is how these ideas were shaped by engineers' organization of data sets. Rainfall data for engineers became what historian of science Orit Halpern (2015, 108–10) calls "material for storage" or data that makes explicit the complex assemblages of infrastructures, calculative technologies, practices, capital, and machines required for design. If design for embankment damming had always been about preserving its structure to stop erosion, with rainfall data engineers could now anticipate the dam's peak or base water supply.

Good design involved engineers assessing how an embankment dam's structure was affected by rainfall in real time versus by month, season, year, or decade. For his part, Russell mounted rain gauges in the EDWC and compared their outputs to the rain gauges at the Georgetown Botanical Gardens' agricultural laboratories (Wolstenholme 1953). Engineers' focus on the particularities of rainfall data required that they become familiar with reading rain gauges and learning, by experience, the best places to mount them, be it in rivers or within the dam itself (Robertson 1903). They were trained in being both producers and consumers of data: capable of discerning patterns in water supply by collating rainfall data into multiple data sets. Within this framework, water accumulation and its distribution are the goals driving embankment damming.

The EDWC remained engineers' crowning achievement into the early twentieth century. But in January 1934 the EDWC's dam was for the first time compromised by flooding from both a rainstorm and high tide. Heavier-than-average rainfall and abnormally strong winds led to simultaneous flooding in Georgetown, surrounding East Coast villages, and the upper reaches of the mining camps in the colony's interior region (A Sufferer 1934). With many ground provisions and rice fields inundated, food shortages occurred, evacuations were mandated, and a corps of administrators and militia rounded up cattle and disposed of carcasses to stop the spread of disease. Rural residents reported that flooding intensified when sections of the EDWC's dam were breached, causing thirty-foot cracks along its embankment. Estates and villages organized labor gangs to raise sections of the EDWC's embankment dam's walls and plug breaches with fallen trees. Nonetheless, rural residents waded through water for weeks, lived "through a situation fraught with terror," and inhabited a place inundated like "waterfalls" (A Sufferer 1934).

The governor appointed a flood investigations committee to assess damage to the EDWC's embankment dam and its adjacent waterway, the Lamaha Creek. Parting with Russell's design approach of beavering, the committee underscored the obvious: "It is abundantly clear that this Creek into which all surplus water flows is not capable, in times of excessive rainfall, of giving sufficient relief owing to the encroachment of bush [forests and pegasse] on either side of the Creek and considerable silting at the mouth where a bar has built up. It is considered essential, in order to avoid a repetition of the damage which recently occurred, that an additional relief canal be constructed leading direct to the sea" (Second Legislative Council 1934, 3). Within weeks of the investigation, engineers created plans to heighten the EDWC's embankment dam's walls and to build the storm relief canal.

The head engineer on the commission noted, "It is evident that the practice of cultivating dams is a *contradictory factor.* . . . This practice [heightening the dam's walls] not only lowers the [dam's foundation] but loosens the top layer of soil and allows water readily to percolate through and thus destroy their efficiency" (7; emphasis added). While the head engineer hoped that the storm relief canal would provide a means to quickly release floodwaters, he still recognized that the EDWC was structurally insecure. In addition to the storm relief canal, the head engineer suggested that the EDWC should be expanded and, if funds were available, more embankment dams built to support it (9).

The 1934 flood investigations committee and Russell viewed the EDWC's dam differently. First, the committee realized that heightening the EDWC's embankment dam's walls with more pegasse was not the best possible solution for repair. Second, the committee narrated the EDWC's past in a nonlinear progression. Excessive rainfall created the possibility for repeated disaster, but engineers' efforts to modify the EDWC were also in this respect a never-ending task. For the committee, past disasters were not events that ceased to exist with the formulation of new dam designs. Rainfall counts were data that helped engineers retain a memory of the EDWC's past structural failures and their capacity to haunt present and future design efforts.

The plans for a storm relief canal also proved to be amenable to experts other than engineers on the committee, including the politician E. A. Lukhoo, founder of the British Guiana East Indian Association. Lukhoo argued that with the construction of a canal, the governor could establish more settlements for time-expired indentured laborers near the EDWC (Second Legislative Council 1934; see also British Guiana Constitutional Commission 1954). At the same time, he noted the dismal reality that even with fortified lands they would run into debt paying for the maintenance of the canal and associated pumps.

Lukhoo argued, "If you sell your lands several times over again you would still not be able to meet these obligations" (A Sufferer 1934). Lukhoo was seemingly invested in securing the long-term interests of Indo-Guianese as settlers, but he recognized that this could not be achieved simply through better embankment damming but rather through broader social reforms.

The 1934 flood investigations committee and Lukhoo's critique of it might be understood as anticipating the political crises and reform movements that were slowly emerging in the wider British West Indies at the time. A series of labor protests, riots, strikes, and looting swept through Trinidad, Jamaica, Saint Vincent, British Guiana, British Honduras, and Barbados from 1934 to 1938. Working and living conditions for the poor had become deplorable across the British West Indies, sparking criticism from Black and Indian Nationalist leaders abroad about the lack of social reforms Britain had enacted since the end of slavery (Fraser 1996). A committee chaired by Walter Edward Guinness, First Baron Moyne, was appointed to investigate these events (West Indies Royal Commission 2011). In preparation, the West Indies Development and Welfare Organisation and research councils were established to fund academics from the British metropole and the West Indies to complete social science studies, specifically about the labor disturbances (Bush 2013).

Over the course of fifteen months, the West Indies Royal Commission held numerous public forums and completed 370 interviews. The final report concluded that West Indian economic development was being blocked by the supposed moral and cultural failings of the West Indian family unit—particularly households headed by single Black mothers. These conclusions, steeped in European middle-class worldviews about respectability and social reproduction, also assumed that material betterment was conditioned by West Indians themselves (Austin-Boos 1997). In its quest to uncover a West Indian understanding of political personhood, *The Moyne Report* reduced the complex demand for social reforms to the economic agency of the individual.

The West Indian envoys representing the commission included men from a variety of political, class, and racial-ethnic backgrounds. Other than being of West Indian ancestry, the characteristic that drew them together was the "command, however rudimentary, of the language and culture of Imperial Power" (Guerre 1971, 154). They argued that the colonial office, "once an exceedingly philanthropic institution" that oversaw the abolition of slavery, "had yielded to the idea of pecuniary profit and colonial exploitation" (136). Playing the long game for a referendum on independence, envoys openly debated whether a federal body should administer free trade between the colonies and agricultural marketing organizations (West Indies Royal Commission 2011, 256–60).

Historians widely herald the West Indies Royal Commission as a turning point in the further integration of a cohort of local Black and Coloured technocrats into colonial state bureaucracies throughout the British West Indies (Beckford and Levitt 2012; Crichlow 2005).[4] In other words, the West Indies Royal Commission was a first step in laying out an agenda for what could be described as "applied" postcolonial technoscience with an emphasis on the agricultural sectors and some on tourism and mineral extraction. With independence, local political elites and technocrats would become responsible for overseeing social reforms, particularly in land settlement. Yet *The Moyne Report*'s recommendations, in some instances, did not take into account the suggestions of those engineers already working in the colonies. The commission might have taken great steps to create opportunities for professional mobility across race, class, and political affiliation. But the report was ambivalent about the ways to improve, or at least better support, engineering sciences in the colonies.

Take the 1934 flood investigations committee's recommendations for the EDWC's storm relief canal, which was completely bypassed by the Moyne envoys. They proposed that engineers in British Guiana halt EDWC land settlement schemes until more extensive soil and river surveys were completed. The report summarized, "The British Guiana system does not involve one great outfall like the Fens of Eastern England, the problem of silting at the various small outfalls, with comparatively small discharge and low silt-removing power, is an extremely serious one" (West Indies Royal Commission 2011, 307). The Moyne envoys' prognosis was grim. Either the cost of drainage would "be undertaken as an irrecoverable Colonial charge" or royal engineers would have to be permanently stationed on Guiana's coast to manage flooding, even after independence (307–8). Taking the Moyne conclusions to heart, engineers saw no immediate need to move ahead with dam constructions.

They would wait another decade until a royal inquiry into riots and the shooting of a laborer at the Enmore sugar estate in 1948 provided a rationale for land reforms and thus for more damming. The colony's consulting engineer, A. H. Hutchinson, and his team completed the Boeraserie Conservancy along the Essequibo River in 1949 and then turned their sights to completing soil and river surveys along the Mahaica, Mahaicony, and Abary Rivers as advised in *The Moyne Report*. Along these rivers, Hutchinson planned to expand the EDWC's network of canals with the agriculture works project, the Mahaica-Mahaicony-Abary (MMA) Scheme (Spencer 1950). Relying on an approach called river-basin damming, the MMA Scheme was planned to include an interconnected system of dams along each of the three rivers. The dams were to "spread across the rivers, to join the land on the higher land on both sides [of the dams] and thus form a shallow reservoir" (Clark 1953, 202). In addition, the dams would be designed to overlap with the irrigation and drainage grid of an existing small rice estate, which was started in 1942 and covered eleven thousand empoldered (and diked) acres, of which four thousand were cultivated (Hutchinson 1950).

This river-basin perspective on embankment damming put the 1934 flood investigations committee's recommended plans for the construction of the EDWC's storm relief canal once again on the back burner. Engineers assumed that with the river-basin approach they were taking a more integrative stance on design: embankment dams did not have to be completely impermeable. They required only a consistent monitoring of erosion and water levels that could help see through needed social and political reforms for the colonized (Spencer 1950).

Can the Mosquito Remember?

While embankment damming offered the colony opportunities for development, it also posed the well-known risk of malaria to Hutchinson and his team of day laborers. For decades malaria had been the leading cause of fatalities on sugar estates. But by the early 1950s, the colony experienced a rapid increase in population, particularly among Indo-Guianese, due to malaria campaigns.

A Rockefeller Foundation–sponsored malariometric survey in 1946 showed that the vector *Anopheles darlingi* had long ago adapted to the coast's irrigation and drainage grid. As Dr. George Giglioli (1948, 49), the head researcher on the survey, noted, "The breeding places of this dangerous mosquito on the coast are nearly exclusively man made: Irrigation canals and smaller ditches, rice fields, and cane fields in flood fallow." The grid fueled Giglioli's sense of wonder about *A. darlingi*. He spent as much time counting larvae as he did counting canals. "The hydrological problem," he noted, was further magnified by the "average width of an irrigation canal which is fourteen to twenty feet, with a depth of three to four feet. The enormous development of the irrigation network—there are approximately sixteen miles of full section canal per square mile of cane cultivation—is best judged by aerial views" (39). These exact figures and his topographical perspective were not just evidence of his obsession with mosquitoes. Giglioli and his team used these figures to identify the distribution of larvae, which they correlated to the number of child splenic enlargement cases at area hospitals. With these cases in mind, they targeted rural districts at the household level for DDT spraying.

The preparations for the spraying and for the dosages were intricate. Nozzles, guns, filters, and pumps had to be manufactured in the colony to conform to the various chemical emulsions used for the survey. The stream of the guns simplified and lowered costs for spraying across space—canals, open pastures, and buildings. Through these spray campaigns, Giglioli recognized an emerging aesthetic. He passionately noted in his field report, "No schemes of development can be implemented, maintained or exploited throughout the tens of thousands of empty square [miles] which are the Colony of British Guiana: *Homo sapiens!*" (Giglioli 1946, 52). The irrigation and drainage grid merely exposed the nightmare to the light of day: permanent human settlement of the coast was a perilous enterprise.

Giglioli proved that engineers, particularly Russell, had been mistaken and had misdiagnosed the coast's floodplain. There was not an absence of ruins in the colony. Russell's attention just happened to be too narrowly focused on human memory of engineering and dams. Whether by accident or design, Giglioli argued that mosquitoes were reliable witnesses to the colony's settlement. He hypothesized that because mosquitoes were the main cause of plantation labor fatalities, their breeding grounds could partially explain the dramatic shifts in the colony's racial demographics. What's more, mosquitoes' habits of marking territory corresponded to the changing realities of not only rainfall but of engineers' designs for embankment damming. And Giglioli's insights were not particular to British Guiana.[5]

For instance, Timothy Mitchell (2002) argues that the web of events stirring British-inspired damming in early twentieth-century British-occupied Egypt was parasitic: mosquitoes (*A. gambiae*) sucked the blood of capitalists, which inspired innovative agronomists to develop markets in pesticides. The '"main-spring' that powered the movement of capitalist history" seemed to reside in the exchange of ideas between engineers, scientists, entrepreneurs, and colonial officials about methods for killing mosquitoes (30). As Mitchell shows, these exchanges were haunted by a remainder: the idiosyncrasies of data collection and the famines and deaths vectors caused. Mitchell uses parasites as metaphors to evoke a critical distinction between the strategy and tactics of dam design. Mosquitoes may be affected by damming, but engineers are the figures who decide when and how they engage the movement of capital across the world.

In this way, an intimate dialogue between engineers and mosquitoes emerged in the British Empire that allowed engineers to recognize the insects as essential partners in dam design. Engineers in British Guiana designed a grid that created *A. darlingi*'s breeding habitat while *A. darlingi* killed off engineers' labor supply of Indo-Guianese, who maintained this very habitat. *A. darlingi* was a "para-site," in George Marcus's (2000) phrasing, offering information that helped engineers better understand the spatial relations between infrastructure systems, technology, race, and expertise. This point was not lost on Giglioli. Upon completing the surveys, he recommended that sugar estate owners build mobile shelters to protect drains and water from toxins. His recommendation contributed to a decline in infant mortality from a rate of 176 deaths per one thousand live births in 1946 to eighty-two by 1948, a 21 percent increase in the colony's overall population by 1949, and the elimination of *A. darlingi* from the coastal region by 1951 (Seecharan 2005, 372). Historian Clem Seecharan argues that this human and more-than-human "demographic revolution" paved the way for a nationalist political front for the PPP, one that had an "Indian sensibility" for agricultural development (379).

With this data in mind, Giglioli believed that the Rockefeller campaign would simultaneously improve flood management, agricultural development, and public health. His attention to a dying racial demographic, Indo-Guianese, made the influence of the Rockefeller Foundation on British Guiana just as politically significant as in other places of the decolonizing world plagued at the time by human overpopulation (Parmar 2015). The challenge for engineers in British Guiana, Giglioli contended, was to figure out how to make embankment damming amenable to both human and mosquito memory. But if Russell's naturalistic metaphor of beaver damming was any indication, rarely do human and more-than-human forms of memory seamlessly chart a single path toward the future.

By the end of the antimalaria campaign, work on the MMA Scheme came to a halt. In 1949, Hutchinson received more funds from the International Bank for Reconstruction and Development, an agency institution of the World Bank, to complete surveys of land and rivers for the MMA Scheme's three dams. But the surveys were delayed for months when sugar barons obstructed legislation in British Guiana's parliament, fearing that the scheme would cost too much and take away cheap Indo-Guianese labor from sugar estates. Hutchinson allegedly grew disillusioned and "eventually resigned in disgust," leaving the project stalled until the colonial governor could find a new consulting engineer (Smith 1962, 92–93).

Embankment dams were intended to help engineers like Hutchinson manage an irrigation and drainage grid that became indebted to an Indian sensibility for agricultural labor and expertise. This grid was built, however, on top of rivers that are life forming and life taking, whether approached from the question of disastrous flooding or of engineers' access to rainfall data. Indeed, the subsequent decade of stalled elections and apaan jaat violence that engulfed the colony on the eve of independence speaks to the racial political tolls and casualties that inform embankment damming. But for all the forms of racial inequality and political uprisings attributed tragically to embankment damming in the British Empire and Guiana in particular, engineers never took for granted the EDWC's fragility. They understood that their primary job was to figure out not if but when the next disaster would happen.

Benevolent Servants

In the late 1950s, Hutchinson was replaced by a Guianese engineer of Portuguese descent, Robert F. Camacho. He completed degrees in the colony, which led to work as the colony's director of drainage and irrigation (1957–61), followed by time in British Yemen where he became a senior engineer for Sir William Halcrow and Partners of London, the firm hired to complete the MMA Scheme project (St. Stanislaus College 1968). Given this experience, he was responsible for completing plans and field surveys for Stage One, damming of the Abary River. In the Stage One report, Camacho (1961, 1–3) explained that the dam was a realistic venture if only because of the meticulous record of rainfall data engineers had kept since Russell's time. The data showed "abnormal" periods of dry and wet weather in the East Coast region, which led Camacho to believe that riverine areas with fairly deep pegasse were "well-nigh impossible to drain" and should effectively be avoided in design efforts (Clark 1953, 203). The Abary River's deep pegasse led Camacho to design for the dam's minimal storage capacity (42). Once again, pegasse was an inspiring resource for dam design. But it was also a burden for Camacho, a well-seasoned engineer hired to fill the technical vacuum Hutchinson's departure created at the Ministry of Agriculture. Camacho's hire was an affront to the British colonial governor's idea that locals were too feeble, uneducated, and perverted by communist ideology to see through decolonization (Palmer 2010). At the same time, Camacho's observations of pegasse proved telling of the obstacles the colony would continue to face if engineers' employment catered only to the whims of apaan jaat and sugar barons.

Camacho used a differential equation, Manning's formula, that estimated the changes in flow (velocity) of water in open channels due to topography, tides, and the elevation of the Abary River's basin. He viewed these calculations as a way to "govern flood relief by *practical* considerations" by designing dam embankments, channels, and banks that were "purposefully oversized and extremely flat" (Clark 1953, 228–38; emphasis added). Because of the East Coast region's "periodic fluctuations in climate," Camacho refused to implement additional design measures to heighten the walls of the EDWC's embankment dam (228–38). He recommended instead that the MMA Scheme should be designed and managed like India's Damodar River Valley Corporation, with engineers conducting periodic soil and land surveys to monitor the dam's stability (Camacho 1961).

The MMA Scheme introduced a new role to rainfall, along with soil survey data, in dam design (Spencer 1950). Namely, it introduced the possibility that data sets are a social convention engineers use to build consensus about the history of a dam's flood catchment and that the spatial scale through which engineers narrate this history matters to their integration into global alignments of technology transfer between former colonies and Britain. Therefore, the plans for the MMA Scheme did not originate only in development planning but also in the need for and increased importance of archival practice in the professionalization of the engineering sciences.

This is no small claim. Designing with multiple river basins in mind was a distinctively American invention first conceived by engineers managing the Tennessee Valley Authority (TVA) (Lilienthal 1944). They envisioned using the water from rivers for various purposes, from irrigation to flood management to hydropower. The history of the TVA's influence on the formation of high-modernist aesthetics and planning in the decolonizing world, particularly in colonial India and its Damodar River Valley, is well documented (D'Souza 2006).[6] If by historians' accounts TVA-style damming has been little more than an export commodity (Ekbladh 2002), the MMA Scheme also demonstrates that engineers learned to conceive of rainfall data as a natural resource. By this I mean that engineers were willing to apply rainfall data to all sorts of activities that had very little to do with flooding. For instance, Camacho suggested that engineers should use rainfall data to build structures for activities including mining and to coordinate other kinds of data collection (e.g., soil and land surveys). But rainfall data were not always benevolent servants.

Rainfall data were also tethered to a range of technical and bureaucratic protocols in order to become useful. In his tome *Dams and Other Disasters* (1971), TVA engineer Arthur Morgan explains that Army Corps engineers resisted the TVA model when it was first proposed. Along the Mississippi River, levees, not dams, were their preferred choice for flood management. Morgan (1971, 266) argues that because engineers did not travel to the "top catchments" of rivers and set up rain gauges, they had developed a reliance on dams for irrigation alone. One engineer complained that river-basin damming "was like the 'combination tool,' the joy of the inventor but the despair of the user." Yet with attention and the commitment to collecting more rainfall data, Morgan argued, engineers could learn to anticipate disasters with engineer review boards, independent of the Army Corps, which could periodically monitor the network of dams.

Similar attitudes toward rainfall data informed the MMA Scheme's management. Technical boards composed of sugar and rice barons, agronomists, engineers, surveyors, hydrologists, politicians, and soil scientists were hired to oversee dam construction and planning activities and were responsible for reporting to the Ministry of Agriculture. In turn, board meeting minutes became the point of reference for the development of farmer-based water associations and protocols for when engineers should open sluice gates in the event of a flood.

This stratified approach to damming and flood management had a dual effect. On the one hand, engineers became dependent on other technocrats' data for flood management. On the other, their work became hyperspecialized and relevant to the general public, if only when disaster struck. For instance, from the late 1950s into the early 1960s, *Timehri*'s articles focused on hinterland settlement, health, and forestry issues rather than coastal engineering projects. Clive McWatt (2010) attributes the topical shift partially to editor Vincent Roth's time serving as a colonial surveyor in the hinterland and to a fire in 1945 that destroyed the Agricultural Society's museum in Georgetown. And so, by the end of *Timehri*'s initial circulation in the late 1960s and the colony's independence, the editorial board published only two articles related to irrigation, drainage, and sea defense and held only one public lecture on these topics. Meanwhile, engineers' musings about dam design were increasingly relegated to the pages of development and policy white papers.

Many engineers during Guyana's postindependence period found themselves in a bind. Between 1970 and 1985, the Ministry of Agriculture developed marketing campaigns that were state owned and operated. But during these years, the financing of dam construction was still dependent on foreign loans. This meant that contracts for foreign engineering consulting work were limited by individual engineers' personal relationships with firms rather than by state diplomacy. The ministry started numerous projects, including one with a British firm that helped engineers create a hydraulic model that detailed drainage coefficients for both dams and sluices. With these data, they planned to upgrade most of the country's main water outlets with mechanical-diesel pumps instead of gravity pumps. But of the thirty-two pumps, fewer than half were installed, and only two dams were dug: the Tapakuma Conservancy (1974) and the Abary Conservancy of the MMA Scheme (1985). Most engineers of the socialist generation I interviewed attributed the partial execution to the lack of hard capital the state had and not to thin soil or land surveys. Other than the problems the state faced shoring up aid and loans from development agencies, the engineers attributed the incomplete damming to a more pernicious problem in the way Burnham envisioned the relationship between apaan jaat and engineering expertise.

Many speculate that Burnham prioritized funding for the Ministry of Works and Hydraulics's sea defense projects over the Ministry of Agriculture's damming projects because Indo-Guyanese remained the majority racial labor pool in agriculture. The inequitable funding contributed to engineers' informal stereotyping of the profession: sea defense has been labeled a so-called profession of Black expertise and irrigation and drainage a so-called profession of Indian expertise. Nonetheless, few engineers have settled on offering me a single explanation for why racial stereotyping persisted under Burnham. Was he exceptionally apt at negotiating racial cleavages in professional status and voting? Did he have ambitions that exceeded sugar, with a plan to slowly re-reinvest in public infrastructures for other industries, such as commercial manufacturing, mining, and maritime trade? Or were his policies more pragmatic than ideological, given that by the end of his tenure he was successful at brokering foreign loans for sea defense and less so for agriculture? The archive and oral histories I have encountered suggest a combination of all these possible explanations. What's more, Burnham's adherence to a style of Afrocentric socialism, modeled after Tanzanian president Julius Nyerere's ethos of *ujamaa* (brotherhood), only further complicates matters.

Whereas Tanzanian engineers sought training from their socialist and communist counterparts in Germany and the Soviet Union, this was not the case for Guyanese engineers (Burton 2020). A handful of Guyanese engineers participated in degree-granting programs in Cuba, while many more trained throughout Britain for their postgraduate degrees.[7] Guyana's approach to engineering originated in a blend of cautious skepticism toward the West and attempts to provincialize Afrocentricity in a multiracial society. In this respect, Burnham's vision of ujamaa was driven by the rivalries of political elites who supported the party and the loyalty of engineers who played their roles as "Black sea defense experts" and "Indian irrigation and drainage experts."

In turn, racial stereotyping created an atmosphere wherein engineers treated socialism as a kind of "secular faith" in good science (Andreas 2009; Znamenski 2021). They learned to approach their craft through practical decision-making that created space to hope for political change or at least to imagine a future in which race did not define the means and ends of expertise. And all would agree that the long period of Burnham rule (circa 1966–85) contributed to the costly and inconsistent maintenance of the EDWC.

The neglect of the EDWC exposed that apaan jaat was a variable that shaped engineers' efforts at flood management. As Kwame A. Appiah (2019) argues, racial identities matter to the formation of social collectives, setting the terms by which people articulate accountability to one another. For Guyanese engineers, apaan jaat has never been a convincing motivation for their work across engineering agencies. Instead, they have come to interpret the EDWC's fragility and damming more broadly as making self-evident the limitations of apaan jaat to support their efforts at holistic engineering projects.

One engineer who worked on the Abary Conservancy explained to me at length the difficulties he and other engineers faced:

> We went through a period when there wasn't much money. And things were really bad. When things started to go bad financially, we still had the infrastructure, which was good, but we did not have money to maintain the infrastructures. When you nationalize major industries in your country, the big corporations and superpowers of the world tend to pressure you, and I think that's what happened to the government. It

all revealed that we had more work to do than money. So if you aren't maintaining adequately, things get progressively worse. It meant that farmers were not able to pay for their irrigation and drainage rates, and they were calling for services. Some were saying because they weren't getting adequate services they wouldn't pay. Well, if you don't pay you can't get services! And if you are not maintaining your infrastructure adequately, something is actually happening; it's getting worse. Coupled with that a lot of engineers left the country. We had brain-drain. I don't think we ever saw the recovery of that. Only after the 2005 disaster have people come back. Many were trained abroad. . . . But it's only right now that we have started to recover.

This engineer's comments return to the question Russell and *Timehri* editors posed when the EDWC was first imagined and planned: What are the stakes of living in a world where racial politics are tightly coupled to the state's demand for technoscience and settlement?

This engineer suggests a style of government whereby a lack of racial trust among state officials, politicians, and engineers can facilitate the neglect of infrastructure systems to the point that their decay appears to be uncontrollable and inevitable (see also Subramanian 2019). Take, for instance, another engineer's description of a river defense project he completed, pro bono, with a friend during the socialist era:

You can't divide the issue of design from the realities of the day that knock you to the ground. When we were working on a project, funding was there, but as we came down to the end they [the government] terminated the contract; the government wasn't available to pay outside consultants. They [foreign consultants] left, and we were working in an inadequate environment. So we had to innovate. We did river defense using timber sheet piling. There's no way anybody was gonna do that, then or now. So let's say there is a breach, and you can just get timber sheet piling to build a wall, but you should have used steel. But that's what we could afford. So that's what we did.

In the midst of terminated contracts, design does not proceed from data alone; instead, it emerges from the sociomaterial, economic, and political resources at one's disposal. This engineer explains that irrigation and drainage infrastructures have their own temporality, but so too do the design techniques that inform their cycles of construction and maintenance (Gupta 2018).

In interviews, engineers spoke at length about the importance of engineering field reports, especially in the context of doing impromptu design activities. Many—Afro-Guyanese and Indo-Guyanese alike—filed duplicates of the reports away in boxes at their homes. Others had a more overt political investment in private archival systems and thought it was their civic duty to protect reports from a purportedly corrupt and/or shortsighted state apparatus. As other scholars have noted, because of their diagrams, formulas, and maps, engineering reports carry inherent characteristics of immutability and mobility (Knox and Harvey 2015; Latour 1988). Engineering reports undergird and give meaning to engineers' professional sense of authority. But as the case of the EDWC also reveals, engineering reports do not exist only for engineers to design. They also exist to be preserved for other engineers to reference. Thus, the transformation of engineering reports into archives is a fundamental activity for the reproduction of knowledge exchange and a sense of fraternity within the profession.

Today, state-sponsored engineers I know admit that the Ministry of Agriculture has yet to track down all of these socialist-era reports. Without these reports, it has become easy for them to view the PPP neoliberal administrations (circa 1992 to 2015; 2020 to the present) as governments reinstating an Indian sensibility for engineering expertise. By this they mean not only that the racial demographics of engineers have appeared to skew toward an Indo-Guyanese majority (although there are no actual statistics to prove this) but also that the state now cares more about flood management. Even so, the Ministry of Agriculture openly relies on the anecdotal knowledge of retired engineers from the socialist era to contextualize work on older structures, including the EDWC's enhancements. In short, apaan jaat gives shape to engineers' sense of the amateur or unprofessional at the same time that it drives engineers' desires for climate adaptation.

From the engineers' perspective, climate adaptation is an accumulative process that draws on and modifies their past efforts at dam design. The specific activities of data collection, surveying, and archiving reports link dam design less to issues of individual ingenuity and will than to engineers' collective experiences of working for the state. In turn, engineers treat climate adaptation as a partial effect of the historical forms of racialized exclusion and divisions of labor in the engineering profession since the EDWC's construction in 1880. Engineers, in other words, challenge settler colonialism through an investment in counter-racial thinking.

If the historical facts of race and racism can be identified and circulated by engineers, then the universalizing project of dam design needs to be not discarded, but rather reconstituted on a different basis. Engineers attempt to do this daily by explaining to the public aspects of the EDWC's safety, soliciting funding for projects, and conducting field inspections. Climate adaptation simply reminds us of the urgency of this agenda and the limits of apaan jaat to see through into the future the country's continued settlement.

What makes the EDWC case so striking is that engineers had many opportunities—and the premonition perhaps—to modify the design measures of embankment damming well before the 2005 disaster. Engineers' proposals after the 1934 flood are a case in point. The commitments to seeing through these modifications, however, were challenged by efforts at decolonization and, later, the emergence of apaan jaat. And if flooding is an important mechanism for helping engineers to call out and counter the racial politics of the state, then the EDWC's life history is still being written.

▼

4   COMPENSATION AND RESETTLEMENT

▲

The EDWC's Hope Canal cost over GYD$4.1 billion (US$19.7 million). What made it so expensive was the maintenance work engineers had to do to address the pegasse at the construction site (*Guyana Times* 2016). Even so, an independent auditor found that the project was deliberately underestimated by engineers and that it would need a taller than average embankment to protect the residential areas nearby.

Intended as a storm relief channel for the EDWC, the six-mile canal cut through Hope and Dochfour, two predominantly Indo-Guyanese cash-crop farming villages. Homes and provision grounds the state deemed vulnerable to flooding had to be moved, and farmers were compensated with funds provided jointly by the Ministry of Agriculture and the Ministry of Housing. The canal's construction affected fifteen households, or thirty title-holding farmers, and required that they resettle a few hundred meters from their original lots. Alongside the state providing millions of Guyanese dollars in compensation, engineers planned to realign secondary drainage for the farmers' new provision grounds.

Farmers were skeptical of this new arrangement because they feared that the Hope Canal's pegasse embankment could fail if and when there were torrential storms. They also believed that the state deemed the project realistic only because it was willing to "buy the Indian small man" or secure Indo-Guyanese votes by providing generous compensation packages. The protection of land rights was a secondary priority for farmers. They were more concerned that apaan jaat, rather than sound technical measures, was shaping the Hope Canal's design.

Compensation for the Hope Canal grapples with the relationship between race and vulnerability to climate change and with farmers' aspirations to decouple the two. An agreement between multiple parties, compensation for land resettlement is a form of payment that acknowledges a loss but not necessarily in ways that will maintain livelihoods and needs into the future (Roy 2005). Compensation is the critical political fault line in climate adaptation projects: what the future entails for the resettled is as much a matter of reinvesting as it is a difficult and sometimes impossible task at making predictions.[1] The farmers argue that whatever comes after the Hope Canal's construction—another disaster, less flooding, different farming opportunities, and so on—is radically underdetermined by the state.

The claim that the state is "willing to buy the Indian small man" gestures to a political imaginary about the possible (the what-ifs, the maybes, the probable, and the speculative). Farmers' reference to the possible is not about a single identity in the name of, say, land rights or tenure, but rather a commitment to activities or to doing things to enhance drainage. Farmers viewed themselves as essential to the EDWC. So, while they will never know for certain if state ministers and engineers believe they are "Indian small men," they act as if the state is making this racial claim while aspiring to a different mode of human engagement. For the farmers, compensation has set in motion practical activities that involve making visible the nonlinear trajectories and sociomaterial inconsistencies of apaan jaat. Their simultaneous refusal of apaan jaat and commitment to climate adaptation enacts a kind of counter-racial thinking.

Proximity

Located twenty-five miles from Georgetown, the sparsely populated villages of Hope and Dochfour include a mix of freehold and leasehold settlements on what were once sugar and coconut estates. The EDWC and adjacent savannah form the northwest border of the villages' backlands. Both villages were where freedmen took part in the village movement by collectively purchasing land known as Plantation Northbrook several miles away.

In the late colonial period, Hope/Dochfour reemerged as home to one of the Caribbean's premier coconut estates. It included a processing plant alongside workers' logies and provision grounds (see figure 4.1). By the early 1970s, Burnham's administration took over management of the estate. But its nationalization strategy was centered around sugar, with little economic planning funneled toward the remechanization of coconut trees. As Eusi Kwayana, a prominent activist and former member of the original PPP coalition (before the 1959 split), explains, Burnham "introduced compulsory labor at Plantation Hope, a coconut plantation. . . . At Plantation Hope he lorded it over the people. . . . He sent typists, office workers, professionals into the

FIGURE 4.1.
Photographs of mid-twentieth-century Hope Estate logies hanging in engineers' field office

cane field in 1977, to break a sugar strike. They messed up the cultivation. They knew nothing about it [coconut]" (Naipaul 2003, 76–77).

Residents and former workers of Hope Estate have continued to debate whether the socialist government ever owned it or managed it for a private investor. Either way, they all refer to an estate manager by the name of Sankar, a member of an Indo-Guyanese family that incorporated its countrywide rice and coconut operations in 1975 (Rahman 2016). Within a decade, the estate went under, and some of the land was reused for housing. Workers at Enmore, a nearby sugar plantation, and squatters were encouraged by the state to resettle the area. Unless special arrangements were made, residents with rights to colonial-era logies maintained freehold titles, and newer residents took leasehold titles with Sankar Limited.

Consistent with this historic pattern of restricted resettlement, Hope/ Dochfour remains fairly small in population today. The village-level census completed in 2002 counted sixteen residents in Hope and 368 in Dochfour.[2] Across the two villages, 190 residents self-identify as male and 194 as female. The villages are racially heterogeneous, but the clear majority, 205 people, self-identify as Indo-Guyanese, while 116 self-identify as Afro-Guyanese and 62 as Mixed Race. The main occupations are farming and teaching, with a majority of the population reported as underemployed. By 2008, the population had grown by one hundred, when residents of Joe Hook and Grass Hook—villages in the Mahaica ravine deemed by engineers as severely flood prone—were relocated to Hope/Dochfour's backlands. With the support of the welfare organization Food for the Poor, the Ministry of Housing sponsored the construction of forty houses. The relocated families were not required to pay for land lots. However, they were expected to pay an annual rent on lands the government issued for farming. And in 2015, the Ministry of Agriculture announced its aspirations to revive coconut mills in the area.

While the irrigation and drainage grid has long coordinated social life in Hope/Dochfour, it provided residents little direction during the 2005 disaster. Due to what residents call its low land, flooding occurred for six weeks across the villages. In addition, the majority of residents could not return to their provision grounds until two or three months after flooding subsided. They traveled to a neighboring village called Ann's Grove for help during the disaster. A larger village on high land, Ann's Grove has schools and a church that the national Red Cross and the CDC used as shelters to distribute flood relief supplies. But problems arose when people living in bottom-flat homes in Hope/Dochfour reported having difficulties traveling to shelters. Many residents of Ann's Grove responded by volunteering with both agencies to ensure that people from across the three villages received aid.

The Ann's Grove residents who volunteered described their work as improving on the efforts of the two agencies. They collected basic demographic information and helped do wellness checks of residents stuck in their houses. In interviews with me, they described their work as not community motivated but, rather, inspired by their commitments to help individual households. This distinction between the individual household and community was significant in two ways. On the one hand, they did not want to be perceived as privileging the needs of Ann's Grove residents, a predominantly Afro-Guyanese village. If the volunteers could track which households received flood relief supplies, they argued, no one village received more or less than its fair share. On the other, they perceived their work as a symbolic effort to monitor outside agencies that did not have a firm understanding of local interests.

Yet the extent to which concerns about racial discrimination informed volunteers' understandings of intense flooding, as opposed to disaster response, is a bit less clear. Volunteers were satisfied with the decisions of local state officials to organize an emergency crew of garbage trucks to retrieve waste from shelters and private residences. Despite these efforts, however, volunteers were well aware of the flood hazards around them. Given the proximity of Hope/Dochfour and Ann's Grove to the EDWC, the floodwaters took on a distinct character relative to places farther away from the embankment dam. While many eventually received flood relief supplies from the Red Cross and the CDC, it was water in backyards—its stench, color, and volume—that shaped their attitudes toward intense flooding. As Melanie, an Afro-Guyanese and self-described housewife of Ann's Grove, explained to me:

> Normally when we get flood, we get it today and by tomorrow it's off. But that flood wasn't going anywhere, so we marked it, and it was there all the time. I stayed in my house and only went out to do assistance [with the CDC/Red Cross] while others had to go to shelters. The worms were coming up from the pit latrine in my yard. And there wasn't any need for long boots. It was beyond long-boots stage. So we were told we had to line our feet with coconut oil. A whole six weeks, and you know we tried to stop the kids going into the water. The smell of the water was awful. And nothing came to you [other than what the CDC/Red Cross provided], so you had to think about when to use supplies.

At least it was a little cool because it was constant rain, but there was no day without rain. Maybe that's what kept the water so long. The water was there, and it had nowhere to drain. The worse rain I've ever saw in my life.

If Melanie's description of her home is any indication, people were not confident that they knew all the things that could happen during intense flooding or how to respond. A few weeks after the floodwaters subsided, Melanie and other volunteers were recruited by the Guyana Human Rights Association (GHRA) to spearhead a civic group to clean up debris. The GHRA civic group held periodic meetings that focused on lobbying local state officials to dredge canals.

Other than its work with the post-2005 disaster cleanup, the GHRA was known for monitoring elections, organizing on behalf of Amerindians for land and social services, and successfully forcing the state to sanction a Canadian mining firm after a tailings dam broke and leaked waste into the Essequibo River, killing hundreds of fish in 1995. Even though the GHRA prided itself on being a politically neutral body, none of the volunteers I know spoke of their time with the GHRA as being different from serving on other village-based civic groups. They agreed to work with the GHRA more because of its national political influence and less because of its explicit investments in human rights law or conventions. With the help of the GHRA, intense flooding justified a range of new technological and knowledge interventions in the name of cross-village partnerships.

But when the Ministry of Agriculture announced its plans in 2008 for the Hope Canal, the GHRA civic group decided that they could no longer focus their grievances around lobbying local state officials. Members reached out to Hope/Dochfour farmers to join the civic group. The farmers were concerned that the new project would distract engineers from attending to derelict and clogged drainage canals in the areas they believed were already making seasonal flooding intolerable. The GHRA civic group's new attention to the Hope Canal and the specifics of drainage sheds light on the lived reality of climate adaptation as shifting the sociomaterial production and organization of flood knowledges. Even for those like Melanie, with little to no intimate knowledge of drainage, there was strength in numbers. As she noted:

The GHRA decided to respond [to the Hope Canal] and somebody called us, and that's how we started. But you know, you can find that it can be a bit political in Ann's Grove. When it comes to election, people claim to be this or that race, but when floods come, everyone is one.

Myself, I'm not attached to anywhere. And I want to just see the area grow. A lot of people in the community talk against the canal. But in this area we are the small men, so we had meetings at Hope/Dochfour and Ann's Grove saying this canal is not needed and that other places' drains can be opened up. And then we went ahead against it [the Hope Canal], and that was it.

Melanie suggests that small men are the most efficient people to coordinate and assess the best activities for climate adaptation.

The figure of the small man is prevalent in Guyana. Perhaps the most famous expression of it was during socialism, when Burnham launched the Make the Small Man a Real Man campaign. He envisioned the campaign as a means to galvanize community development through cooperative efforts. The Ministry of Agriculture initiated several projects to improve the livelihoods of small men or farmers (both men and women) who owned roughly one to twenty-five acres of land (Ford, Lallbachan, and Ramnarine 1985, 11). In reality, however, projects were marred by corruption and left many farmers in debt (Hintzen 1989; Raghunandan and Kistow 1998). And while small men today still speak of corruption eating away at the internal channels of government, the debt small men accumulated from the socialist era persists but has morphed into a problem of social accountability. The Ministry of Agriculture's policies in recent decades have focused on investments in agricultural marketing campaigns for the microbanking of farmers' food/market stalls in rural and urban Guyana. But, as Caroline Shenaz Hossein (2014) notes, racialized practices of clientelism, with some Indo-Guyanese creditors refusing to loan to Afro-Guyanese farmers, inform these relationships across the public-private sector, thereby limiting the opportunities for all small men to engage the agricultural market writ large.[3]

Melanie speaks against the grain of these exploitative histories. She refers to herself as a small man. This statement is less a claim about property ownership or occupation than identification with an epistemic community. Melanie diversified her role as a housewife by learning about drainage and using this knowledge to create new political networks. She argues that intense flooding provides a temporary reprieve in Ann's Grove and Hope/Dochfour from apaan jaat. But she recognizes that small men are vulnerable to flooding as long as the state disregards their expertise. Small men, in other words, are a product of people working against a racialized configuration of intense flooding, technoscience, irrigation and drainage infrastructures, institutional agendas, and gendered bodies.[4]

Small men are not born with that identity, nor are they exceptional people who can single-handedly resist or right the wrongs of the state. They instead, following Mimi Sheller (2012, 2), acknowledge that "power operates precisely through unmarked but situated knowledge," and they circumvent conventional definitions of political agency by producing new epistemic relations to intense flooding. As Sheller notes, land has been a key site of political struggle in the Caribbean since slavery, whereby objects such as trees, houses, and infrastructure systems provide vantage points about identity and belonging beyond the state's written archive. Melanie and other small men articulate such a vantage point by mobilizing new flood relations and claims to expertise for climate adaptation.

"Just the Faithful Ones Are Left"

Whatever Melanie learned about drainage with the GHRA civic group was informed by the belief that the Hope Canal is not the only or best solution to address intense flooding. If in Guyana following the 2005 disaster, drainage has become an essential feature of small-man identity formation, then climate adaptation is entangled in broader processes of land management and not only in the engineering sciences. Since the socialist transition, the state has diversified its investments in agriculture. While sugar remains tied to the mixed private/state-owned Guyana Sugar Corporation Inc. (GUYSUCO) estates, trade agreements with Venezuela, Europe, and other parts of the world have supported the productive earnings of privately owned rice mills. The idea is that by expanding Guyana's international rice market, other international markets for cash crops will follow or can be redirected to grow food markets within Guyana. While many of these mills are located in Guyana's West Coast region, programs for rice on the East Coast have been piloted in the MMA Scheme. These programs target farmers with medium- to large-scale estates, many of which are owned by Indo-Guyanese, whose families benefited from the land reforms of the preindependence period in the 1950s. For small-scale farmers, however, opportunities for growth remain tied to annual state-sponsored marketing programs.

In Hope/Dochfour and the extended Ann's Grove area, the majority of farms are small scale and grow crops other than rice. Following the success in the MMA Scheme, the villages were incorporated into Water User Associations (WUAS). In 2004, the National Drainage and Irrigation Authority (NDIA) passed an act that registered WUAS as nonprofit businesses with jurisdiction over secondary canals, sluices, outfalls, and the like. Through

WUAS, farmers pay fees and are expected to participate in the planning, design, and operation of irrigation and drainage. Because WUAS operate as self-sustaining businesses, they are distinct from institutions such as community development councils popular in rural Guyana or the water boards envisioned in the original 1950s MMA Scheme plans.[5]

Despite allegations that fees were not being collected across the country's nine certified WUAS, an NDIA audit found that between January 2011 and June 2015, WUAS collected over GYD$1.1 billion (US$5.3 million) (Nigel Hinds Financial Services 2015, 10). Activities of WUAS are based on water schedules provided by the NDIA. And while the WUAS may be predicated on farmers' participatory engagement, they still operate as hierarchical institutions. Farmers rely on subtle tactics to gain leverage within the WUAS. As one Hope/Dochfour farmer explained to me, "We have benefited from the water schedule. When the rice farmers [in nearby villages] need water, we get water for our estates. So one rice farmer gets water, he would own like one hundred or two hundred acres of land. But you, a small man, you have four or five acres, so you can take a little more [water] here and there."

For this self-professed small man, it was important to learn when to abide by the water schedule, request a favor of rice farmers, or simply take water. While this microlevel decision-making is widely acknowledged and accepted among farmers, it also means that small men are adversely affected by extreme changes in weather. For instance, WUAS partner with the NDIA and other state institutions when there are droughts or floods in order to help monitor the EDWC's water levels. In 2013, a series of intense floods led the NDIA and the Ministry of Agriculture to propose another program with the WUAS that would require they use fees to help fund the operational costs of the EDWC. These bureaucratic arrangements further reinforced the self-sustaining business model of the WUAS by encouraging farmers to value water as a commodity and to value less so their knowledge of drainage processes.

But the realities of intense flooding make no room for such distinctions in daily agricultural practice. Many Hope/Dochfour and Ann's Grove residents argue that it has always been the case that "the boys who drop out of school early" find it hard to find agricultural work. Residents pointed to not only the 2005 disaster but also the floods of 2006, 2008–9, 2011, and 2013 as evidence of the structural economic difficulties farmers confront because of climate change. With every flood they notice "more abandoned plots grow up with a lot of weeds." Some reported to me that they invested over GYD$1 million (US$4,788) in seeds in 2013, and within a month of that year's flood, they lost everything. It takes more time to recover from a flood because of the heavier rainfall experienced throughout the wet season. In turn, farmers now equate a slower pace of life and a diminished cash flow with climate change.

"Just the faithful ones are left here," one Hope/Dochfour resident explained to me. For everyone else, gold mining in the interior has become an alternative form of employment. Those now gold mining describe it as predictable and therefore lucrative despite the time away from family and the risks (e.g., banditry and accidental deaths due to drowning in pits or faulty equipment). Both men and women have joined mining crews or do monthly rotations as clerks at shops in mining camps. This pattern of employment is, admittedly, not altogether new. Beginning in the postemancipation era, labor in the mining sector was typically performed by Afro-Guianese, even though planters enacted legislation that discouraged them from mining during the harvest (Josiah 2011). Today, however, both Afro-Guyanese and Indo-Guyanese are forgoing agricultural work altogether in Hope/Dochfour and Ann's Grove. This means that the threat climate change poses to residents has not only economic effects but racial demographic ones as well. For the "faithful ones" who stay and farm, their understandings of drainage are symbolic of a plantation economy partially crippled by climate change.

Disclosure

When the Ministry of Agriculture began surveying a site for the Hope Canal in early 2009, the GHRA civic group wrote letters to the ministry to express their concerns. While the ministry held a town hall meeting, the GHRA civic group was frustrated by the lack of information the ministry disclosed about the canal's design. They claimed that the ministry only provided information about engineers' plans to update hydraulic models and ongoing work repairing the EDWC's embankment. A letter dated 2009 and signed by "Mr. Forde and Residents" noted, "History has recorded the deaths of millions who lost their lives in countries through failures of levees, dams, embankments, earthquakes. The record of facts will be supplied. I did speak with one of the local engineers for the canal project, and I asked how are they going to build on six to seven miles of pegasse land and he made mention of geosynthetic [geotextiles] means. I thought he meant by geomantic, geomancy, or voodoo means" (Forde and Residents 2009).

Forde suggests that geomancy and engineering are compatible ways of knowing the world. But pegasse, in this instance of climate adaptation, helps people delineate the geography of a canal and compels a specific mode of shared belonging, or humanity. He notes that community fact checks are no match for unwieldy pegasse and openly queries at what cost Guyanese will become another statistic in the history of the "recorded . . . deaths of millions who lost their lives in countries through failures" of engineering.

From late 2009 into early 2010, the Ministry of Agriculture, Ministry of Housing, and Ministry of Lands and Survey sponsored meetings to discuss compensation packages for those who would be resettled due to the Hope Canal. Of the thirty farms affected, the majority were headed by Indo-Guyanese men (*Stabroek News* 2010a, 2010b). The farmers would receive a one-time payment to cover their move and the titling of a new housing lot and provision grounds. They had to provide a transport title or land tax receipts to receive the payment. Near the new housing lots, a gravel road would be developed along with improved drainage for their provision grounds. The compensation package was negotiated by a private-practicing lawyer and former parliamentary cabinet member of the PPP. At one of the meetings, he explained that the compensation packages were scientific because they were similar to those he brokered for farmers relocated for the construction of a bridge in the country's West Coast region (*Stabroek News* 2010a). Despite his degrees and letters, the lawyer purported to be well versed in the plight of farmers.

While the lawyer pieced together a deal, Ministry of Agriculture officials had ambitions that some funds for *future* projects related to the EDWC–Hope Canal could eventually be obtained from the newly launched LCDS. Partially sponsored by the investment fund of the United Nations Program on Reducing Emissions from Deforestation and Forest Degradation (UN REDD+), LCDS, at least initially, used forests in the interior region toward the specific aims of carbon sequestration accounting projects and sustainable mining. Alongside participatory forest mapping exercises, the state set up consultation meetings with Amerindian communities that have settlements where these projects were to take place (Mentore 2011). Many perceived some of the initial consultations, particularly as they related to distinctions between mining activities and collective land rights, as not providing enough time for communities to consent (Bulkan 2016; *Kaieteur News* 2010a). With these consultations and objections in mind, LCDS took on a racial character, with the state under scrutiny about its commitments to the 2006 Amerindian Act. A number of well-known Guyanese environmental consultants felt equally interested and became involved in LCDS planning to ensure the protection of Amerindian land rights.[6]

Sensitive to the national media's coverage of LCDS planning, ministry officials at Hope Canal meetings highlighted the benefits LCDS would have on farmers. For instance, the ministry launched an LCDS-inspired campaign called Grow More Food.[7] It would provide farmers with flood- and drought-resilient seeds and education programs about how to cultivate them. Ministry of Agriculture officials looked to reassure farmers that the Hope Canal was a fair deal as long as they became involved, as Amerindians presumably were, in LCDS. The ministry attempted to use coastal flooding events to index low-carbon development at a national scale. Thus, the community focus groups and informational sessions for the Hope Canal compensation defied stable relations between apaan jaat and resettlement.

The farmers responded to LCDS by taking issue with the *timing* of the negotiations for the compensation package. They questioned why the ministry requested them to move before the canal's feasibility study was completed and why there was a rush to build the Hope Canal if other LCDS initiatives were already in the pipeline. These questions were unsurprising given that some farmers did not have originals or copies of transport titles and therefore feared having to undergo a long bureaucratic process to receive payments. With the negotiations scheduled to be completed within a few months, before a feasibility study could be concluded, farmers argued that the ministry was in violation of Article 13 of Guyana's constitution, which requires the government to "establish an inclusionary democracy by providing increasing opportunities for the participation of ordinary citizens and their organizations in the management and decision-making processes of the State." The Ministry of Agriculture countered the farmers' complaint, insisting that their engineering assessment reports following the 2005 disaster already justified the canal (*Stabroek News* 2013). The farmers nonetheless remained skeptical, calling on the ministry to suspend planning and payments until a feasibility study was completed.

During its long construction (circa 2008–15), the Hope Canal was represented in the national media and political propaganda as a powder keg for debates about social entitlements and apaan jaat. A local newspaper known for its plain speaking and critical stance toward the state published the editorial "Striving to Build a United Country," with a photo of engineers taking surveys of the Hope Canal construction site (*Kaieteur News* 2014). The editor outlined things to look forward to in the coming years, including the Hope Canal's economic prospects alongside an end to race-based politics.

Members of the coalition Afro- and Indo-Guyanese opposition party, A Partnership for National Unity, attended Hope Canal negotiation meetings

with the intent of representing farmers' economic interests. A few years before a national election cycle the party created a manifesto that outlined
why the Hope Canal would not benefit all farmers: "We have no confidence
that the Hope Canal will probably not [sic] solve the problem of flooding
but has the capacity to create a greater flood hazard on our East Coast in
case of failure. It is also clear that the PPP's support for farmers in all areas
is particularly poor even for the rice industry which has now become our
second biggest GDP earner" (A Partnership for National Unity 2011, 20). But
while the political establishment(s) took issue with the nuances of GDP, the
farmers viewed no real stake in debating the value of land or crops given
their 2005 disaster experiences. The farmers instead requested that the Ministry of Agriculture release more information about the canal and said that
they would benefit from and appreciate the input of the ministry's engineers
along the way of the canal's construction.

The release of information to the public, the farmers argued, fulfilled
the bare minimum implied in the constitution's Article 13 and the citizens'
right to inclusivity in state projects. And so, over several months in 2010, the
University of Guyana held public lectures warning of the canal's danger, and
private citizens descended on Hope/Dochfour offering legal counsel and engineering advice to farmers. The ministry, however, still did not feel moved
to complete a feasibility study. Denied such a study, many farmers concluded
that the Hope Canal was being built for political reasons. In all, the payments
farmers received amounted to roughly GYD$1 per plot of land, or GYD$70
million (US$335,210) in total (*Stabroek News* 2010b).

In interviews, farmers admitted to me that they were cautious, character-
izing the payments as generous but shortsighted because they were based in
talk of race. They spoke of needing to "organize like those Amerindians in
the bush" to prove their expertise to the state. This gesture toward a mutual
vulnerability with Amerindians settled in the interior was striking: it suggested that the right to consent (whether understood as Amerindian customary land rights or as guaranteed under Article 13 of the constitution) was
embodied through not only the individual settler but the national terrain
itself and flood processes.

On this point, farmers continued to write letters to local newspapers explaining their discontent with the canal's design and, to a lesser extent, with
the terms of their compensation packages. Along with a number of retired
engineers, farmers wrote that other embankment dams should be built to
take pressure off the EDWC. A channel called the Kofi Canal located on the
other side of the EDWC could be utilized to release excess floodwaters from

the EDWC into the Demerara River. They argued that the Demerara, which was larger than the Mahaica River, was a safer, reliable natural spillway into the Atlantic Ocean. In many ways, farmers, engineers, and Ministry of Agriculture officials hold very similar perspectives on climate adaptation. They all recognize the inherent risks of canals and large-scale damming but nevertheless view them as the most effective way to minimize the impacts of intense flooding on people. Their differences lie in their convictions about whether pegasse is a worthwhile investment for building these irrigation and drainage infrastructures. This distinction, they all realized, was more than just technical. It ran the risk of further inciting political anxieties about apaan jaat and who could be counted as making a national commitment to climate adaptation.

Mati Norms

Race as a tool citizens and states use to demarcate, or at least make judgments about, compensation is not unique to climate adaptation. In many environmental justice and human rights contexts, particularly those related to toxicity and genocide, compensation is understood through the lens of (un)intentional injury that disproportionately affects a racial population (Bullard 2000; Clarke 2019). But within the field of compensation for climate adaptation, evaluations of race are explicitly linked to forms of expertise intended to mitigate known or unknown threats—that is, the expertise involved is less about labeling people as racialized victims of X event(s) than of creating space for eradicating racial inequalities that contribute to vulnerability. This is a slight distinction. But it is one that has powerful implications for how people view themselves as entitled to compensation and whether they view state officials or engineers as actors who can help them achieve it.

Thus, the farmers' annoyance with the state's race-based approach to compensation was lofty but not unprecedented. Ethnographic scholarship on Guyana is ripe with studies that examine the relationship between race and egalitarianism. In his study of competition and the socioeconomic structure of plantations, Chandra Jayawardena (1968, 413) contends that egalitarianism is defined in two ways: equality based in social rights and "the equality of men" based in intrinsic human worth. This distinction is important, Jayawardena argues, because while historical events such as slave emancipation and decolonization might be steeped in rhetoric about human equality, they have not necessarily brought about social rights for all. Plantation workers are most preoccupied with preserving a social order based on an idea about the equality of "men." They believe in this idea to resist racism perpetuated by the wider society and to create solidarity despite differences in work status, ethnicity, and race. Jayawardena acknowledges that this sentiment of solidarity, which was historically recognized by both Afro-Guianese and Indo-Guianese, was expressed with the concept of *mati*—a derivation of the word *shipmate*. Jayawardena argues that for Afro-Guianese, the concept was coined and put into wide use during enslaved Africans' Atlantic crossings. For Indo-Guianese, on the other hand, it was first used when indentured laborers recognized Hindu caste identities as creolized (or influenced by British culture) and, in some instances, erased—through plantation interactions with Blacks, Muslims, and Whites (416–18).[8] Jayawardena's ethnohistoriographic insights are based on fieldwork in the moment following the constitutional crisis *and* the internal fracturing of the PPP (418). Especially for Indo-Guianese plantation laborers who were the electoral base of the PPP, the failure of the party and unions to represent their interests was a blow. These realities, Jayawardena notes, only reinforced their belief in mati and the dire need to "act in masse" (422).

Apaan jaat, however, had yet to completely reshape the trajectory and demands of the engineering sciences. By that time, the colonial governor and ministries had hired only a handful of local engineers as *lead* project managers on irrigation, drainage, and sea defense projects. Most of the highly trained and skilled local engineers were either just finishing postgraduate degrees abroad or serving as apprentices for the ministries. After the British head engineer quit the MMA Scheme project, the colonial governor was under pressure to recruit a local/non-White engineer to replace him (see chapter 3). From this perspective, mati norms preserved a certain kind of interracial solidarity that could potentially provide a model for highly skilled workers, such as engineers, if they ever felt threatened by apaan jaat. Similar to Walter Rodney's concept of the working people (see chapter 2), the concept of mati reenvisions plantation societies from the racial worldview of Guyana's non-White settlers.

This is no small feat, as Brackette Williams's (1991) seminal ethnography would reveal a generation later in Burnham's socialist Guyana. What Williams calls ideological precepts do not merely shift with the rise and fall of state regimes. Instead, they run in the veins of humans or, at least, stoke fear in them when a racial epithet is slurred. Williams demonstrates that contestations over mati norms are not necessarily based on how those within the community evaluate property, wealth, or profit between racial groups. Rather, mati norms require one to become aware of subtler distinctions: "The problem was not success, but instead how to know when one had moved beyond the mati category, how to accomplish that move without breaching the local moral code, and how to claim the status implied in such accomplishments without alienating and angering one's neighbors and relatives" (96). For Williams, negotiating mati norms is a distinctive feature of what is means to be human in Guyana. Williams writes, "As human beings, all persons are ideally deserving of some unspecifiable degree of respect, cooperation, and concern from others simply because they are human. Human equality transcends historical experience, locality, kinship, and status" (99). But Williams cautions, following Antonio Gramsci, "all criteria are part of an ideological field, aspects of which are also potentially divisive because they suggest differentiation and inequality" (100).

Williams is not alone in this insight. The promise and peril of human equality are an explicit theme woven through much of Caribbean ethnohistoriography. It is a theme that highlights the empirical importance of studying the region, as Michel-Rolph Trouillot (2002) argues, because it is an ethnographic site of the world's first modern hybrids. From this perspective, the transatlantic slave trade and its related postemancipation racialized systems of indentured labor ushered in state projects to manage cultural and racial mixture (Mintz 1974). These systems made Enlightenment ideologies of freedom and personhood dependent on the lived experiences of enslaved Africans, not merely on the principles of liberalism (Buck-Morss 2009). Human equality had been transformed into something related to the law, along with one's sensibility for knowing how it feels to be treated as less than human because of race. In this sense, human equality has been analyzed in Caribbean ethnohistoriography around people's efforts to live with respect and dignity while holding out for a utopian future (Freeman 2014; Wilson 1969).

Still, anthropologists' doubts about what counted as human equality in mid- to late twentieth-century Guyanese ethnography persisted. By Jayawardena's and Williams's accounts, many resisted identifying with mati norms even though they still felt aggrieved by state institutions that showed an unwillingness to ensure basic rights. For instance, the 1964 race riots that ushered in national independence and the military's use of violent tactics to quell union activity in the agriculture sector (predominated by Indo-Guyanese) and the mining sector (predominated by Afro-Guyanese) created a repressive political atmosphere for all. This is what Raymond Smith (1995) means when he describes life in Guyana as "living in the gun mouth," where the fear of racialized violence is ever present, even for those racial groups who believe they hold power. Thus, despite scholars' attention to the flattening and strategic positioning of race in mati norms, they have tended to describe race as an empirical experience of exploitation and its ethnically and culturally specific forms of marginalization. In doing so, they have not addressed how race may also become a symbolic relation for articulating redress.

Mati norms, in this respect, may also provide a useful ethico-political framework for understanding *why* the Hope Canal compensation packages divide people instead of bringing them together. For the Hope/Dochfour farmers, the compensation is shortsighted because they view themselves as having never been without drainage skill sets or flood knowledge. Instead, they have been imposed upon by the EDWC and engineers for different reasons at different moments (e.g., the formation of WUAS versus the Hope Canal). Their expertise is historically produced through both bottom-up and top-down processes, underscoring the limits of racial biopower and hegemony to justify climate adaptation. They do not treat the drainage system as a self-evident tool for promoting agricultural livelihoods, as the state assumes, but they also do not regard their knowledge of drainage as distinct from that of other Afro- or Mixed Race small men in Hope/Dochfour and Ann's Grove. Within this lived experience of climate adaptation, where counter-racial thinking and compensation are mutual efforts at consolidating power, various embodied forms of vulnerability to climate change come to light. In other words, farmers are more than small men; they are survivors of disaster, bricoleurs, political provocateurs, village members, and efficient water takers. But above all, like engineers, they are not prophets. They struggle in various ways to adapt to climate change while turning to pegasse-laden canals and EDWC embankments to give them some clue about what climate change has in store and new ways to organize across villages to monitor drainage.

It is worth noting that the farmers who warned me that the state was trying to "buy the Indian small man" did not view themselves as being racial or overly concerned with perpetuating apaan jaat. They believed that they were revealing the true consequences of the canal's design. For instance, they expressed concerns about insecurities, such as lost crops or washed-out roads, due to the canal's potential failure. The farmers recognized the problem of the color line the compensation packages enacted. They did not assume that their compensation was the end point of climate adaptation. This is because they developed other practical activities to monitor the disturbances the Hope Canal and intense flooding were causing them. But these practical activities are grounded in human acts of sensing as well, and so they have just as many limitations as engineers' EDWC modeling and design operations.

When I visited the Hope Canal in its final phase of construction in July 2014, it resembled a river (see figure 4.2). For six miles, its slight bend and uneven embankment made the handful of houses and road that ran parallel to it appear as if they were accidental bystanders. The houses were on stilts, and the road was elevated. If I had not known I was walking along a partially completed canal, I would have assumed groundwater in Hope/Dochfour always charted its own path. But there had been little rain in the past few months, which meant that somewhere along the canal's six-mile stretch, engineers were hastily building.

Many of the farmers resettled for the canal acquired new lots near where engineers had found large amounts of pegasse and reinforced the canal with geotextile. In this respect, pegasse served multiple purposes in Hope/Dochfour. But farmers knew it best as a nutrient for crops. It supported all types, including coconut, tubers, melon, squash, bora (Chinese long beans), pepper, *boulanger* (eggplant), and okra. In particular, coconuts were an important food staple as well as an index of property. Farmers treated coconuts as a central feature of their diet and economy because coconut trees

FIGURE 4.2. Hope Canal in 2014

were located in the house yard or kitchen garden, whereas other cash crops cultivated on provision grounds required more labor.

Farmers relied on what could loosely be described as a collaborative network to sell their crops at one of Georgetown's big markets. The Doodnauth-Dass family manages one such network on Thursdays. Roy, the eldest son (pictured in figure 4.3), who is in his thirties, used money from the Hope Canal compensation package to buy a minibus to haul crops to and from Georgetown. Alongside his teenage cousins, nephews, and a family friend, he drives to farmers' homes to pick up crops in Hope/Dochfour and parts of Ann's Grove. The farmers pack each type of crop into separate rice mill bags. Roy asks for the types of crops they are selling, while the others load the bags into the minibus (see figure 4.4). They never weigh the bags but inform farmers about the number and quality of other crops Roy is collecting for the week. By late afternoon, they drive to Georgetown to drop off the crops. At the market, they meet with a vendor and collect money for the past week's drop-off, touch base with a city constable to record their new drop-off, and pick up market workers who need a ride back to Hope/Dochfour. If there is any room left in the minibus on the way back, Roy drives along the public bus route to pick up passengers.

Some of the money Roy receives from the vendor is used to cover the Doodnauth-Dass family's travel costs, and the rest is split among the farmers who contribute to the week's drop-off. In this way, each farmer bears equal risk and opportunity—or can be guaranteed an income even during a period when sales are weak. Trust is integral to these exchanges. The farmers rely on Roy returning with not only money but also a few words of reassurance that the vendor is still interested in working with them. Roy's female relatives usually have the task of bookkeeping, double-checking line items and sales for the week.

The bookkeeping ledger, as measuring apparatus, provides an account of not only the income the family generated from the new business but also, as Roy explained to me, the commitments he put into attracting more residents to work with the family and the losses he could expect from intense flooding due to either rainfall or the partial realignments in drainage. Given these commitments, Roy was equally interested in keeping vigil over the Hope Canal's construction. "I never have to keep numbers. You just know. It's all in here [my head]," he joked as we sat on a shaded bench in his yard and stared at the canal's embankment. He was describing the crop yields lost since the canal's construction began. Although it was 2014—over four years since farmers moved and were compensated—neither the canal nor its secondary

FIGURE 4.3. Roy Doodnauth-Dass standing on the Hope Canal embankment

FIGURE 4.4. Roy's cousin loading crops into the family's minibus

drainage channels were complete. Roy's provision grounds were now under the constant threat of flooding because the area's original drainage system was cut off from its regular path for the canal's construction. Without a reliable drainage system, he and other farmers experienced intense flooding when it rained, and crops were "drying up in no time" when the sky was clear.

He noted that he often "didn't get through" when he tried contacting the ministry for specifics about the canal's construction time line. Along with describing the grief he experienced because of the piecemeal construction,

Roy offered a critical appraisal of climate adaptation and the value of keeping a bookkeeping ledger to record his profit:

> It's like this: say they [the ministry] take this piece of land and there's a coconut tree. I make GYD$5,000 [US$24] per month on this coconut tree. And now to cultivate back a piece of land and put back a coconut tree, it would take you about three months. Now you calculate it by month, and that's how much they are supposed to pay you. This canal is taking the barren food we have, which is our backbone. See, with cash crop, it's our normal thing. We take it to the market and sell to get the family going, and everything. But too with some other crops like these, coconut, this crop is our backbone, it comes from our fore-parents, come to us and this probably might be our savings. And so you know if we fall short, our crop—whether the dry or rainy season—we have something to raise us.

Although he received a lump compensation payment of GYD$2.1 million (US$10,056), Roy was still preoccupied with securing his future. Apart from potential changes in weather patterns, the canal itself informed how Roy perceived climate adaptation. On the one hand, he understood climate adaptation to be synonymous with a virtual land grab, with the state dispossessing farmers of their property. On the other, he increasingly perceived farming as dependent on one kind of cash crop: coconut. By recognizing the spatiotemporal limits of climate adaptation projects, Roy uses the bookkeeping ledger to draw a boundary, or an agential cut, between the market value of his crops and his lived experience of flooding and drainage (Barad 2007). The Hope Canal's pegasse-laden embankments have now made him skeptical about the water flow on his land. He wonders whether he can make a good life for his family.

Even when he is able to salvage a crop, Roy faces difficulties simply working next to the canal, which has an embankment over twelve feet tall. A towering structure, it not only lays the canal's path but is a useful resource that helps Roy decide where to plant crops. The ministry initially wanted to relocate farmers' provision grounds to lands that were at a lower elevation than their original lots. This land would have been more difficult to drain, so Roy led engineers to an area in the backlands that he knew had a higher elevation. The engineers ultimately agreed with the suggestion and relocated provision grounds to that area. His suggestion brought about an impromptu exchange of knowledge incited by eroding terrain, drainage, and the elevation of land. In that moment, Indian small men such as Roy became the guides facilitating the canal's construction instead of following the lead of engineers.

Roy assumed that the new location would work as long as he and others received new secondary drainage. But they had yet to receive it, so he resorted to using the canal's embankment to measure the height of floodwaters on his land and places where he could dig makeshift trenches. These encounters with the embankment helped him reconcile the discrepancies between daily work on his land and engineers' design and construction efforts he observed over the years. Given the extra work he put into drainage, he became preoccupied with monitoring where parts of the embankment show signs of too much wear. He and his father would walk parts of the embankment looking for eroding areas that often were composed of vegetation and other remains such as mollusk shells (see figure 4.5).

For Roy, farming was a matter not simply of work but of devotion to pegasse as a resource for articulating a critical appraisal of race in climate adaptation. He took pride in gesturing to other identities, particularly being an evangelical Christian, to explain why he stays on his land despite its problems. He grew up Hindu but became involved with the church in Ann's Grove after a North American congregation visited. Besides Sunday services, annual retreats were a highlight for Roy because the congregation hosted prayer and social activities that brought people in from all walks of life. At one of these retreats he met his partner, an Afro-Guyanese woman, and some members of his extended family also converted. Since becoming a Christian, Roy describes farming as purposeful and centered on making time for God.

FIGURE 4.5. Roy's father inspecting pegasse soils overrun by mollusk shells

Farming in Hope/Dochfour after the 2005 disaster is less a conviction about the value of land than an effort he calls "honest living": finding the will to reach out, partner, and exchange knowledge with others when he cannot rely on himself. For instance, after flooding in 2013, Roy had low expectations for Christmas profits and expected that he would have few resources to buy gifts for his children. While he recognized that the rainfall that year was extreme, he also surmised that because engineers had yet to complete the new drainage canals, the flooding was worse than usual. He noted that despite the flooding, he found relief in attending the *jhandis* (Hindu thanksgiving rituals) of neighbors and family members. He also found relief in daily life by traveling along the Hope Canal in a rowboat he and his father painted with the slogan "Try Jesus." Engineering and religion were becoming parallel lifeworlds for Roy, generating relations of care between coconut trees, pegasse, Jesus, and Hindu prayer flags.[9]

But living honestly or having religious devotion does not make it any easier to ignore the apaan jaat fray. While Roy was grateful for the compensation and new land, he still interpreted the canal construction as a divisive political process. He explained at length:

> Part of this canal is politics. Because, years ago, the government say we do this. It just be we the government, we don't want something the previous government left, we don't want to be *anybody legacy*, we want a name for ourselves. And also its money making too because you build this, you give a friend a contract. So yes, they come in and gave us compensation. OK, good. If they [the government] feel like coming they will have a meeting. But you tell them your view and how you are feeling, like you here taking notes and everything—nothing happens. It just goes like that. Because they come, they come just because of the politics. They feel because we are like you, Indian. We are in power. We will give you security. But when they are gone they don't care about you.

Roy regarded the Hope Canal as enacting a chain of events over which he had very little control even though he was an essential player in making it a reality. He suggested that climate adaptation creates a public debate about whether it is morally right for the state to use a language of compensation to rewrite the history of the coast's drainage. Similar to other modes of environmental governance, including conservation and ecosystem services, climate adaptation is indebted to galvanizing rhetoric about the prior structures of social and economic power to articulate an assemblage of the now (West 2016). Roy suggested that everyone—politicians, engineers, state officials, and farmers—knew that the Hope Canal was a tall order with few guarantees.

I asked Roy to clarify what he meant by "power" and if that had anything to do with how residents in the village vote in elections. He noted:

> Ann's Grove is more like Negro people, so PNC. And here [Hope/Dochfour] it's more like a mixed community. Here it's kind of mixed PPP and PNC. And though we are Indian we aren't like that [PPP]. Here's why. Like for me, I never vote. And most in this community don't vote, because we don't feel like we are treated the way we should. We would say, man, "I want this to happen and I will vote for his party." But here, they will promise you something and come and campaign and do this and it won't pass, so why would we want to put you in power? The same people that come here and tomorrow they are in power they won't talk to you. They won't listen. You can't reach these people. Even the minister of agriculture is silent. We farmers—*we are* agriculture. And he's not there. You understand? You say tomorrow is Wednesday, he's out, never available, the permanent secretary is gone. Even the engineers come with their assignment and just have their work. They come in and don't ask of our land, and come in and just dig. It's politics and power, man.

"Politics and power" are coupled realities but, indeed, not identical ones. Roy's decision not to vote is a strategic refusal of the stereotype of the Indian small man as a docile servant of the PPP and irrigation and drainage infrastructures. At the same time, he finds comfort in a racialized narrative about the political distinctions between a place like Ann's Grove and Hope/Dochfour. He erases the complexities of his racial status within Hope/Dochfour as a partner and father of a *dougla* (Mixed Race, Afro-/Indo-) household. He knows that it pays to show a public face as an Indian small man. This contradiction creates the conditions for Roy and others to "make new sense of their situation [and] forge alliances" in ways that help them articulate critical insights beyond binary terms (Li 2019, 47). After all, farmers "are agriculture," whether they manipulate pegasse for cultivation or rely on it to monitor the Hope Canal's structural stability.

Racializing Tropes

Engineers have a complicated and, at times, nerve-wracking relationship with pegasse. They recognize that it can hamper their design measures. For this reason, pegasse is a helpful explanation and, in a few instances, an alibi for why they view their work as not determined by apaan jaat. But as Roy remarked, it is another issue altogether whether ordinary citizens believe or have faith in the work of engineers. Perhaps the biggest challenge the state faces is convincing ordinary citizens to cosign for, or at the very least not stand in the way of, climate adaptation projects in Guyana. One of these tactics involves state agencies, such as the Ministry of Housing, framing compensation for resettlement as a collective effort that alleviates the nation's vulnerability to climate change. This tactic may not require much nuance on the part of a postcolonial and postsocialist state such as Guyana, where apaan jaat has played a role in performing difference and establishing legal systems of labor, property, and land. Apaan jaat produces a certain history about the coast's irrigation and drainage infrastructures and the expertise of the people who have drained and reengineered coastlands. Referring to compensation in racialized terms, the state therefore treats climate adaptation as a kind of litmus test of its commitment to social welfare for all citizens.

Despite the initial conflict over the interpretation of Article 13 of the constitution, the state has since encouraged farmers like Roy to provide feedback to engineers about the EDWC's drainage system and the Hope Canal. In turn, farmers have become implicated more than ever in the EDWC's operations, even as the state recognizes their land as expendable in its broader plans for LCDS. The state assumes that any racial-ethnic group is susceptible to becoming a population in need of compensation. There is, in other words, nothing exceptional about Indian small men and the crisis of apaan jaat that climate change has intensified in Guyana. With every climatic event (such as drought, torrential rainfall, and dust storms) that threatens the country, the state continues to offer new frameworks for justifying why climate adaptation projects are necessary for the continued settlement of the nation.[10]

From this perspective, compensation for climate adaptation functions quite differently from other racialized modes of governmentality that are explicitly concerned with displacement-resettlement. Paul Silverstein (2005, 365) argues, for instance, that European state immigration policies tend to treat non-Western immigrant populations as possessing incommensurable racial differences that challenge the integrity of the nation-state: "This racial categorization amounts to the construction of a new 'savage slot' . . . through which immigrants are constructed as the European nation-state's abject, and anthropology's increasingly preferred, exotic other." In climate adaptation projects, however, the savage slot is not a category the state fears but, rather, is one that it embraces.

To receive funding for climate adaptation, the state first declares to its citizens, international lenders and the United Nations Intergovernmental Panel on Climate Change (UN IPCC) that it is committed to drawing up plans that enhance the livelihoods of all citizens. Moreover, the label *savage* that Silverstein argues is central to contemporary governmentality is not reserved for any one type of racialized citizen in climate adaptation. The figure of the savage is the state's *preferred* citizen, in need of state-sponsored expertise for infrastructural and/or land management.

For this reason, the clearest path for pursuing climate adaptation involves cultivating a hyperawareness about racial inequality. Such hyperawareness is shaped by words, images, and affect invested in pursuing alternative modes of human engagement. Pursuit in this iteration is marked by the duration of time it takes for someone to visualize a shift between the present and the future. Breaking the narrative continuity between racial inequality and conflict, pursuit creates moments that seek to decouple race from power. Specifically, climate adaptation pushes against what Michel Foucault (2003) identifies as the modernist image of race war, or a population defending itself against degeneration, whether as a consequence of xenophobia or ethnocentricism (see also Rasmussen 2011). But when Foucault and other scholars treat race war as the only end point of modern racial politics, the concept tends to assume a narrative of universal history salvaged and told from the perspective of the victors.[11] There is perhaps another way to conceive of race beyond this master trope to engage the pursuits of people attempting to avoid racial inequality into the future.

In climate adaptation, images of race war are unsettled by images of the potential absence or the representation of racialized subjects living, striving, and working toward "zero." Following the insights of number theory, "the view of zero as a position in a structure performs as well with respect to the Ontological Constraint. Zero is to be conceived of as a *position in a (relevant kind of) structure*, much as the other numbers" (Barton 2020, 3828; emphasis added). Climate adaptation makes space for racialized subjects to think beyond race war while cultivating new ethical practices for thinking zero.

Rather than zero as a mere index of future death or mass extinction, climate adaptation also treats zero as undergirding a sentiment of measured optimism: zero communities excluded from consultation on flood hazards; zero people left behind when it floods; zero engineers and farmers who migrate. The fear of small numbers has diminishing returns in climate adaptation. These are future scenarios that make climate adaptation worth investing in even as apaan jaat proves relentless.

But accounting for zero is not the only factor that goes into feeling, pursuing, and doing climate adaptation. It is also important to note that climate adaptation seeks to make explicit how some racial groups may become overrepresented in practices of calculation, measurement, and design. An unintended outcome of compensation for climate adaptation is that when the state targets all citizens, it is at risk of continuously unearthing citizens' past grievances of being excluded. In turn, those citizens who do not find compensation or resettlement very prudent or advantageous may deem the state deeply offensive, bigoted, racist, or flat-footed in its response to climate change. Thus, the alternative to the state's multiculturalist attempts at climate adaptation compensation often circulates in the guise of counter-racial thinking.

As farmers' struggles to slow down the Hope Canal's construction make evident, counter-racial thinking is not in opposition to the EDWC per se but is in opposition to apaan jaat as a guiding principle of the state's modes of address to citizens. Their opposition suggests a more general point: people's lived experiences of race are not indebted to a single domain of knowledge. Not only the engineering sciences but also the social sciences, biological sciences, natural sciences, the arts, and religion, for instance, have all played a part in the way people tell stories about race and confront it in daily life. Images of Earth—its land, water, minerals, soils, and atmosphere—are captured in these stories and differently signal the configuration of race as a planetary subject of politics (Spivak 2005). Counter-racial thinking in climate adaptation makes this point evident while creating space for people to treat some knowledge forms as more important than others to explain race and its dehumanizing effects.

And yet, counter-racial thinking may offer only a momentary instead of a permanent disruption to the inner workings of apaan jaat. This is an especially fair critique in light of the management of unknown climatic risks alongside the ambivalence many non-White Guyanese have historically had about their identities as settlers. Their ambivalence raises questions about how counter-racial thinking challenges not only racism but also liberalism's model of the propertied citizen that climate adaptation seeks to compensate.

To start, this ambivalence has been shaped by an emerging transregional geography of racialized land grievances in Guyana. Many have argued that the current efforts by the state to incorporate Amerindian communities into plans for LCDS have the potential of repeating colonial-era state practices of settlement/bare life that privileged the development of mining-logging camps over basic infrastructural development (e.g., roads, water, and electricity) in the interior region writ large. Likewise, the state's management of coastal front lands has been described by many Guyanese in recent years as on the brink of collapse. Located adjacent to the sea, front lands are some of the most difficult in the country to manage for cultivation and housing. With slave emancipation, most front lands were bought by freedmen during the village movement. Today, those lands are informally referred to as African ancestral lands and have been inherited, with or without transport titles, by many who no longer reside full time in the country. In their absence, African ancestral lands have been at the dual risk of sea-level rise and of reappropriation for private and state development. In 2017 the state, along with the African Cultural and Development Association, established a commission to create an inventory of lands bought after slavery and to compensate Afro-Guyanese who have lost land. Originally the commission included Amerindian lands as part of its inventory, but the partnership failed to materialize after some state officials and Amerindian activist groups called for separate hearings (Wilkinson 2017).

Many of these land disputes, similar to those involving the Hope Canal, are never litigated in court. Some lawyers contend it is because disputes are hatched out on the ground in much more civil and effective ways between land officials, engineers, and landowners, while others argue that Guyana is not a litigious culture because people fear political retaliation or racial discrimination. Collectively, the Hope Canal, the LCDS Amerindian land disputes, and the African ancestral lands inventory reflect that climate adaptation unfolds in ways that draw Guyanese toward noticing the more-than-human in order to renounce apaan jaat. Floodwaters, eroding pegasse, rising sea levels, and carbon flow are nonlife forces that inspire counter-racial thinking. Climate adaptation, in other words, is one instance of what Elizabeth Povinelli (2016) has called the rejection of the boundary between life (organic) and nonlife (inorganic) as the distinguishing feature of liberal citizenship.

Beyond Guyana's Indian small men, critical appraisals of compensation for climate adaptation have depended on the expertise of other racialized subjects across the planet. Perhaps the most noted are Tuvaluan climate refugees, positioned by the United Nations as the world's first peoples to "speak for an entire planet under threat" (Farbotko and Lazrus 2012, 382). Their ability to speak for an entire planet assumes that other nation-states have already failed to respond in an adequate way to climate change. Moreover, their migrations (or potential migrations) in this planetary iteration become decoupled from past transnational migrations, including the transatlantic slave trade. In a similar vein, the White, male Appalachian coal miner, long coded as a prototypical all-American subaltern, finds his life chances cut short by miners in fast-developing, coal-dependent states such as China, South Africa, and India. Indeed, racializing tropes of climate adaptation can often index global hierarchies of resettlement and displacement that make locales such as coastal Guyana appear marginal to political imaginaries of climate adaptation. But while these tropes metastasize as the planet gets hotter, so do people's commitments to climate adaptation and debates about its viability.

5

There were moments during my fieldwork when engineers reminded me that their work required numerous compromises. Only after watching the course of a river, cloud, or tide could they find a rhythm. Over the years, some picked up habits such as smoking to pass the time before instructing laborers to dig. Others rested in field offices, opting to fill out budget reports until enough time had passed to begin leveling the EDWC's embankment again. Sometimes at the end of the day they kept each other company at rum shops before reluctantly going home to settle into a different rhythm. They believed that there was a profound relationship between nature and technology that made *science* only a partial descriptor of engineering.

Their compromises were not a great surprise. After all, I spent a lot of time hustling to get clearance from state ministries to do my research. With the numerous calls and trips to various offices, I assumed that I was doing something wrong. "Floods?" I heard as state officials grudgingly stamped my papers. "We have engineers for that. You aren't an engineer; they do that work." Part of their hesitation about granting me research clearance stemmed from the fact that the study of coastal flooding did not fit into any existing bureaucratic slot for research fees. But they eventually gave in after the Environmental Protection Agency took note of this loophole and decided to redefine its category of environmental research to include coastal sites. Even within state channels of research clearance, efforts persist to distinguish the value to the nation of interior versus coastal settlement.

I should have been, or so I was told, at the University of Guyana's Amerindian Research Unit, making inroads on studying the mining industry's impacts on the national economy. Or even better, I should have been studying Amerindians and land stewardship to provide the country invaluable knowledge about its culture. After I recounted my hustle to obtain a research permit, George Simon, a prominent Lokono (Arawak) Guyanese artist and archaeologist at the university, explained to me, "With floods, you can conquer a lot. It would be great if you could find a love story in floods." He gave this advice before leaving to take teaching contracts in another part of South America. His departure was etched into my memory as a reminder that climate adaptation often comes with a lot of sacrifice.

I was at first leery of George's love story proposition. As I understood it, he wanted me to figure out how people forge attachments to a place for long periods of time despite the odds. This seemed hard to justify about a research topic so overdetermined by political divisiveness.[1] Yet I came to realize that George was not wrong because climate adaptation has been a practice that requires engineers to deeply care for, rather than abandon, the EDWC. They do work very few are qualified for and in environmental conditions that would make even the most ardent conservationists rethink their commitments. By choosing to stay and combat floods, engineers produce love stories: narratives about the methodological opportunities, challenges, and fieldwork operations that contribute to settlement.

Engineers recognize that the troubles pegasse creates for them and the EDWC cannot be tackled alone. In an effort to anticipate the EDWC overtopping or eroding, engineers have partnered with other experts. To date, they include military personnel affiliated with the CDC who were the first responders during the 2005 disaster, implementing a flood early warning system. Engineers provide CDC staff insights about where the EDWC could fail, and the CDC staff provide engineers insights about the time and resources needed to respond to such a scenario. These engagements reveal that climate adaptation rescues engineers' affection for a thing—in this case, the EDWC—from being overdetermined by possession (Berlant 2011b). In turn, climate adaptation unfolds not only as a practice in prediction but also as a desire composed of intersecting agencies, materialities, bodies, scenes, and milieus. Engineers, CDC staff, and pegasse encounter one another in often subtle but consequential ways to develop new drainage arrangements for the EDWC.

I take these encounters as my ethnographic object or entry point for tracking love stories. Venturing into an ethnography of love stories, I ask how climate adaptation challenges the material-infrastructural norms of coastal settlement in Guyana. Since the 2005 disaster, for instance, engineers have found that the EDWC's embankment dam's internal drainage channels are more complex than they previously thought. These channels, essential to flood management, have eroded and become clogged over the centuries, putting a strain on the EDWC. Sometimes glossed as simple load-bearing foundations, soils have an engineering value that is often credited as merely pragmatic, as detailed by engineer William Russell in the late nineteenth century. But soils—as strata, objects of erosion, and fluvial sediment—are also agents that shape technical engineering activities in diverse ways. Engineers now use other kinds of construction material, such as geotextiles, to reinforce the EDWC. As they build with these materials, they learn to question the relevance of measuring apparatuses, such as hydraulic models for damming, while developing new ones, including the flood early warning system.

To this end, the Hope/Dochfour farmers' efforts at counter-racial thinking do not unfold in a technical vacuum. They parallel engineers' production of love stories, even as engineers decide to sideline, or at least selectively engage, the expertise of Hope/Dochfour farmers. Love stories hinge on difference, subsuming the Other into worlds of engineering. With this in mind, I find it helpful to treat love stories as a subgenre of counter-racial thinking, which experts trained in the engineering sciences create to demonstrate their commitment to the safety of the general public. Engineers' partnerships with CDC staff, for instance, often involved conversations about pegasse and, to a lesser extent, apaan jaat. I read such silences not as signaling elitism or an obliviousness to race. Instead, the silences evoked a sensitivity to the broad range of ways in which their work comes into tension with more-than-human flood hazards that disrupt the disciplinary gaze of apaan jaat. Following Rudolf Mrázek (2002, xvi), engineering has the capacity in particular moments of national formation to "[break] through—or at least scratch—the otherwise smooth surface of [people's] behavior and language." Climate adaptation, in other words, lays bare much more than the legacies of race and settlement; it sustains relations of encounter, desire, and expertise.

Guyana's Ministry of Agriculture negotiated with the World Bank for funding the multiyear Conservancy Adaptation Project (CAP). For the World Bank, CAP was its first project in the Caribbean to target infrastructure for climate adaptation. The project was expected to produce hydraulic models and usher in a framework for knowledge transfer whereby engineers across the Caribbean would share hydraulic data and technical dam information related to climate change. The timing of CAP was significant, as the World Bank previously had been in the business of directly targeting economic development projects rather than environment or infrastructure (Sande Lie 2015). With CAP, the World Bank created a portfolio to launch separate climate change action and global infrastructure facility programs worldwide, including a similar dam project in Suriname.

As one might expect, what followed CAP negotiations were months of reviews, consultations, and contract bids in Guyana. The Ministry of Agriculture solicited both local and foreign engineering firms to bid on projects to create hydraulic models. With advances in computer programming in the 1970s, hydraulic modeling has since involved engineers streamlining data related to water velocity alongside fluid mechanics (Arndt, Roberts, and Wahl 2000). The engineers I worked with, in a self-conscious slippage that indexed a blurring of theory and practice, often used the term *flood model* to talk about hydraulic models. Before the 2005 disaster, for instance, the ministry had successfully produced a hydraulic model of the EDWC with help from the US Army Corps of Engineers, whose water balance study focused on the long-term rainfall patterns and water flows into the EDWC and modeled scenarios for irrigation water services (Morton and Guzmán 2014; Quintero, de Beer, and Lochan 1991) but analyzed little about the impact of storms on the EDWC's internal drainage channels.

When CAP started, the ministry was short on computer software and staff with skills in advanced modeling, so it decided to solicit support from the British engineering firm Mott MacDonald. With experience working on MMA Scheme–related irrigation and drainage infrastructures in the early 2000s, Mott MacDonald looked to square the circle of past, present, and future hydraulic modeling operations in Guyana. At the same time, their bid cleared space for two local private engineering firms to work with the ministry to continue physical repairs and constructions on the EDWC.

The approach to CAP hydraulic modeling developed from one simple observation: the EDWC does not have a level slope. This insight was not obvious to Guyanese engineers or to Robin, Mott MacDonald's British engineer consulting on CAP, because there were no existing bathymetric assessments of the embankment dam. In an interview, Robin recounted to me the difficulties associated with the EDWC's topography: "It was always very low-lying land. If you look at the digital elevation model we made, it shows that the original drainage went out to the Mahaica River and it would have all been floodplain, so engineers did not excavate that. There's been excavation of channels but no large-scale excavation to create a reservoir. The EDWC, with its total length of the embankment, is quite an unusual structure." Robin conceded that it is difficult to model the EDWC's elevation and that accounting for it requires engineers to identify the EDWC's internal drainage channels.

Take, for instance, the measurements required to produce a digital elevation model of the EDWC. A surveyor affiliated with the US Geological Survey took numerous LiDAR (infrared) surveys of the EDWC from an airplane. The technology works by sending a laser light signal to the ground and measuring how long the pulse takes to return, which is dependent on the type of terrain detected by the plane's laser range finder. With these coordinates, the surveyor created a model depicting the EDWC's vertical datum or elevation at various points. The surveyor found that the embankment dam is low-lying compared to the higher-elevation or multiple peaks that have formed in the middle of it to create drop-off points that drain water into the EDWC's flood catchment. Engineers' LiDAR surveys revealed not only that the EDWC is organized by measuring practices; the sheer force of floodwaters can also radically alter the EDWC's coordinates.

To better understand this problem of "multiple peaks" in the EDWC, I take a cue from Helen Verran's (2001, 39–47) critical analysis of numbers as "decomposing" figures. As Verran understands it, technoscience assumes that things in the world can be described and compared with measurement units. For instance, such measuring practices as scientific assessments and surveys tell stories about how numbers are produced in the everyday routine of laboratories or field sites. She explains, "Numbers are familiars that seem to 'do' us as we do 'them'" (30). They are transactional entities that take part in charting connections between humans and things. I interpret Verran as arguing that measuring practices enact a sort of haunting—that is, they have the potential to reveal the multiplicity or nonorigins of numbers.[2] In the case of the LiDAR survey, the vertical datum reveals that humans and more-than-human forces have not equally contributed to the physical formation of the EDWC throughout its existence.

If Robin is right that the EDWC's original embankment naturally compressed over time, then LiDAR surveys provide an incomplete view of the EDWC's internal drainage channels. To resolve this issue, Robin turned to hydraulic modeling for a richer analysis of the EDWC. Building the model required that engineers mount water-level monitors and automatic water sensors in the EDWC to measure water inflow and outflow over multiple wet seasons (circa 2008–10). With this data, Robin solved finite differential equations that took into account water levels, discharges, and velocities at various elevations within the EDWC. He referred to the model in qualified terms: "Everything is interlinked, so the flow at one point is dependent on what is happening at another; it's a simultaneous set of equations that the model solves."

He modeled for an overall calibration of extremes: fifty-, one hundred–, one thousand–, and ten thousand–year rainfall events with scenarios for changes in sea level and rainfall patterns. The model showed that even a fifty-year event contributes to water levels in the EDWC that are unsafe and that the most efficient way to lower water levels involves building a new canal adjacent to the EDWC. These scenarios, Robin noted, were rough estimations. He explained to me at length that the model's "grid spacing" was not detailed enough to capture the "true grid" of the EDWC's internal drainage channels:

> I think with an approach to modeling you have to be able to deal with different scales. One of the difficult things with 2D [two-dimensional] models is that most of the flow in the EDWC is occurring within small channels. And if you have a conventional 2D model, the grid spacing you have could be one hundred meters or 250 meters, and the channels themselves where most of the flows are coming through are much smaller in the EDWC, like tens of meters wide. So you know if you have a proper 2D model, you aren't really picking up the flow properly. As an alternative, we linked a 1D and 2D model where you have a 1D model representing the channel system and you link that in with nodes on a 2D model to represent your drainage channel. But with this you still get numerical instabilities in the interface between your 1D and 2D models. So the approach we adopted for CAP was a more pragmatic approach; I would call it a pseudo-2D model. We couldn't model a grid that could give us the whole conservancy, to show a true grid.

Scaling up hydraulic models is an indeterminate process (Haff 2013). Robin's "pseudo-2D" modeling approach reveals that the EDWC's small channels or subchannels are much more interdependent than engineers previously thought.

His approach created what I would call *channels of authority*. Even if Robin could identify subchannels, which would be most important to the EDWC's overall function? Many engineers in Guyana would argue that those connecting to the Mahaica River are most important, but this choice assumes a storm occurs during low tide. A problem engineers faced in 2005 was that the extreme rainfall in January occurred during high tides, so the sluices of canals could not be lifted to drain water. Or, one might imagine that extreme rainfall occurs during a cycle of shore accretion or mudbank migration from rivers, when canal outfalls are more prone to being silted and clogged with mud. There are a finite number of scenarios and material-epistemic arrangements under which the EDWC system can adequately drain.

When Robin spoke to me about the EDWC, he was quick to note the numerical instabilities in other hydraulic models he has developed, as if to make sure I did not assume that Guyana's flooding woes were outside of the norm. His modeling included work for dams located on the Caspian Sea, a landlocked water source that is highly sensitive to changes in sea level and rainfall. After running scenarios of a Caspian Sea dam system, Robin noticed a short period when there was a sea-level decline. At first Robin was confused by the outputs until he considered that in the 1990s, Russian engineers were developing the area's aquifers for dams and thus reversed trends in the region's rising sea levels. "So now," he maintained, "we have to constantly reconsider [the data we are using], what is going on in that [dam] system despite climate change."

From the view of hydraulic modeling for climate adaptation, dams appear to engineers as overdetermined sites of vulnerability. There is no way to study dams without recognizing that an essential part of their character has to do with the ways engineers negotiate measuring grid space. In the case of the EDWC, any discussion of its subchannels slides into one about scalability in which past and potential future disasters are analyzed and the dam's subchannels become the figures that plot the strength of its drainage system. For instance, the pseudo-2D modeling approach identified Hope Village as the *only* site from which water could be effectively pumped for the EDWC's storm relief canal, which suggests that hydraulic models could invent localities as much as erase them in order to make climate adaptation possible.

Still, engineers constantly worry that a subchannel in the EDWC will erode and morph, blocking water flow in one area of the EDWC while the rest of its system keeps flowing as if nothing happened. Or a section of the embankment could collapse, reconfiguring the EDWC's elevation and therefore causing water to drain slowly to create a new subchannel. These are emergent events that have their own histories and often unfold unseen, outside the logics of equations (Nirenberg and Nirenberg 2011).[3] There is no way to imagine these events simply as mathematical in the abstract; engineers instead treat them as reckonings with an unruly world.

Then what good is modeling to the messy worlds of climate adaptation projects? I pose this question not to gloss over the contexts, conventions, and infelicity that grant models their force in the world (Callon 2010; MacKenzie 2008). Rather, I pose it to highlight how and why engineers might turn to other activities to justify climate adaptation and to note that modeling offers only one perspective for imagining its possibilities. Engineers rely on hydraulic models to map the EDWC's drainage channels and predict their function during a storm. At the same time, hydraulic models generate scales of analysis that inhibit them from seeing other geomorphological processes that contribute to drainage channels' transformations over time. So there are indeed fugitive ways of knowing in climate adaptation, which lend themselves easily to invocations of the subterranean or flood knowledges so far overshadowed by hydraulic model outputs but nonetheless fundamental to the EDWC's future.

All Is Subterranean

During the 2005 disaster, Flagstaff—the EDWC's headquarters—was the place where engineers monitored water levels. By the start of CAP, it was a drop-off point for construction materials and equipment. "We'll just have to see where we dig," said Bert Carter, a retired engineer, as he drove Philip Allsopp, another retired engineer, and me to Flagstaff. Full of interest, Bert was taking bets on why a meeting was being convened by the Ministry of Agriculture. He and Philip thought it was unnecessary because the Hope Canal had already taken off with reasonable success. I too was unsure about the need for the meeting because all I could see from the back of the pickup truck were a number of excavators hard at work digging.

When we arrived, a group of engineers was already huddled around a table assessing blueprints. Most knew Bert and Philip and so were eager to tell them about the bottomless pit of pegasse along the northeast edge of the embankment that was causing delays. According to the hydraulic model, this section of the embankment, where soils transition from a mix of pegasse-clay to savannah, is the ideal site for the Hope Canal. They debated whether to take another borehole sample to ascertain the depth of clay in the area. Bert and Philip were a team, playing the roles of consultant and consoler, providing the others insights about the EDWC's cycles of decay and resilience. After about an hour of reciting hydraulic model outputs, everyone agreed that it was best to do more drilling. I had come to know borehole musings as standard intergenerational and fraternal rituals around EDWC constructions. Musings quickly morphed into curiosity, when an engineer turned to me and asked whether the University of Guyana was now training female engineers. If so, today was an ideal day to be on site (see figure 5.1).

It turned out that the engineers and I were inspired by similar, and perhaps interrelated, geological paradoxes. We had stumbled across something we thought to be of tremendous importance and about which little was known in the professional worlds in which we moved. I had become involved in tracking a present history of climate adaptation. Meanwhile, engineers were becoming more involved in surveying pegasse or the matter that was making climate adaptation particularly difficult. In 1927, British Guiana's first geological survey declared "the sedimentary nature of the coast gives distinctive rise to the artesian conditions on which the coastal water supply depends" (Bleackley 1956, 1). Clays and white sands are the oldest sediments dating back to the Pliocene. Pollen spectra provide detailed records of a period when river levels were very high, blanketing a large swath of both savannah and mangrove forest (Plew 2009). At the same time, sea levels shifted with glacial

FIGURE 5.1. An engineer standing next to the EDWC

events, causing an absolute sea-level rise that moved the coast inland and developed the pegassy conditions (peat) found in the present day (Williams 2003).[4]

Engineers in Guyana do not tell many tales about uniformitarianism or the history of Earth's evolution from the perspective of sediments (cf. Bjornerud 2006; Szerszynski 2019). They might be important geological agents who realign soils for a living, but engineers are not indebted to geology.[5] As one might expect, because pegasse is composed of vegetative matter, it is lightweight. It is almost like a liquid when wet and very hard and brittle when dry, making it quite difficult for engineers to discern sheer strength or the strength of a material against structural failure. Laboratory tests have shown that compressing samples causes diagonal cracks to appear, and engineers can use these disrupted planes to model pegasse's failure rate. The tests offer a snapshot of pegasse at a certain point in time, a vision of soil particles in friction.

But why would engineers care about these minute distinctions between particles if it is nearly impossible to avoid stress on the dam's foundation? That was, in effect, the question addressed by the MIT-Harvard lecturer Karl von Terzaghi from the late 1920s into the 1940s, when he described the world as experienced by soils (De Boer 2005). Analyzing soils under pressure of a consolidation machine, Terzaghi (1943) showed that soils have a physics based on particle mixture. He noted that soils with high water content (such as peat) can congeal into arrangements that can become waterlogged. Subsequent earth pressure tests and professional rivalries led Terzaghi to observe Nazis bombproofing buildings in order to develop his methods. As Terzaghi himself noted, real soils behave differently from those idealized in the laboratory. Soils are not only makers of racialized worlds but also matter that can split them into pieces.

Under CAP, engineers also attend to the interplay of soil worlds and its racialized legacies, and they do so in a way that builds on Terzaghi's theory of soil mechanics. They make inferences about soils based on both their load-bearing capacities and locations relative to drainage channels. This means that soils help engineers fold the EDWC into processes of knowledge production and exchange beyond hydraulic modeling. Soils are both engineers' research objects of climate adaptation and forms of evidence that document humans settling the coast and how it happened.

There are a number of clever ways engineers improvise to engage pegasse and to become (more) responsive to its shape-shifting forms as research objects and evidence. One example is devising strategies for walking to make the EDWC's terrain a bit more predictable. The engineers told me to follow them and step into the footprints they left behind in mud. If there was no mud, I slowed my gait, gaining traction from entangled shrub roots or savannah grasses. Other times I tried to quickly discern clay—usually matter bearing gray, light brown, or red hues—and steered clear of pegasse's dark brown–black globs. We were aligning our bodies with soil particles, but we knew of very few methods for sensing these alignments as a whole. With every step, we pushed and conspired with a world we could never completely inhabit.

Pegasse creates its own atmosphere, bringing an aesthetic dimension to borehole drilling. While engineers relied on rudimentary visual observations of the color and texture of soil to guide these drillings, they also depended on sound. For instance, engineers completed cone-penetrating tests to identify soil compositions near the Hope Canal site. When the cone is pushed into the ground, it chugs like a locomotive. One engineer reflected:

> Borehole one, ten meters: chug. Borehole two, fifteen meters: chug, chug. Borehole three, twenty meters: chug, chug, chug, and so on. And so when you go off, you go to the computer and it gives you this beautiful curve. But that's not the problem. Who is going to interpret that? You have to assume that the machine was right . . . and hopefully the machine is in calibration. Because apparently at different locations [at the EDWC–Hope Canal construction site] you have to have some feel for the terrain, and 'cause we aren't in sand [a surface with little to no friction], you have to decide when to use a different cone for drilling. So you have to have some awareness of pegasse and what it does to the machine.

Borehole drilling allows engineers to reconfigure the dimensions of the EDWC's drainage in real time because it does not require a division of expertise between building infrastructure and knowing the natural history of soils. It is an activity that persists as a reminder of engineers' uneven ways of knowing drainage in Guyana. Engineers read back into pegasse all that is excluded from their hydraulic models.

For instance, an awesome phenomenon of hot weather and pegasse is fire. Unlike the floods that wet weather and pegasse produce, fires cannot be registered via borehole drilling. This is because pegasse fires are often sparked not only by parched soils but also by vegetation. Pegasse fires burn low to the ground, creating a lot of ash, compared to the large flames discernible for miles that are spawned by sugar cane harvest burning. Despite the burn, engineers attest that pegasse fires wreak less havoc than floods on the EDWC. As one engineer explained, "Where a pegassy side burns out in the heat, you can sometimes get a 'catchment area' on the dam itself, so you get a lower buildup of soil over time, a place for water to go, and we try to rebuild the embankment from that." Fires, engineers know, bare the traces of the worlds they transform (Pyne 2001). And, like floods, fires are more than properties of the earth. They are events that shape the entangled pathways for human and soil futures.

For months as engineers investigated the EDWC–Hope Canal construction site, they expanded their borehole drillings to adjacent areas of the EDWC's embankment. They found too much pegasse and too little clay. Not interested in abandoning CAP altogether, they kept drilling and filled as many areas of the embankment as they could with clay to restabilize it. With these newly excavated sites, they reevaluated, albeit within a few hundred feet, where to keep digging the Hope Canal. The pegassy areas near the canal became what engineers called provisional surveillance sites or places to monitor what pegasse was doing to the EDWC's embankment. As far as engineers were aware, this dual method of excavation and surveillance was never before attempted on the EDWC, a reminder of the ways pegasse inspires engineers' methods at climate adaptation. But more to the point, the method demonstrates that soils, and to a lesser extent hydraulic modeling operations, were guiding engineers' understandings of the EDWC's overall drainage.

Engineers' measured rebuffs of hydraulic modeling show how climate adaptation strategies can depend on more-than-human agents shaping new possibilities for human action. Following Stefan Helmreich (2011, 138), pegasse-clay soils "athwart theory"; they help engineers "tack back and forth between seeing things as explanation and taking them as phenomena to be examined." This dynamic is central to how engineers' decisions about measurement are made in climate adaptation when models prove immediately unhelpful and new logistical procedures need to be enacted. A view from the EDWC–Hope Canal construction site reveals that climate adaptation emerges from engineers' urgent need to use pegasse to draw flexible distinctions or boundaries between the empirical and the theoretical.

Another Skin

There is, however, very little naiveté here. Compared to mid-twentieth-century TVA-inspired damming, when engineers assumed they could avoid pegasse, CAP operates in a world where pegasse is a matter that cannot be ignored.

Thanks to pegasse, borehole drilling loosely props up CAP's research program. As the EDWC's head of operations, a man nicknamed Horse, explained to me:

> You have to have physical presence [when dealing with the EDWC]. After the 2005 disaster there were a lot of calls from the ministry reading that data, telling me the dam would overflow and that I had to get people walking on the embankment. But sensors might not see everything. Monitoring the dam is like a military routine. It's like when you have heavy rain or like high tide [and] you have to move. When you walk the dam, you look for any sign of leakage. If it cracks, you can see it split open. And if it's overtopping, you can see it overtopping. As soon as you see it, you have to start fixing it daily or else it [water] will just wash it away. We set our own rules and time lines to what the embankment is doing.

Wet season to dry season, day to day, and hour to hour, this field operation— monitoring dam leakage—is hard work. The Ministry of Agriculture hired about a dozen laborers to train under Horse. They lived in the EDWC, far off in its back end, in wooden barracks that had been renovated from the original colonial structures used when the EDWC was initially planned. The small single rooms, furnished with bunk beds, were sparsely decorated, dimly lit, and not easily converted into living spaces. The bare necessities were all men could afford to enliven the spaces. Transistor radios helped them make contact with the outside world, and tattered government propaganda posters on the walls helped them stay committed to the EDWC, despite the isolation and boredom that engulfed daily life.

By maintaining the EDWC, the laborers made compromises in their personal lives that in many ways proved their love for or attachment to the dam. They rotated every two weeks, sacrificing family and lucrative work to learn how to read the EDWC's terrain. Days were long. Mornings were occupied by watching fish, rattlesnakes, anacondas, ants, savannah deer, and ducks maintain habitats on or in the EDWC. Animals scavenging, foraging, and building on the EDWC's embankment helped laborers identify which areas were susceptible to erosion or infringement. The laborers' insights about animals were structured by nighttime walks on the embankment or canoeing during the quiet early hours to listen for water trickling from cracks in the dam. At the end of the two-week rotation, when many are emotionally exhausted and some are feeling isolated, they rush into town or negotiate with Horse to do different kinds of work.

These field operations demonstrate that pegasse normalizes the often awkward, irksome, mundane, and messy material realities of the other essential work on the EDWC: the construction and alignment of the Hope Canal's embankment. Geotextile reinforced the canal's embankment. The laborers spread the fabric across the ground, pulling and tugging it as if they were making a bed (see figures 5.2, 5.3, and 5.4). Creature-like in their movements, they waded in craters and crevices, contouring their bodies low to

FIGURE 5.2. Laborers unfolding rolls of geotextiles

FIGURE 5.3. Laborers pulling geotextiles

FIGURE 5.4. Laborers folding geotextiles

the ground to fold the fabric to get it snug and fitted to the soil. Excavators stood in as convenient referees in this fight, pouring tons of soil on top of the fabric, redistributing the geotextile's grip in places where the laborers struggled. They repeated this process five days a week for the four years of CAP and interrupted their work only during inclement weather.

While geotextiles—an umbrella term for geomembranes—are delicate, they are malleable enough to respond to changes in soil compositions over time. Indeed, they can mimic the lives of soils. The Dutch first incorporated geotextiles into the construction of dikes damaged by the North Sea flood of 1953. To reinforce the dikes, sandbags composed of geotextiles were placed along their front ends to protect them from water pressure. French engineer J. P. Giroud (2006) used the term *geotextile* for the first time in 1970, at an engineering conference where he proposed that the material could act as a barrier or skin to stop water leakage. He based the term on longitudinal field observations of a dam's embankment lined with geotextile and its exposure to water, wind, and sunlight.

An emphasis on the ways in which geotextiles could be modified for design purposes led Giroud to invent a classificatory scheme of keywords for geotextile skins. *Geomembranes, geotextile cushioning, geonets, geoliners, geocomposites*, and so on became technical language. Touted as an alternative to the costly task of building with metal planks and concrete, geotextiles are described by engineers as having a smaller carbon footprint (Kelsey 2014). Only in recent decades, engineers in Guyana explained to me, has there been a turn worldwide to geotextiles for the construction of inland dams, as the engineering industry becomes more committed to environmentally low-impact construction. Building inland dams with geotextiles is engineers' desperate plea to soils to help them manage flooding, as earthen dams prove increasingly vulnerable to climate change.

Even so, the turn to geotextiles is not a mere claim about the evolution of engineering. At borehole drilling sites, I learned rather quickly that to elicit conversation with engineers I had to talk about CAP's supposed exceptionality. As if to preempt and guard against criticism, engineers often followed up the word *pegasse* with a sigh, along with the disclaimer "We never work with it; we try very hard to avoid it" or the statement "You know 90 percent of our canals are built on clays." Pegasse can divide and rearrange the boundaries of climate adaptation in often subtle ways that rework engineers' understandings of climate adaptation from simply technical matters into a project that challenges the historical-physical arrangement of coastal settlement. One engineer noted:

> We want this [CAP] to be done in two years, you know before the next big flood. So whatever it is that we are doing, you'll have to get an accelerated approach to withstand the loading of the embankment. So you know, we can't wait like the slaves did when they built this thing [the EDWC]—wait for twenty years and wait for things to compress and to be suitable. So, this [geotextile] is an evolution of machinery, to make things quicker. And you know that I'm a civil engineer, I'm not an environmentalist, but based on what I have used in my career, I'm comfortable with my preference to use the fabric, and maybe at some other point we'd decide to use other materials too.

Pegasse undergoes distinct transformations in technical value in light of climate adaptation. Engineers now think of pegasse as forming and taking shape in a shorter time span than they did previously; likewise, they view it as forcing them to build drainage in more efficient ways. This efficiency is what apparently distinguishes contemporary engineers from the category of the slave. This engineer collapses distinctions in racialized human labor by treating the pegasse he encounters in the field as having its own agency.

He believes, nonetheless, that geotextiles offer a turning point in the coast's history of engineering because the EDWC's maintenance is informed by a cautious skepticism about hydraulic models. Geotextiles, in other words, uproot normative racialized boundaries of expertise or the geographic divides between White foreign engineers and Guyanese engineers. He also acknowledges that geotextile building activities prove useful but *only because of* engineers' experiential encounters with pegasse, whereby expert habits, numerical assumptions, and morale are necessarily adjusted to the new threat of intense flooding. Soil particles are thus never simply objects to be enumerated and are instead entities that prompt certain ways of knowing the EDWC. The "matter and meaning" of soils as load-bearing structures do not "pre-exist" but are reconstituted through engineers' assessments about the contingencies of race in various facets of climate adaptation methods and measurements (Barad 2012, 6).

Ventriloquism

Pseudo-2D hydraulic modeling has increased the sophistication of measurement once considered impractical in Guyana. As a practice, hydraulic modeling emphasizes a dam's structural uniformity instead of its gaps or misalignments in design. For this reason, it cannot mirror the moves made by engineers and laborers in the field, who resist totalizing claims about borehole drill tests and the readings of "beautiful curves." Engineers are attentive to the profoundly contingent nature of CAP. They learn to work with and appreciate the EDWC's unwieldy slopes. They remain skeptical about the hunt for the EDWC's true drainage channels, with which they are ultimately involved as they dig the Hope Canal. And they are in no hurry to treat soils and geotextiles as equivalent technologies. But they find that it is much easier to call a truce somewhere in the middle between an ecocentric and an anthropocentric approach to engineering.

If engineers cannot guarantee the EDWC's drainage, then the physical boundaries of the EDWC's flood catchment are also prone to flux. With the public awareness campaign and the animated film *A Bird's Eye View of the EDWC*, the Ministry of Agriculture outlined the logistical problems engineers face managing the EDWC's flood catchment. The film is narrated by "Rocky," a Canje pheasant (*Opisthocomus hoazin*) and Guyana's national bird—a species that, when on the coast, resides in the EDWC. Flying over a map of the EDWC, Rocky explains the importance of the EDWC to humans as well as the difficulties he faces evacuating his home when it floods. The EDWC's main drainage channels light up as he flies over, as if his flight pattern verifies engineers' work whether from ground, water, or air. Unlike the mosquitoes of millennia past, Rocky notes that more heavy rain will force communities in and around the EDWC, including Canje pheasant flocks, to migrate to new homes as far away as Georgetown.

Rocky was spun from the imagination of a British hydrologist. Hired by the ministry to write CAP's final project report, Isabella Bovolo had prior experience producing hydrological surveys for rivers in Guyana's interior region. With CAP, she found herself newly obligated to coastal geographies and the rather opaque spatial arrangements that climate adaptation research demands. "Somehow," she explained to me, "I had to communicate the obvious to people while reassuring them." Working for the first time alongside visual animators and the ministry's marketing team, Isabella was up for the challenge of communicating science rather than only doing science. But she admitted that making this distinction was hard to sustain. She worked under the demands of a tight schedule (just over half a year), compounded by the holdup of data from laborers at the EDWC and the personalities of various state bureaucracies. Her participation in the project was highly sought after and valued by the ministry because she taught at Newcastle University, world renowned for interdisciplinary hydrology studies. Alongside creating the Rocky character, she encouraged junior engineers at the ministry to enroll at Newcastle and to complete master's theses that outline technical recommendations for embankment dam failure (Thorne 2014).

With the birth of Rocky, engineers were no longer the only people experimenting with other kinds of engineering activities to circumvent the shortcomings of hydraulic models. *A Bird's Eye View of the EDWC* demonstrates that hydraulic models are not granted the same importance or value across various phases of climate adaptation projects. Instead, to mobilize and sustain expert commitments to hydraulic modeling, the ministry treats *A Bird's Eye View of the EDWC* as an act of ventriloquism (see also Corren 2010). Through animation, the film disavows models of their magical status as the producers of scale, gesturing to the open-ended and complex engineering activities that go into maintaining the EDWC. Rocky speaks in the name of engineers, charting the gaps between nature and technology, engineering and hydrology, past and future, and knowledge and nonknowledge.

Rocky reminds the public of the floods that have yet to come.[6] In this sense, it was important that the ministry disseminate the cartoon widely, airing it on television on weekend afternoons between local political programming and on its YouTube page. Through a story about how intense flooding manifests in Guyana, *A Bird's Eye View of the EDWC* demonstrates translocal expertise or skill sets that focus on the relations between the circulation of people, natures, and things. But climate adaptation is made in ways that, by definition, also presume to stabilize certain expert alliances and not others.

The challenge for engineers was deciding where and how long to continue their research on the EDWC's drainage system. During the 2005 disaster, villages in close proximity to the EDWC were flooded out when engineers decided to release excess water into the Mahaica River. This was an area engineers believed could be flooded out again, even with the construction of the Hope Canal, so the state ultimately decided to resettle people in Hope Village (see figure 5.5). The people who moved became known as Guyana's first "climate refugees" (*Guyana Chronicle* 2015). Engineers justified the resettlements by arguing that the EDWC's flood catchment is rapidly expanding because of the increased occurrence of torrential storms and therefore is in need of close monitoring (*Guyana Chronicle* 2012). The resettlements have allowed engineers to continue using the Mahaica River as a drainage channel for the EDWC.

These resettlements reproduced a number of overlapping material and institutional arrangements. At first glance, engineers might appear to be involved in an endeavor that is strictly a procedure in normalizing preparedness through modes of prediction. Their decision to resettle people, however,

FIGURE 5.5. Mr. Sankar, a displaced farmer and "climate refugee," standing in his new kitchen garden at Hope Village

was not based on hydraulic model outputs alone. Instead, it was also informed by observations engineers made in the field during the 2005 disaster and while doing soil surveys, borehole drillings, and construction. From this perspective, climate adaptation in a more inclusive sense relies on methods that facilitate the construction and dismantling of research sites, migrations, and flood catchment ecologies. Through such efforts, climate adaptation projects become highly productive of all kinds of discursive material desires for coastal settlement that crosscut strategies at hydraulic modeling.

Vetting

Kester Craig never seemed to mind his time at the EDWC, which was a stark departure from his daily office work at CDC headquarters in Georgetown and his past military training. Since Guyana has never had a major military operation other than negotiating border disputes with agitated Venezuelan militia, intense flooding has had the potential to make the CDC relevant. Having served just over a decade as an officer, Kester was on the cusp of promotion when the CDC was solicited by the United Nations and the Ministry of Agriculture to help engineers develop a flood early warning system. This partnership, however, was easier said than done.

I first came to know Kester after a week and a half of informal vetting. My introduction to the CDC was quite different from my introduction to engineers, who identified my papers and affiliation with the University of Guyana as enough proof for me to tag along. With Kester, papers were not enough, which meant that vetting was a process of both distinction and appraisal. I was shuffled between approval meetings with the UN official on the project, a Tajik disaster management consultant who had prior experience implementing UN reconstruction projects in the early 2000s of the American-Taliban war in Afghanistan. "I know your type," he told me. "You want to come in and tell us our project is wrong." His guess was as good as mine—and for that matter, as those of engineers, animated Canje pheasants, and hydrologists.

After a few weeks of scrutinizing my American accent and training in a social science, he and Kester decided that I could be of potential value. They wanted me to help interview and inform state officials about the flood early warning system, which they described as similar to my own research—making small talk. I could not disagree.

Weeks quickly turned into months, as we and other CDC staff attended meetings with state officials from across the Environmental Protection Agency, the private sector, and the ministries of health, hydrometeorology services, local government, and public infrastructures. A standard form provided by the UN framed Kester's interview questions, which ran the logistical gamut: Did you have enough supplies to help alert the general public or for staff to work during the 2005 disaster? How long were staff absent from work? He also posed leading questions that assumed ineptitude: Does your office have a disaster plan? Were you able to contact the Ministry of Agriculture to get updates about the EDWC and its water level? Such questions prompted ministry officials to recount redemptive narratives about coming to terms with bureaucratic oversight and openness to reform, presumably along the lines of partnering in the future with CDC staff and engineers.

Much of what Kester expected surfaced during these interviews: frustration about too few resources and lack of communication between ministries. He invested in a number of activities to quiet their concerns, such as convening meetings at the CDC headquarters where ministry officials developed standard operating procedures for floods. These procedures included creating filing systems and archives whereby each ministry would catalog flood hazards related to their ministry work. Kester and his team sought information technology specialists to create databases, drew up flow charts of ministry responsibilities for flood response, and, with land management specialists, produced maps of the coastal floodplain and its population density.

These data sets and diagrams were intended to approximate flood scenarios that originate from the EDWC. At one meeting, for instance, discussion morphed into debate about which cabinet officer of the Ministry of Agriculture would communicate updates to other ministries about the EDWC's water level. Initially, an engineer suggested that it did not matter who at the ministry made these announcements. But a meteorologist was quick to note that discerning the duration of a flood is dependent on more than just drainage. Storms can and do shift paths. They swell and dissipate in ways that do not always parallel ministries' organized protocols on the ground. The meteorologist suggested that wind, air pressure, rain, and clouds can make monitoring the EDWC's water levels *during* a storm a moot exercise.

For the meteorologist at the workshop, there is very little fixed about classification. She was not using the term *water level* as a referent to a specific drainage channel in the EDWC, as engineers would. Rather, she spoke of the term in reference to a storm's potential to disrupt bureaucratic arrangements through which the EDWC is managed. This distinction underscores a fundamental point of climate adaptation. The ineluctable blend of nature and technology in the practice of drainage challenges the idea that climate adaptation is a mere effect of human sciences and its taxonomies. More than evidence of storm systems, floods often push back and reorient algorithms of drainage.

"It May Be No Coincidence"

One day I traveled with Kester and some laborers by motorboat across the EDWC. I was warned that the ride would be bumpy. Although I sat near the front, to even out the weight of the boat, water still splashed from all sides. The sun beamed down on us that day, drying our damp skin, hair, and clothes. The mix of the sun's suffocating heat and the motorboat's choppy rhythm made it difficult to gauge the boundaries between our bodies and the EDWC's surface. The laborers were eager to show off newly repaired embankments, while Kester insisted that we also visit the EDWC's sluices. He figured that the sluices were command points, or sites important for reading water levels and communicating early warnings about flooding. Water level readings at Flagstaff were insufficient for providing ministries enough lead time for response. Kester envisioned, instead, that at each sluice, laborers and engineers could analyze local storm conditions, make decisions about when to release water, and then inform relevant ministries as needed.

Kester's approach to the flood early warning system departs from the engineers' hydraulic model in two ways. First, it relies on techniques of measurement embedded not only within the physical space of the EDWC but also across state officials' practices engaged with the EDWC. Second, it creates a demand for what Peter Galison (2001, 8) calls expertise that emphasizes monitoring "vulnerable targets." Galison argues that this kind of expertise originated during World War II, when American and British planners designed strategies for bombing campaigns. Vulnerable targets were often classified as infrastructure systems. This meant that planners had to learn to perform "inverted vision" or analyze how the weapons the enemy used to destroy the Allies could be turned against the enemy's own oil rigs, power plants, roads, or dams (13). Staff at the CDC have also developed a capacity for inverted vision, by analyzing how the EDWC's floodwaters transform communication between engineers and other state officials.

At the same time, CDC staff acknowledge that climate adaptation depends on modes of self-reflection that find potential in the collapse or even the erasure of such techniques as inverted vision. Far from environmental determinism, the all-too-destructive realities of intense flooding led Kester to express anxiety about the flood early warning system. Similar to engineers' sobering encounters with pegasse, I heard him once greet state officials at a workshop with the announcement "It may be no coincidence that the worst flood within living memory occurred so recently!" Kester believed that the mere feat of Guyanese surviving disastrous flooding does not prove that climate adaptation projects work—only that they have the potential to be modified.

This was a proposition that the CDC staff took seriously, in both coordinating workshops and mobilizing research programs. They hired a Japanese consulting firm to help develop the flood early warning system. The firm provided a file of background reading materials, including the 1934 article "Natural Disasters and National Securities" written by Torahiko Terada, a renowned Japanese physicist whose attention to the "physics of actual phenomena" departed from the quantum theory mechanics that shaped the Japanese military's atomic ambitions during World War II (Beatty 2001, 83). Recounting a flood in the Kinki region, Terada writes, "It wouldn't be wrong to say that the man-made structure that stands against nature was the cause of such disasters" (quoted in Beatty 2001, 2). Climate adaptation energized new routes for knowledge production about the EDWC: a Caribbean-meets-East knowledge exchange that paralleled methods for hydraulic modeling and the retelling of flood histories. The CDC's turn to a flood early warning system is a reminder that different technocratic activities generate different scales of analysis of the EDWC and its flood catchment. Climate adaptation has a tendency not only to disorient expertise but also to invite its reinvention through appeals to still other ways of understanding floods. But as CAP participants' work on the flood early warning system becomes more and more complex, those ways of understanding can diverge rather than converge, creating tensions that undermine an allegedly synthetic enterprise such as CAP.

Staff at the CDC experienced this tension when they visited villages in the EDWC's flood catchment to inform residents about the flood early warning system. Fieldwork that began in an effort to valorize the system quickly turned into an effort that further exposed complications with it. These villages were located far from the head of the EDWC and so were outside the relocation zone engineers identified as the Mahaica River's most flood-prone areas. But given the Mahaica River's relatively flat terrain, its sediment and velocity are highly susceptible to change as sea levels rise in the Atlantic and regional rainfall patterns shift (Narayan 2006). This means that the Mahaica River creates its own patterns of climate adaptation, even as it coproduces and subtly recalibrates the drainage of the EDWC.

Well before the CDC arrived, most residents had already devised responses to the river's changes. They had put house foundations on stilts. Those with small garden plots slightly built up the land and dug side trenches around their land to keep river water at bay. Their trenches also supplemented the already heightened earthen embankments engineers had built along the Mahaica River. Yet across properties, faint watermarks on trees and barn doors were still visible. They gave the impression that stilts, trenches, and embankments were not enough. Personnel from the CDC responded to the watermarks by focusing their workshops on educating residents about the flood early warning system while helping them devise community maps and flood evacuation routes. The CDC's notion of climate adaptation shifted, as they recognized these residents' interpersonal connections to the river alongside the narrowing pool of resources they attributed to the river's transformations.

Important players managing this narrowing pool of resources are farmers who, unlike those in Hope/Dochfour, have enough money to hire hands to care for land while they run a small business in Georgetown or visit family abroad. These well-off farmers greeted and engaged CDC staff as they had with other state-sponsored projects in the past: through intimate and reciprocal patronage relationships indebted to home-cooked meals and bags of freshly picked produce. Kester relied on these farmers to encourage other village residents to attend workshops, which meant that when few residents showed, he had less confidence that information about the flood early warning system would circulate.

But even when residents attended and gifts were graciously offered and received, the river created logistical obstacles. Residents with enough knowledge of the Mahaica River guided CDC staff on boat tours. Swamps, piranha-infested banks, and steep embankments often stood in the way of CDC staff taking surveys and documenting the distance between a river's edge and homes or roads. The information residents provided CDC staff did not always resonate or synchronize with the broader aims of CAP. Farmers, for instance, have become adept at identifying distinctions in types of floodwater. It turns out that when the Mahaica River's water is blackish in color, they know that engineers have drained fresh water from the EDWC into the Mahaica River. This human-made water flow is less predictable than when it is high tide and salt water inundates their land, turning the Mahaica River clearer and the land salty.

The focus of CDC staff and village residents on the Mahaica River helped them recognize the subtle variations in the boundaries of the EDWC's flood catchment. At the same time, the Mahaica River's seasonal flux is indifferent to the technocratic modes of organization, measurement, and observation that inform the flood early warning system. It is true that the Mahaica River and EDWC have a coproductive relationship. But the Mahaica River possesses its own modes of communication and occupation that often simply ignore the EDWC. These moments bring into being a flood catchment that is potent: a site that makes for disrupting historic human efforts at settlement along the coast.

Rerouting and Rearticulating Expertise

The desire for settlement that engineers, village residents, and CDC staff all possess underscores divisions in expertise as well as efforts to translate various love stories about the EDWC. Engineers, for their part, articulate love stories through descriptions about how they use soil-oriented design methods, such as building with geotextiles. At the same time, CDC staff articulate their own love stories after engaging engineers. They primarily use love stories to describe their investments in communicating information about storms and rivers to ministry officials and village residents living in the EDWC's flood catchment. But in the context of CAP, these theoretically translocal love stories have absorbed and been transformed by a new set of experiences with pegasse and rivers. Climate adaptation, therefore, is rarely borne out of convenience but more often out of the necessity of recognizing the power of the world to challenge and reshape technical paradigms, identities, and social commitments.

Since the 2005 disaster, engineers have attempted to use love stories to adjudicate conflicts that arise over measuring apparatuses and flood observation techniques. They have gathered scientific evidence of climate change in the name of accommodating the EDWC and keeping it operational. But difficult soils have transformed and, in some instances, challenged the scales of analysis engineers rely on to model hydraulics to predict flooding. As Robin, the lead British engineer on CAP, made clear, engineers' efforts to scale down hydraulic models to the level of a dam's internal drainage are nothing new in the field of hydraulic engineering sciences. But within the context of climate adaptation projects, this expertise is given new meaning because of the flood early warning system. With the system come divisions in expertise that do not neatly map onto engineers' sustained commitments to transnational networks of data and their collection. It is also unclear whether it matters if expertise in countries such as Guyana, with a hybrid of national engineering approaches, is ever routed back to those countries of origin. In 2014, for instance, the Ministries of Agriculture and Public Infrastructure held a joint press conference announcing interest in consulting with Dutch engineering firms to model flood scenarios for Georgetown. Many interpreted the contract bid as an insult or slight to local engineering firms and others, including American and British firms that had worked with the ministries in recent decades (Persaud 2015). Others questioned the composition of the Dutch engineering team, wondering how master's students from the University of Delft could be qualified to consult on and complete such a monumental project.

The disputes over the bid suggest that particularities of pegasse's sheer strength and porosity will continue to shape engineers' efforts to reimagine the flow of the EDWC's drainage and its enhancements. Climate adaptation, however, is more than an effort at prediction—a narrative device that informs most risk policy contexts (Stengers 2000). Despite all their efforts at flood assessment, engineers and related colleagues in Guyana have become good at telling other kinds of stories. In particular, they are good at telling love stories or accounts of their ongoing frustrations with such measuring apparatuses as hydraulic models and their efforts to reinvent and repurpose field observations. These love stories have come to serve more than a technical role: they have put engineers in a position to challenge the legacies of apaan jaat on the engineering sciences as well as on coastal settlement. But the extent to which engineers and the CDC staff always stick to these love stories and circulate them beyond the confines of their group(s) is a separate issue. They also face difficulties deciding whether they can learn to become accountable, not just to each other but to the broader national public.

▼

▲

The flood early warning system provides engineers with a sense of support and the CDC staff with a sense of purpose. Likewise, the topographies of the EDWC and the Mahaica River are inseparable, demonstrating that intense flooding can create the conditions for networks of expert communication. But how and why do engineers and CDC staff become committed to these networks? If the flood early warning system informs the ways they communicate before a disaster strikes, then the system requires a variety of planning activities (Lakoff 2017). Staff at the CDC were responsible for such activities with the writing of the "Guyana Flood Preparedness and Response Plan" (national flood plan). Numbering over thirty pages, the document outlines the CDC's role in coordinating shelters, the distribution of flood relief supplies, and the completion of disaster-damage assessments. At its outset, the national flood plan was a relative anomaly in the history of the CDC because it demands extensive partnerships with nonmilitary branches of government.

The plan is fueled by the concerns of engineers and CDC staff that climate change compromises the EDWC. They have sourced a variety of data sets not only from the 2005 disaster assessment and engineering reports on the EDWC but also from health, communications, transportation, and housing agencies.[1] However, when combining data sets generated from different agencies, considerable challenges emerge, many of which are related to the essential localness of various institutional protocols, technoscientific instruments, and data collection. The new standards, classificatory schemes, and labels CDC staff have implemented to organize information in the national flood plan might be one way around this problem. When two or more expert groups collaborate, their efforts are driven by the demand for data sets to move easily between people, organizations and machines and from one data format to another (Edwards et al. 2011). Those involved in the national flood plan hold each other accountable by reflexively engaging in conversations about the limitations of measuring apparatuses and thresholds for the EDWC's operations.

This reflexivity is particularly important in climate adaptation contexts because data sets used for interventions are often deployed to explain exceptional occurrences rather than the norm (Walford 2015). Guyana's national flood plan ties the interests of engineers and CDC staff to a shared notion of accountability: the willingness to take action to manage the EDWC and the circulation of data about it. They also seek to convince not only themselves but the Guyanese public as well that the national flood plan is essential to the EDWC's adaptation.

Guyana's national flood plan demonstrates that a crucial method for convincing people of climate adaptation's efficacy is through the militarization of technoscience. By this I mean that the technoscientific practices, data, and objectives of climate adaptation are reinforced by military spending and resource support. Theories of climate change are due in large part to how Euro-American states funded technoscience, particularly for earth sciences research, to fight the Cold War and shape the realignment of state and parastate territories (Edwards 2010; Sabin 2010; Weart 1997). With present-day climate adaptation projects, however, the reverse is the case. Militaries now apply their expertise to climate change to highlight the shortcomings, failures, and contingencies of state-sponsored technoscience and its related political coalitions. From this perspective, the militarization of technoscience has as much to do with experts cultivating a professional collegiality and accountability as with states deploying climatological information to avert military conflicts (Oreskes and Krige 2014).

The military conflicts they might wish to avert are often internal, driven by vulnerabilities in the guise of the biopolitical—especially race but also gender, class, ability, and generation—that could become further aggravated by people migrating to find safer places to live in or outside their countries of origin. In an effort to avert potential military conflicts, technoscience-military collaborations involve experts presenting themselves as neutral witnesses of climate change as they disseminate information to help people adapt. They train and perform duties in a way that deemphasizes explicit appeals to their identities and differences, unless they deem such appeals necessary to save lives.

Yet they also recognize when such neutral performances are insufficient and leave much unaccounted for in their efforts to appease people's concerns about climate change. In the particular case of the EDWC, the majority Afro-Guyanese CDC staff have become invaluable colleagues of Guyana's multiracial staff of engineers. The CDC provides a show of epistemic political support—a public face—against scrutiny about the EDWC's fallibility. Their combined efforts manage (or at least make palpable) the often-fine line between racial conflict and counter-racial thinking in climate adaptation.

The "Human Resources" of Disaster

The CDC was established in 1982 under the jurisdiction of the prime minister to manage all types of disasters, including floods, droughts, earthquakes, and fires. Although not legally designated a military agency, active and retired members of the Guyana Defence Force, the main branch of the military, have historically constituted its staff. When the CDC was founded, the PNC socialist state reaffirmed its commitments to the Non-Aligned Movement, which many historians argue was a response to its loss of popular democratic support from across racial groups (People's National Congress 1979; Taylor 2015; Thomas 1974).

With the PNC's legitimation crisis, political violence intensified and contributed to the rise of a "police state" (Carto 2012, 52). The Guyana Defence Force created a penetration model of national defense whereby civilian loyalty and obedience to it were enforced by political doctrine instead of direct force (Nordlinger 1976). Burnham transformed the military into what Chaitram Singh (1993, 221) calls a "people's militia." Several paramilitary organizations, including the Guyana National Service, were established, and internal Guyana Defence Force agencies, including the Education Corps, were charged with the political indoctrination of troops (Singh 1993). Many Guyanese I know recall the emergence of the police state in paternalistic terms. They have memories of Burnham riding on horseback through villages, firing state officials for leaving work to stand in breadlines, and putting restrictions on imports such as milk, split peas, potatoes, sardines, and flour—the ban on the last of these particularly affecting Indo-Guyanese subsistence diets of roti. Additionally, the police state was believed by many to be both racially and politically motivated (Scott 2004). Burnham did not meaningfully recruit or fully integrate Indo-Guyanese into the military, an important factor that contributed to his continuing support from within the PNC party (Singh 1993).

He also justified the buildup of arms to prove that he could counter the critiques of local leftist political opponents while positioning Guyana as a Caribbean state that commanded respect and importance in the global Cold War arena (Puri 2014). The majority of these arms went to militias managing ongoing border disputes with Venezuela (Colchester 1997; Singh 1993). The Guyana Defence Force training of both men and women was centered on arms exercises in the interior region that helped protect Guyana's Army Corps of Engineers developing roads and airstrips.[2] Yet these cross military-engineering arrangements were short-lived. A case in point was Burnham's attempt in 1974–75 to build a hydroelectric dam for an aluminum smelter in the Upper Mazaruni River basin with the support of the World Bank and the Swiss company Alusuisse. The Akawaio community in the basin opposed resettlement for the dam, and Venezuela escalated border tensions, sending a letter to the World Bank claiming that the dam infringed on its territory.[3]

In response, Burnham used the soft force of foreign actors to challenge Venezuela. In 1974, he made the high-profile decision to allow the Peoples Temple to establish a church near the border. A multiracial religious movement that tied socialist ideals to Christianity, the Peoples Temple was founded in the United States by the White evangelical preacher Jim Jones. Despite accusations that Jones used cultlike mind-control tactics, the Peoples Temple membership flourished, particularly among Black congregants when services spread to the San Francisco Bay area. Urban recruitment focused on Jones performing spiritual healings, giving sermons about capitalism as the Antichrist system, and strategizing with recruits to move the church abroad to Guyana, a country they believed espoused racial equality. Jones signed a land lease under the condition that he would further Burnham's Feed, Clothe, and House the Nation program through the development of pilot irrigation and drainage schemes in the interior. Engineering works were once again envisioned as having the potential to bring about a new social contract in Guyana. But Jonestown ended in despair. In reality, the Peoples Temple resembled less a multiracial commune of settlers than a state within a state, with Jones eventually ordering the mass suicide in 1978 of his 918 congregants

(Kwayana 2019). In the aftermath, Burnham claimed to have been unaware of the inner workings of the temple and deemed its brand of socialism—a foreign, Western imitation of Black Nationalism—and tactics antithetical to the strategy of Guyana's national security and settlement in the interior.[4]

With the PNC's political fallout around the escalation of foreign attempts at settlement-invasion, the CDC was left to clear up its mess. The CDC grew out of a model of postcolonial and Cold War militarization that converted disastrous events and rhetoric about anti-imperialism into racial political currency. Its responsibilities as an agency revolved around enhancing staff's skill sets in the "human resources" of disaster management (Velasco 2014, 70). The staff learned to bear witness to the people, events, and things that contributed to national unrest or, worse yet, disaster.

With liberalization, the CDC's jurisdiction was moved from the prime minister to the Office of the President in 1997. This administrative move overlapped with a national surge in gang-related violence and gray economies that some scholars argue has spun the Guyanese military and police into a fraternity fractured by distrust (Kwayana 2019; J. Mars 2009). Many Guyanese had reason to fear a coup d'état in the last two decades following prison breaks by members of a high-profile gang (2002), the murder of a state official (2006), racially and politically motivated village massacres (2008), and the expulsion of American Mormon missionaries after the government feared that some were meddling in political affairs (2009). While a coup never happened, British and American contractors were solicited to aid the reform of the Guyana Defence Force, with the intention of ridding the military of unqualified leadership (*Stabroek News* 2007).[5]

Through all of this, the CDC remained relatively insulated from critique and the corrosion of public trust for a few reasons. First, between 1982 and 2004 in Guyana, the only recorded climatic disaster was the 1997–98 El Niño. Given that the drought conditions affected farmers' irrigation water more than the country's potable water supply, many perceived the event as mismanaged by the Ministry of Agriculture and not by the CDC. Second, the military's reliance on special operations units (sometimes known as a phantom squad) has been widely associated with antinarcotics and white-collar crime investigations.

But with the 2005 disaster, public trust in the CDC was tested, and the agency responded in 2009 by agreeing to work with the UN Development Program to write the national flood plan. Fewer than ten CDC staff regularly contributed to the project. The majority of them were seeking exposure to skills in project management and community relations. There were also three decorated majors and colonels who wanted slower-paced work that would help them ease into retirement. Levels of ambition, interest, commitment, and education varied; all of those involved were male and Afro-Guyanese, with the exception of one Mixed Race officer, a female officer, and the CDC's director general, who was a retired Indo-Guyanese colonel. They had diverse military backgrounds, but all would say that they looked to their past military training in developing the national flood plan.

Still, CDC staff were not always confident about the plan's relevance to climate adaptation. Yes, the sea is rising and there has been an increase in torrential storms in Guyana, but in what ways do these processes matter to them, if at all? If the plan is a document for flood preparedness and response, the CDC staff now presumably care about what engineers are doing—not only during a disaster but also before and after it. The combined attention of these experts to the EDWC's potential to overtop with water and its embankment dam to erode set the ground for provocations about a world under pressure and the way that pressure comes to affect them. Climate adaptation, in other words, has a tendency not only to disorient boundaries of expertise but also to reinvent the assumed relations of accountability that inform it.

The EDWC Files

The CDC's headquarters is unassuming. Located in the heart of Georgetown, a block from the Atlantic Ocean, on Thomas Lands (a national park), the structure—consisting of fewer than ten rooms—is easy to miss. Thomas Lands is also home to other nondescript military buildings, a stadium and sprawling park, a handful of schools, trade union buildings, and a strip sold for commercial use as a fitness center and race car track. Its entrance has no security guard to greet visitors. But when I made my initial visit in 2009, a military briefing was being held in the front office, so someone was there to direct me to Kester, the CDC head managing the national flood plan at the time.

After spending over twelve years as an avionics technician for the Guyana Defence Force, Kester found that the national flood plan provided an opportunity for broadening his career goals. Originally from Georgetown, he was intimately familiar with the lack of job opportunities that awaited him in the mid-1990s after completing school. So he joined the military, which offered a reprieve for young Afro-Guyanese men like him, as it had for members of the prior generation who did not have the means to migrate or who decided to ride the wave of socialism. For both generations, the Guyana Defence Force provided class mobility while transforming the way they imagined migration forced and unforced, brain drain, and modes of self-conscious survival.

When we first met, Kester was completing an online bachelor's degree in emergency and disaster management with the for-profit American Military University. Earning these credentials would help him navigate the professional worlds of humanitarianism, engineering, and NGOs that had become central to climate adaptation in Guyana. But he wondered to what extent these credentials and professional networks would pull him further away from the life he had grown accustomed to as a well-liked technocrat in Guyana's military. He aspired to stay with the CDC, become its director, and hire others to help with the load of climate adaptation.

"You see this box? All the papers in it need to be archived; we haven't gotten to [filing] it all," Kester explained to me in the CDC's conference room. He plopped the box onto a desk, causing papers to fly everywhere. The majority of the papers were from the Ministry of Agriculture, detailing analyses of flooding near the EDWC, the real-time repairs engineers made to it, and its water levels during the 2005 disaster. Kester hoped that the EDWC files would eventually be organized into a digital archive once the CDC hired more staff and purchased more computers. The digital archive, Kester explained, would make it easier for CDC staff to keep track of not only what happened to the EDWC but also what engineers were thinking and doing during the disaster.

Following this explanation, I better understood his demeanor when we went to various state ministries to collect information for the national flood plan. Kester often used the interviews to test out his understanding of floods to see if it corresponded with engineers' concepts. During the interviews, his understanding of floods shifted from simply information he needed to add to the EDWC files to a resource for imagining disaster preparedness and response activities. Take, for instance, an exchange Kester had with a National Drainage and Irrigation Authority engineer:

> KESTER: So one of the things we are trying to identify is the window in which we [the CDC staff] have to act to get the emergency plans in place—like for restocking supplies or opening shelters. We are trying to identify that base time. How long does it take for rivers to peak and pose a problem? Do you have that information?

> ENGINEER: I can speak of . . . let me take one of the most vulnerable areas in Guyana. As you know, on the coast you have the Mahaica and Mahaicony riverine areas. The mere fact is we are below sea level. We always have this ponding effect. As the sea coast is here [he lowers his

hand] in Georgetown and as you go further south there's a natural rise of land. so you have this runoff when it rains. So to deal with all this we have the EDWC, to pick up all these backflows and to store it during a heavy storm and to discharge it at a strategic location, and it's also being used at other times for irrigation. The fact is we have this . . . just . . . ponding, a ponding effect.

K: For example, but what happened in 2005, when you have the excessive rainfall and the dams were being topped? What was being identified about what caused this? And in terms of how long it took before flooding? We are picking up [hearing] that some people [state officials] said it took three days for water to get on the land at somewhere like eighteen inches.

E: On the land?

K: Yes, on the land. So that's the time we are trying to identify. Because for the CDC, if it's three days, then we could have a two-day warning based on a forecast. Then we have two days to move, to get people and animals onto higher land.

E: Well, I can only speak about what the records say. I think it was no longer than thirty-six hours, so actually a day and a half.

K: So between the rain falling and the floodwaters. It was intensified in a very short period.

E: I think it accumulated thirty-three inches in a short duration. I would have to check with Hydrometeorological Services again. Take, for example, the Mahaica and Mahaicony areas. That rainfall had a direct impact on the EDWC. We had overtopping . . . water spinning over the dam in 2005. I think if you take the length of the dam, forty-two or forty-three miles, 10 percent of the dam had water overflowing. The storm was just excessive. And I tell you, what we are doing is a major investment, and this brings me back to how we are adapting. We are building a relief channel . . . the Hope Canal. And you know this major investment is for the EDWC. And, um, the baseline for us to design for it to function, when we run this model it runs up to 2005 flooding, and that has become my design storm.

Kester pressed this engineer to identify a "base time" for flood warnings, as he wanted to get a detailed understanding of the inconsistencies between engineers' descriptions of rainfall and modeling operations. What's more, the engineer acquiesced, recognizing the relational authority of the CDC staff to engineers because of the EDWC's tendency to overflow with water in some places of its embankment dam and not others.

Kester believes that engineers' descriptions of rainfall data as a mere index of the EDWC's water levels are insufficient for flood warnings. He needs more information about what engineers call stage readings of rivers or a "base time," so he coaxed the engineer to be more precise about when he reported seeing flooding versus the EDWC overtopping. Knowing where and when to "discharge water from the EDWC at strategic locations," as the engineer explains, is essential to Kester's notion of base time.

Within the context of climate adaptation, disaster preparedness and response can originate from engineering interests. The motivations behind flood warnings may indeed build on Kester's need to identify an accurate base time. But Kester's motivations are more than technical. In the above interview, he is also envisioning that CDC staff act as what I would call *accomplice witnesses*, helping engineers observe the EDWC's adaptation as its drainage responds to swollen rivers over time. Engineers could no more imagine data collection, hydraulic modeling, or field observations without the CDC than the CDC could imagine itself as an agency responsible for a flood early warning system. The EDWC assessments that both Kester and the engineers make "do not happen in the abstract"; they are performative and coconstituted by the measurement apparatuses they use (Barad 2012, 7).

The EDWC files, in other words, produce relations of accountability—or assumptions and a professional ethos about how engineers and CDC staff should share information. In turn, their related practice of archiving and their aspirations for digital archives are not some price to be paid for derelict infrastructure systems or a state's lack of technological investments. The EDWC archives instead mobilize a system of checks and balances oriented toward their more comprehensive engagement with measuring apparatuses, including the EDWC's water sensors and rainfall gauges.

Similar checks and balances have been normalized by the national security agencies of the world's superpowers. The United States, China, Russia, and the United Kingdom have drastically different rates of military spending based on projected impacts of climate change on the operating conditions of their countries' infrastructure systems (Brzoska 2012). Such spending practices among the military and engineering agencies are in marked contrast to those of just forty to fifty years ago.

Historians of science argue that by the late twentieth century, Euro-American states' military support for research in the earth sciences, including meteorology and climatology, rapidly outpaced their support for engineering fields that were not related to weapons buildup (Sagan 1996). Across the Global North and even some parts of the Global South, military patronage affected a variety of capitalist ventures that used the earth sciences in the name of Cold War containment (Hecht 2012). One reason lies in the earth sciences' reliance on forms of experiential inquiry, which helped militaries gain a better perspective on weapons in use across geographic contexts. Another was the assumption that the cumulative effects of nuclear fallout—the most imminent threat of the Cold War—could not be assessed with biological sciences alone. Thus, the value of the earth sciences to militaries since the Cold War has been in global-oriented data sets, particularly those describing the earth's climate systems. But the current understanding of climate adaptation—at least in places where climate change has already had disastrous impacts on infrastructure systems—is that the earth sciences are not always a helpful guide but need to be contextualized with the engineering sciences for immediate planning in military strategy (Rogers 2017).[6] As the Guyana case indicates, even as climate adaptation unfolds in response to known climatic risks, the roles of engineers and the military in knowledge production and exchange shift with the emergence of each new threat.

"Turning Points"

Staff at the CDC reinforce engineers' efforts by passing along highly technical engineering information and protocols to other state ministries. They are a powerful bridge between long-term planning and accidental encounters. A base time that quantifies when ponding or the pooling of water in a section of the dam due to uneven precipitation will occur offers an agreed-upon and trusted reference point for what the adaptation of the EDWC entails in daily practice. Accountability, in turn, is not treated by the engineers and the CDC staff as an a priori goal of their collaborations but as one that unfolds in real time as they strategize to incorporate new methodological perspectives (see also Hoeppe 2014). Their vision of the EDWC's drainage operations is accomplished through techniques of both fact construction and persuasion.

Take, for instance, the frustrations of the Jamaican disaster management consultant contracted by the CDC to help write the national flood plan. He admitted to me that even with countless years of experience in different countries implementing national flood plans, it is still difficult for him to pinpoint a precise language for something he calls a "vulnerable environment." As he explained to me,

> People just think of disaster as an outside story. Disaster management is just when you give people something and send them home. They see the relief and response. But they don't see the mitigation and they don't see the prevention. So we are trying to draw the big picture. But climate change muddles that picture even more, increasing the severity of storms. So now we need to think more of climate change. But, you know, also coincidentally, we [consultants in the Caribbean] have been pushing for a while now climate adaptation measures. Like if you look back—we didn't say it then—but Jamaica's Hurricane Gilbert [1988], that was our turning point to think of all hazards at all different phases. But you know, at the end of the day, people know the environment in a narrow way. So when you go off talking about words like *sustainability* or *development* this and that, you go off on tangents. So we have to tie in various elements to deal with flooding in Guyana. If you don't look after the environment, you have worse disasters, and if you don't respond to disasters, you have a worse environment. It's a hand-in-glove thing.

This consultant suggests that the technocrats, engineers, and state officials who write national flood plans become responsible for acknowledging how and why past strategies (e.g., sustainability or development) have *contributed* to their nation's vulnerability to climate change. Yet he also notes that it is unrealistic to assume that all of these past strategies could or ought to be revised and eventually integrated into climate adaptation projects. Instead, disasters stand in as important "turning points" or events for technocrats, state officials, and engineers to decide which strategies should be engaged and which put to rest. This means that engineering data such as those found in the EDWC files can activate a competing professional ethos about what counts as productive or negligent work in climate adaptation.

For instance, Kester and the three other senior staff members were the only people at the CDC I ever heard reference data about the EDWC in their day-to-day interactions. By contrast, their aides—whose tasks included answering phones, transcribing workshop notes, driving cars, and scheduling events—were integrated into operations that ensured that the entire EDWC files, not just its data, could be circulated and reproduced. When the Jamaican consultant held meetings, the aides became interlocutors of a new kind because they were briefed on specific ecological and meteorological details about intense flooding.

At these meetings, the consultant instructed the CDC staff on how to write disaster needs and damages analyses. His presentations were elaborate. He pieced together information from UN IPCC reports about the potential impacts of climate change on temperature, rainfall, and patterns of sea-level rise in the region. And when he provided national-level insights, he focused on the 2005 disaster's economic impact on the EDWC and its relationship to other infrastructure systems, including water pipes, electricity grids, and roads. The presentations often concluded with a description of his past work with other Caribbean state militaries developing national flood plans.

These presentations produced a double narrative about what accountability entailed for the CDC staff committed to climate adaptation. One narrative depended on reducing complexity in descriptions about the root causes of climatic disaster. The other depended on finding a broader audience (beyond the collaborating expert groups) interested in climate adaptation as policy that was not only an engagement with engineering sciences. As a consequence, the CDC staff take on a role in climate adaptation that is arguably much more expansive and politically consequential than that of engineers. How, and at what cost, the CDC staff believe they can embody this role is another question.

Humanizing Accountability

As a small agency, the CDC did not mirror the demographics of other military agencies in Guyana that, by the early 1990s under the PPP administration, had higher percentages of women and people other than those who self-identified as Afro-Guyanese soldiers (Guyana Defence Force Strategic Review Working Group 2009). This distinction matters because in postsocialist Guyana, Black masculinity has largely been defined by the failure of Burnham as a president to champion prosperity for "all" Afro-Guyanese.

For instance, Burnham's vision of ujamma socialism provided few stable opportunities for the education and employment of working-class Afro-Guyanese men beyond the military, whereas PNC affiliates and well-educated Afro-Guyanese men found employment within state agencies. This class conflict, in turn, carried with it the idea that Black masculinity was divided between two opposing worlds: a culture of technocracy, intended to protect the fledgling postcolonial state, and urban countercultures, particularly Rastafari.

Burnham's national security strategy filled in this cultural-ethnic vacuum. He presented himself as a race man who comfortably sought to hold up a narrative of Afro-Guyanese men overcoming an epic battle of racial degradation to become victors in the moral, economic, and cultural wars of global capitalism (see also Walcott 2009). Consequently, Black masculinity emerged as a category in Guyana that became associated with state-sponsored violence orchestrated through the channels of the military (P. Mars 2009).

Tropes of Black masculinity since socialism have arguably come under new kinds of cultural policing in Guyana, even though they are still troubled by the legacies of slavery and postcolonial aspirations of state building (see also Reddock 2012). The Guyana Defence Force's attempt of more than three decades to racially diversify military ranks and to engage in state–private sector defense contracts with Euro-American security firms (albeit often with opaque methods) is a case in point. The military's growing diversity has mobilized conversations about whether antidiscriminatory policing is possible in Guyana and if the general public can trust that such policing is not oriented toward fetishizing interracial violence or apaan jaat's role in it. These efforts suggest that Black masculinity is not simply tied to the legacies of Afrocentric socialism and race men; it is motivated by competing logics of security, movement, and expertise and their global inscriptions (Haynes 2016; James 2001).

For instance, the Guyana Defence Force has shared no public documents as to how or if it is concerned that climate-related interracial violence (e.g., disputes over land, migrations, or threatened resources) will become a problem in the country. But concerns about where to relocate people living next to the EDWC have already brought about racialized questions regarding the economic and legal status of land and internally displaced climate refugees in Guyana (see chapter 4). Likewise, as these people move closer to and into the environs of Georgetown, the question of how the CDC and related armed forces decide to enforce the climate adaptation of housing and infrastructure systems only becomes more acute. Thus, the EDWC files and climate adaptation offer just one case in which to track the shifting performance of Black masculinity in the military and its operations in coastal resettlements.

By *performance*, I mean two things. On the one hand, when using the EDWC files, the CDC staff are addressing engineers and, more broadly, an international community of climate change–related specialists and disaster consultants. On the other, the significance of the CDC staff circulating the EDWC files is prospective. In place of the stoic armed fighter is a technocrat who wields information not with the intention to silence or threaten force but to create public engagements with technoscience. The main objective of these public engagements is to devise and implement a set of strategies that will instill a commitment to counter-racial thinking in the body politic. Displacing the idea that military actors only have their minds set on quelling racial conflict or race war, counter-racial thinking also signals the fraught conditions under which they are professionalized as experts. Thus climate adaptation projects in Guyana position Black masculinity beyond the historical contingencies of Cold War–era state building or, for that matter, the plantation. It transforms the materiality of Afro-Guyanese male bodies from mere soldier into meaning and message about planetary ecological crisis.

As Achille Mbembe (2017) argues, the figure of the Black Man is central to Western political thought because he stands as the ultimate archetype of expert witness. Mbembe explains, "The Black Man serves as the very kolossos of our world to the extent that our world can be understood as a giant tomb or cave. In this immense and empty tomb, to say 'black' is to evoke the absent corpses for which the name is a substitute of the world" (53). As witness to modern racial atrocities, from slavery to genocide, that have reinforced processes of nation-state settlement, the Black Man has the ability to see from multiple perspectives "life from the beyond" (53).[7] I suggest that Guyana's national flood plan provides a similar vantage point: as a political-technological provocation, it reorients normative assumptions about who has and ought to have access to technoscience and related data outputs for coastal settlement. In doing so, the national flood plan positions Black masculinity in relation to other human experiences of exclusion and racialization that have made coastal settlement in Guyana a difficult or, at least, a compromising task throughout history.

Take, for example, the ways in which Black masculinity is signaled through aspects of the CDC staff's daily work and decorum. Instead of the fatigues customary for the Guyana Defence Force, the CDC staff wear civilian clothing. Their dress is "smart," in the British idiom; they often pass for nonmilitary state officials in slacks and untucked, mandarin-collar linen-cotton shirts. They do not carry weapons, nor do they have a visible fleet of security, as do other military and high-ranking state officials. Their mode of transportation is not top of the line; they move between CDC headquarters, state offices, the EDWC, and field sites in late 1990s Toyota pickup trucks. There is no coordinated effort on their part through, say, pins or name tags to identify as CDC staff working on the national flood plan. Only the military emblem painted on the sides of trucks gives away their affiliation. For all intents and purposes, they do not depend on explicitly talking about or signaling their masculinity to display military force or status. Rather than actively promote themselves as military men, they do work that simply evolves through its milieu. Around practices of recruitment, however, stereotypes of the military and Black masculinity are often visibly reconfigured in the CDC staff's encounters with the general public.

In an effort to establish a volunteer corps, the CDC developed a website to recruit people from across the country to become skilled in community disaster preparedness and response. At the top of the website is the Volunteer Corps logo: an animated tree. The trunk and branches are sketched to resemble a brown forearm and hand with leaves growing from the tips of its fingers. Its roots are submerged in water. The linkage of humans and trees with floods evokes a national landmark: the Conversation Tree, located near the Georgetown seawall.

The Conversation Tree indexes a sandbox tree (*Hura crepitans*) that was originally planted in 1876 to honor the birth of a plantation manager's son. It was eventually destroyed by termites in the 1960s and replaced with a flamboyant tree (*Delonix regia*); when this was uprooted in the 1990s, it was replaced with another. Below the tree logo is a photograph of boys playfully tumbling on top of each other against a backdrop of palm trees and bush that evokes an Amerindian village in the interior. The resiliency of trees and Amerindian male youth persists in the symbolic realm beyond the physical life of the body. The Volunteer Corps web page fits a certain narrative of the CDC staff as reliable collectors and distributors of data for the national flood plan, but it does so by inserting stereotypical images of Amerindian masculinity. The coupled images of wilderness with Amerindian boys suggests that Amerindians are a racial and gendered population that has been marginal and plays an "underdeveloped" role in modern coastal settlement. While this may be the case in terms of sheer demographics and the geographic distance of many Amerindian villages from the coast, it ignores the state's recent efforts at LCDS that are indeed central to irrigation and drainage infrastructure enhancements.

Staff of the CDC provided volunteers with courses in flood disaster preparedness and response that were part technical training and part public relations. Volunteers strategized about shelter management, water safety, and conflict resolution. The training was also pivotal for the CDC staff, as they held induction ceremonies for those who excelled. The first cohort was a racially heterogenous group and was inaugurated in celebration of the International Day for Disaster Reduction, which bore the theme "Women and Girls, the Invisible Force of Resilience." At the same time, the theme suggested that femininity was an ahistorical category, dependent on Black masculinity in a way that women's identities could be restored only through the CDC. By the CDC focusing these sessions on resilience at the scale of the community and household, women wielded climate adaptation expertise by channeling their flood knowledge into the domestic instead of the public sphere. The ceremonies, in this respect, were intended to grant more women a role in climate adaptation but only if their flood knowledge and efforts did not disrupt the public authority Black men wielded in the CDC and, more broadly, in Guyana's military forces.

Such public authority was cultivated and reaffirmed not only through the CDC's national volunteer programs but also through the agency's understanding of race as a factor in creating transnational expert networks. Many of the CDC staff cared about their reputations outside of Guyana and were well aware that the racial dynamics of the country's military, having a large presence of Afro-Guyanese, could influence disaster response in other Caribbean places. The CDC staff member's charisma, in other words, is fueled by a love of country, but he is cosmopolitan enough to make inroads in new places when duty calls or disaster strikes. Like most identities, this one plays on recognizable elements—in this case, elements that could find historical examples in a concept of Black diaspora.

During the early stages of writing the national flood plan in 2010, the CDC staff received word that Haiti experienced a disastrous earthquake. Given the magnitude of the earthquake, they planned to launch relief operations from the Caribbean Community (CARICOM) headquarters on the outskirts of Georgetown. But for logistical reasons, the Caribbean Emergency Disaster Management Agency ultimately decided to launch missions from Jamaica, and the CDC staff and the Guyana Defence Force were left on standby. Initially CDC staff were disappointed that they were not needed, but in daily conversation they talked about being inspired by the prospect of "helping people like us." Their empathy was matched by the Guyanese state pledging GYD$2.1 million (US$10,056) in aid and sponsoring a massive benefit concert on Thomas Lands.

At first it may appear that earthquakes and floods have no relation to each other or, at the very least, that Guyana's and Haiti's disasters are worlds apart. But there was no confusion on the part of the CDC staff. The idea of a raging flood originating from the EDWC or Mahaica River compounded by an offshore earthquake fueled their imaginations about Guyana's possible future. As many CDC staff remembered, the 2004 Asian tsunami occurred just days before the December 2004 storms that contributed to Guyana's 2005 disaster.

Overshadowed by the tsunami, Guyana's event was either simply ignored by international humanitarian organizations or perceived by many foreign nation-states as minor in the planetary history of a changing climate. Fast-forward five years later, and the Haitian earthquake played out in a decisive manner for the CDC staff in their understandings of race and expertise.

The event stood as a training exercise and a subtle reminder of Max Weber's (1968, 1200) insight that in a bureaucracy, "life is focused not on persons but on impersonal rational goals." While the CDC staff might have justified their interest in Haiti because it is a Black, Caribbean country, CARICOM viewed this appeal to racial affinity as less compelling than logistics. The decision by CARICOM demonstrated that the sociopolitical associations of race with disaster that pervade military bureaucracies are not only internally driven by state apparatuses but imposed by outside forces as well. This suggests that the CDC staff acting as experts who care about race can slip easily into unprofessionalism or even unfriendliness, in Weber's sense.[8] In short, the CDC staff face difficulties knowing how to become accountable in climate adaptation not only to citizens, international donors, and other nations but to themselves as well. They are troubled by the reality that the impersonal rational goals of bureaucracy are not enough to survive climate change.

Better understanding of how experts make decisions and act to make climate adaptation happen requires attention not only to race but also to data management. The biopolitical ascriptions of Black masculinity may inform the CDC staff's notions of accountability to the general public and engineers. But these ascriptions are not necessarily embodied through the flesh of the racialized human subject. Engineering data, such as those found in the EDWC files, originate from measuring apparatuses: the more-than-human observations and faculties of flood hazards. Specifically, the EDWC's rain gauges recall not the voice or gaze of the racialized human subject but the vibrations of mechanical and computerized water sensors.

This technological assemblage evokes an idealized image of drainage for the EDWC. At the same time, the EDWC's ponding phenomenon has caused the CDC staff and engineers to reconsider the usefulness of rain gauges and thus the base time for the flood early warning system. In climate adaptation, therefore, military officials experience race and gender through their engagements with technology as much as through explicit pronouncements about the potential racialized violence or military conflict that climate change can underscore. The CDC staff are deeply aware of all this. This is why they put a large amount of time and effort into public outreach to convince a critical national public that they are there to help, even if many of the staff members do not look or vote like them and work for military institutions partially shaped by gray economies, a narco-state, and the afterlives of Cold War violence. Thus, military work is integral to the technoscientific scope of climate adaptation, standing as one of the more explicit human performances of accountability.

"Getting Out ahead of the Flood"

If the CDC staff had learned one thing, it was that climate adaptation develops in fits and starts. Working with engineers and national publics did not always unfold in complementary ways. Strategic acts and practices of distancing were an important aspect of their efforts, as indicated by the discussions about the flood early warning system's base time. While Kester's interviews with engineers did not provide him with a definitive base time for a flood warning, it did offer a general time frame. Following these interviews, the CDC staff decided that seventy-two hours is adequate for what is called in the national flood plan the phase response preparedness system.

The color-coded system details when CDC staff should send out advisories to relevant government ministries about flooding based on EDWC water levels. Yellow is at seventy-two hours, indicating the window when the CDC should receive information from engineers about a potential flood and report the warning to other state agencies. Orange is at forty-eight hours, indicating the window when the level of certainty of a flood has increased and when the CDC holds government meetings at its headquarters to plan relief. Red is at twenty-four hours, indicating the window when the CDC staff prepare and distribute flood relief supplies to shelters. Moving from yellow to orange to red, the system provides a grammar for installing and recognizing danger. Even so, a draft of the plan notes, "The outlined plan focuses primarily on preparedness and response and not on mitigation and prevention. As such it should not be considered or interpreted as a flood management document as its specific mandate is to provide the Civil Defence Commission with strategic guidance in a systematic and sequential manner for preparing and responding to flood events" (Civil Defence Commission 2010, 2). In other words, the CDC alone cannot guarantee flood management even with the EDWC's enhancements.

Strategies of so-called mitigation and prevention originate elsewhere—at the Ministry of Agriculture or Ministry of Public Infrastructure, perhaps. As an agency, however, the CDC finds value in describing when, where, and how its collaborations with engineers fall short or require motivations other than climate adaptation. For instance, the national flood plan identifies at least four causes for the "slow-onset flooding" typically experienced in the coastal region: rivers, the release of water from the EDWC, high tide, and derelict drainage canals (6). The plan also explains that these types of flooding can occur simultaneously, as was the case in 2005. The CDC staff need to be alert to how the starting and ending points of each color in the phase response preparedness system can quickly change during a disaster.

The CDC staff's so-called flexibility gave them a bureaucratic view of flood management, a perspective engineers lacked because they were preoccupied, on a different scale, with the details of the EDWC's pegasse-ridden embankments. In the context of the national flood plan, pegasse facilitates accountability. Here pegasse is referenced by CDC officials and engineers as a resource that helps inscribe relations of collective action and response for flooding in Guyana.

Hence, the Office of the President had to approve the completion of the national flood plan. Basic considerations, including who at the CDC would contact other state agencies during the seventy-two-hour flood alert or what kinds of flood relief supplies would be stored at the CDC, were scrutinized by the office. Multiple meetings were held to edit the plan. But with each revision, new meetings had to be scheduled and other activities rescheduled, which meant that other CDC work was either delayed or rushed. Impromptu meetings often morphed into all-nighters, with staff rearranging daily life—childcare and errands—around conference calls, briefings, and PowerPoint presentations. Camaraderie at these meetings was marked by a fleeting sense of expectation, time, and endurance. As one of the CDC staff observed: "We can't write this plan without the engineers, but we can't act without the president. This [plan] is us getting out ahead of the flood." The flow of data and information in the agency held consequences for the forms of accountability CDC staff possessed or, at the very least, hoped to demonstrate to one another.

Staff at the CDC were not cynical about this chain of command; it allowed them to claim a degree of distance and, ultimately, to distribute responsibility for flooding in a way that kept them from being the sole group of state officials receiving blame when a flood happens. In a number of closed meetings between the Office of the President and high-ranking CDC staff, discussions arose over whether the CDC or the president had the authority to declare a state of emergency. Part of the issue was over how the CDC could avoid blurring lines of communication between state ministries during a flood. The other issue was to pinpoint when CDC staff should coordinate damage assessments of the EDWC and other affected infrastructure systems.

In the end, they settled on the narrowest of definitions: "The authority for declaring a state of emergency under Guyanese law is vested to the President. As such the authority to activate the Flood Preparedness and Response Plan resides with the Office of the President. The activation of the plan by the President will be based upon the advice of the National Disaster Coordinator and the Director General of the Civil Defence Commission" (Civil Defence Commission 2010, 8). The problem of authority grew only more acute as activities were further defined between engineers and the CDC staff. Whereas developing a national flood plan emphasizes dependence and intimacy between CDC staff and engineers, responding to an actual flooding disaster, at least in theory, requires exclusion and a distinct hierarchy of command. All involved were aware that the national flood plan was just that: a plan, a resource for action and, to a lesser extent, for controlling the environment around them.

The Suspicion of Incompetence

At the same time, engineers might also express discomfort with being held accountable to the CDC staff in their daily work. Recall one engineer's clarification that "engineers are not slaves" because they cannot wait for years, months, or even weeks for pegasse to harden before realigning the EDWC's embankment. As an Indo-Guyanese engineer, he did not use the word *slave* with the intent of marking personal genealogy. Employed by a private sector firm, he perhaps had a stake in offering me a pluralist history about the kind of laborer who is responsible for enhancing the dam. In order to adapt the EDWC to climate change, he now needs a flood early warning system. As an engineer, he transforms the EDWC from being mere infrastructure into a site of collaboration with CDC staff.[9] As I understood him, he suggested that contemporary engineers can create a strategy for climate adaptation that may be shaped by race but is not dependent on race.

Still, public scrutiny stretched across the EDWC–Hope Canal project's life span. The Ministry of Agriculture held periodic promotional tours of the EDWC and the Hope Canal for the media in order to show off its accomplishments. But these tours provided only more evidence for private media reports detailing salacious stories about construction delays and contract disputes over building materials and work pay.

Engineers also had to reconcile what they called conspiracy theories about the 2005 disaster. Some engineers were confronted by friends and family who wondered whether water from the EDWC was released into the Mahaica River to save state-owned sugar estates at the expense of small farmers. Others wondered whether Jagdeo ordered the overtopping of the EDWC to flood out bandits to secure votes in the next election. When confronted with these conspiracy theories, many engineers said their goal was simply to promote climate adaptation as a national good. They also sought to explain the importance of the public's role in climate adaptation, such as attending CDC recruitment events or creating flood evacuation routes in their communities.

This is not to say that CDC staff have been immune from critique or scrutiny from other state agencies. In late 2010, a CDC staff member was allegedly recorded conspiring to plot a coup. He and two other military personnel were charged with treason and served nineteen months in prison. They were eventually released when the charges were dropped because of a lack of evidence. After release, they spoke out about the torture they experienced and warned other military personnel not to fall victim to having their human rights violated. One of the accused was female and counted herself as rewriting the geopolitical history of human rights as the first woman in the Southern Hemisphere imprisoned for treason (Munro 2016). For many of us at the CDC, the charges were disheartening, as we wondered about the extent to which our own work files, phone calls, emails, social gatherings, and travels were used as evidence for their arrests. These events reignited my own ethnographic concerns about how climate adaptation was motivated by interagency surveillance to silence apaan jaat as much as to undermine counter-racial thinking.

Thus, getting used to a sliding scale of expert status and accountability was a cornerstone of engineers' and CDC staff's sociality under climate adaptation. Few engineers articulated this better than the older and retired generation sought by the ministry for consulting work on the EDWC. In the context of climate adaptation, their personal archives of old engineering reports took on a new life, serving as important evidence to improve or, as some radically proposed, to terminate the Hope Canal construction. Many held gatherings at their homes and social clubs in Georgetown. Their discussions brought together a wide array of topics about modeling operations, borehole surveying techniques, more robust private-sector engineering review boards, and reform of industry standards. But given copyright licensing agreements, the ministry demonstrated little interest in sharing details about the formulas used for the EDWC's and Hope Canal's hydraulic models. Intervening from a distance and with incomplete information, these engineers sought to give an expressive political voice to climate adaptation.

The pressures of living under the suspicion of incompetence from both the general public and colleagues took on many forms for engineers. To cope, some would talk about a present utopia: a time when it is possible to fabricate life, to obtain what one sets out to achieve by simply "knowing your environment." As one engineer explained to me:

> Strength in your work: it is built through experiences when things like an embankment fail or you find too soft soils [pegasse]; not running away from failure and not modeling. Problems in engineering happen every day. It's not a theoretical thing. It's that the magnitude of things changes. And conditions change all the time, so you have to train yourself to see. So I'll tell you, like, sea defenses are my favorite projects. And you know, there are two tides every twenty-four hours. And that's how I remember all I have to do and when to do it in a day. But that's too how I started to smoke. You know I never smoked before coming back to Guyana [after working abroad]. I can remember waiting until two in the morning watching the tide, waiting for it to go down to start work again. And I think as an engineer, those are the types of experiences that shape you—knowing your environment.

Climate adaptation proves to be just one of the many projects in this engineer's career that has shaped his understanding of accountability. This is because his work, and that of other engineers, has nourished conspiracy theories, the reinvestment in the preservation of archives, and even calls for political reform. In a reversal of fates, engineers find that their credibility and relationship with the CDC are dependent on making clear that they are always in the process of learning how the "magnitude of things changes." The CDC's color-coded flood early warning system is one example of a learning device, and another is monitoring base time. But engineers and the CDC staff also recognize that these learning devices might not always offer them new ways of "knowing the environment." There are distinct (dis)advantages that come with using these technical terms and languages.

In this discursive space, "knowing the environment" has political implications that are indebted to longer postcolonial and Cold War histories of militarization. However, the militarization of technoscience under climate adaptation is not narrowly shaped by angst about containment, new world orders, violent counterinsurgency, or even the balkanization of territory and people (see Parenti 2011). In other words, climate adaptation's political imaginary involves much more than an appeal to national security. It is also influenced by information sharing and its practices of data management: the calibration of data-gathering devices and instruments, digital archiving, regulatory frameworks, and the various publicity inscription practices used to make information (in) accessible (Kitchin 2014b).

This point about the plurality of political interests within spaces of climate adaptation matters because climate change research was once the province of *only* Euro-American superpowers. In recent decades, for instance, a new industry has arisen in the Caribbean whereby consultants with a specialty in climate sciences and meteorology are contracted by states to both collect data and create packaged forecasts to address countries' particular climatic risks, vulnerabilities, and needs. Likewise, climate sciences and meteorology are not the only kinds of technoscience that make climate adaptation imaginable, let alone sustainable. Tracking engineering-military partnerships in the name of climate adaptation provides one way toward understanding why people's commitments to climate adaptation wax and wane, even in the aftermath of climatic disaster. But climate adaptation projects may not always unfold to legitimize expertise; they also might invite its staunch refusal as an organizing model of climate change politics.

In 2009, I met with Margaret at her home in Sophia. "I have to get some glasses," she explained while walking to a kitchen cabinet. She collected the glasses and then made her way to the stove to boil water to clean them. I sat a few feet away next to a window staring at a plastic vat in her backyard. Placed on a wooden platform, it appeared to levitate above surrounding weeds and a kitchen garden. Connected to it were two drainpipes that ran from the house's roof to channel rainwater. "How often do you go to the vat for water?" I asked. "It depends: who's coming over, when it rains, what I'm cooking."

Margaret worries about floodwaters damaging the vat's platform. The vat has to be monitored at odd moments in the course of the day, week, month, year, and especially during the wet season. She is vigilant, just like other Sophia residents. Even Red Cross staff visited after the 2005 disaster and warned of more, if not worse, flooding due to climate change. Margaret grew accustomed to these warnings, with Red Cross staff holding training work-shops about water safety and plastering signs throughout Sophia that read "Evacuation Route."

"I use it [the vat] only if the sky isn't too gray or the rain too heavy," she noted as she poured soda into our glasses. If the sky was gray and the rain heavy, she disinfected water with bleach and filtered it with a rag. Intuition is both a necessity and a pleasure in itself. It spreads fast, even without the help of expert clarification.

Margaret's vat informs her everyday routine and commitments to the Guyana Red Cross. Vats, along with rags and bleach used to filter water, are ordinary things, insofar as they can be found in most Guyanese households. Red Cross training shapes people's understandings of the ordinary—a commonsense assumption about the "constancy of life" (Dumm 1999, 1). For Margaret, the ordinary is experienced through talk, critiques, assessments, and rumors about climate adaptation. But as she suggests, even though the Red Cross has provided help to Sophia residents, she still lives in uncertainty about how her life will be affected by climate change.

So far, I have sketched climate adaptation as a desire for the continued settlement of the nation and the competing measuring apparatuses that make this desire imaginable. Climate adaptation binds people to the expectation of some sort of transformation, a parting with what was once deemed common sense or good judgment. What I have left to specify, however, is how people understand transformation as tethered to ordinary scenes and activities that depict what it is like to become aware that one is living with climate change. Any account of the ordinary requires, as Lauren Berlant (2011a) argues, acknowledging the structural insecurities (e.g., poverty, pollution, racism, or health disparities) that can contribute to the deterioration of a population. As she elaborates, "The genre of crisis is itself a heightening interpretive genre, rhetorically turning an ongoing condition into an intensified situation in which the extensive threats to survival are said to dominate the reproduction of life" (7). Recognizing the failures of many post–World War II welfare-state economic policies, Berlant argues that fantasies of the good life are bound to modes of self-care and self-management. Instead of the ordinary being shaped by knowledge practices alone, Berlant suggests that confessional storytelling helps people make sense of how their everyday lives are forged by continuous disruption (128).

The genre of crisis can also be located in the forms of participatory climate adaptation that Margaret describes above. With the flood early warning system, the CDC became convinced that every community located on Guyana's floodplain can adapt to climate change. The Red Cross was one institution that the CDC believed could provide them support in this effort. The Red Cross took the lead with one of four pilot programs in Sophia. In

2009 and 2010, Red Cross workers trained Sophia residents in Vulnerability Capacity Assessment (VCA). Conceived of in the early 1990s to educate urban communities worldwide about environmental risks, the VCA is the core methodology of the International Red Cross Federation's volunteer network. Its primary activity includes people participating in focus groups and household surveys about flood hazards in the places they live. A mix of preparedness, relief, and coping strategies, Sophia's VCA centered on educating residents about how to use household water management equipment—or vats, septic tanks, and water filtration kits.

In a neighborhood of roughly thirty-six thousand people, five male and fifteen female adults regularly participated in Sophia's VCA training that I attended in late 2009. They volunteered as trainees after the Red Cross staff contacted the head of Sophia's community center. Already members of a community awareness group, the VCA trainees described themselves not only as community advocates but also as people familiar with drainage issues that affect Sophia. They had various occupational, racial-ethnic, and class backgrounds. Some were unemployed, while others held multiple jobs as electricians, vendors, caretakers, political activists, teachers, and low-level government employees. This diversity influenced the knowledge exchanged about flooding as well as expectations about the purpose of water management equipment. Training was led by a rotating group of five staff from the Guyana Red Cross who, for the most part, had very different daily realities from those of VCA trainees. Their home life, work, and leisure were shaped by Georgetown's middle-class environs, although some did have experience as first responders in 2005. The VCA intended to chart a knowledge network beyond a preoccupation with climatic disaster and its root causes. The water management equipment proved to be an important symbolic resource for remapping daily relations between climate adaptation and accountability.

Instead of a focus on climatic disaster, the VCA helps Sophia residents pay attention to how vulnerability manifests in the everyday. This emphasis on the processual rather than the event suggests that climate change has become entangled with how people envision achieving or making a good life. Living with vulnerability is marked less by the sociotechnical demands of irrigation and drainage infrastructures than by specific scenes of a working day, familial duties, and social obligations. Each VCA takes shape generically through a case study of vulnerability.[1] By participating in Red Cross workshops, VCA trainees provide localized accounts of flood hazards at the same time that they attempt to make sense of the political and technical conditions that stabilize them. There is a steady invitation in participatory climate adaptation projects such as the VCA to reject irrigation and drainage infrastructures and state welfare that require centralized management. This marks the arrival of a new kind of governance: one based not in managing the administration of life around risk per se but in reimagining the ordinary. This gap between the imaginary and practice is generative of broader discussions about the ordinary as an analytic for critical climate change studies and the residual spaces for politics it can incite.

The Ordinariness of Vulnerability

With only fifty miles of canals to support Georgetown and its environs, the city's drainage system is overtaxed by pockets of informal housing that have contributed to garbage and piecemeal road development (Edwards, Wu, and Mensah 2005). From the 1950s to 1970 the city's population grew from ninety thousand to two hundred thousand and expanded from two to fifteen square miles (Pan American Health Organization 2003). This expansion was supported by a remittance economy, with migrants renting multiple units within a building to relatives or close acquaintances (Corbin and Aragon 2014). In this respect, settlement in Georgetown has been associated with costs for maintaining drainage to reproduce kin relations and, to a lesser extent, the speculative logics of real estate capital, as has been argued of other flood-prone Global South cities (Ranganathan 2015).[2] And this fact has not escaped the attention of the Guyana Red Cross.

Through exercises in water management equipment and household vulnerability surveys, the VCA does not simply reflect the biopolitical expectation that the household is where flood hazards should be mitigated. It is also a technique for developing skepticism about the world and its related technological, environmental, and sociopolitical pressures (Cavell 1994). Trainees' decision-making about such activities—including how to create water filtration kits or a flood emergency contact list—prompts an unlearning of their dependence on the drainage grid. This means that the VCA produces forms of expertise that cut across not only racial-kin divides, as I detailed with the Hope/Dochfour farmers, but affective attachments to public-private divides as well.

In the case of the VCA, trainees develop trust in water management technologies to protect them from contaminated floodwaters. These technologies help them become hypervigilant of corporeal routines, such as walking or bathing, in order to identify (un)familiar patterns in the surrounding environment. In such instances, clogged canals or broken bridges are things that "pose a set of quandaries" to movement, sensorium, and cognition (Barad 2011, 147). Exercises become key scenarios wherein VCA trainees develop a collective awareness of vulnerability despite their various personal life histories and situations of privilege. Participatory climate adaptation, in other words, is derived from a mobile skill set, or translocal expertise, that VCA trainees can apply anywhere in the event a flood displaces them from Sophia.

It is no surprise that VCA trainees interpret the Red Cross as helping them achieve a good life, even if in the present they experience what feel like intractable flood hazards. Achieving a good life, as Berlant (2011a, 100) argues, is dependent on how people make the most of an environment that repeatedly causes trouble or that puts them in a condition of crisis ordinariness. She contends, "An environment can absorb how time ordinarily passes, how forgettable most events are, and how people's ordinary preservations fluctuate in patterns of undramatic attachment and identification" (100). Similarly, I track why the environment helps people make sense of temporality. I emphasize, however, that for many VCA trainees, the environment is not only an index of time but also a resource for judging when and how ethics and politics materialize across space. These trainees are not content living with derelict drainage, even with continued assistance from the Red Cross. With every new flood hazard encountered through training, they learn to live off the grid and create networks of care that circumvent those of the state and the EDWC. Some of the most telling of these efforts was the construction of minibridges designated for flood evacuation (figure 7.1).

In this respect, participatory climate adaptation projects work in tension with processes of neoliberal development and engineering sciences that have made drainage a difficult and, in some cases, unsustainable reality in Guyana. Trainees actively recognize the strategic essentialisms and politics on which participatory climate adaptation is often grounded or critiqued. They do not forget those stories about climate change that resist grand narratives of catastrophe (Stengers 2015). A staunch refusal to separate engineering and climate data from other ways of knowing, the VCA amounts to an effort to represent, organize, and reimagine ordinary life.

Thus, it is worth following the emergence of participatory climate adaptation projects in Guyana not simply because they fill a bureaucratic vacuum for the state. They also offer a new imaginary of the ordinary as circumscribed less by the geography of the EDWC (or empoldering, for that matter) than by the humble water management equipment that circumvents it. By 2009 the Guyana Red Cross had positioned itself as the main architect of this geography. The program in VCA training built on the 2009 report *Background*

FIGURE 7.1. A typical canal in Sophia overrun with thick vegetation

Document for the Preparedness of Climate Change, completed by twenty-three other Red Cross national societies in Latin America, the Caribbean, Africa, and Asia. The report details the efforts of national societies to use UN IPCC data to spur greater collaboration between state agencies and local communities.

Even "without full scientific analyses on climate projections," Red Cross engagements offer an abiding appeal of immediacy (International Federation of Red Cross and Red Cross Societies 2009, 5). "Humanitarianism in a changing climate," the report argues, is rooted in identifying climatic risks that will affect technologies and resources used for programs such as the VCA (1). As climate change increasingly frames humanitarian sentiment, the VCA is a useful measuring apparatus—easily quantified and statistically represented—for negotiating the terms of participation. As a Guyana Red Cross worker notes in the report, successful climate adaptation is the "expansion of VCA" methods across communities as much as disaster relief practices (9).

The 2005 disaster made evident that such a measuring apparatus was needed in Guyana because the event disrupted neat divisions between public and private aspirations for irrigation and drainage infrastructures. Scholars examining other climate-related disasters, such as Hurricane Katrina, typically portray the failure of infrastructure systems as disrupting normalized understandings of public-private responsibility for goods and services (Somers 2008). This focus on political transaction, however, reinforces the idea that participatory climate adaptation will have obvious civic outcomes and a design that can *supersede* the political hurdles or environment at hand. Instead, participatory climate adaptation requires a politics beyond rights claims and civic government to one that reaffirms the pragmatics of daily life.

For this reason, I caution against viewing participatory climate adaptation as a mere ideological effect of neoliberal development. Analyses that appeal to this teleology assign historical finality where many vulnerable populations seek to assert practical solutions for living with hazards (see also Chakrabarty 2021). Indeed, discovering practical solutions to hazards is a preoccupation not only of those living in postdisaster or marginalized Global South contexts. Bruce Braun (2014, 60) describes parallel sensibilities in England, where climate adaptation involves a "profanation" of technologies, such as fuel gauges and electric cars, to "modulate natural processes" in the everyday. But technologically bounded representations of the ordinary are not the only possible register through which participatory climate adaptation is made legible. Participatory climate adaptation is often directed toward efforts simply to identify what counts as practical activities for maintaining daily life.

Between a Promise and a Trench

Sophia was founded by squatters during Guyana's transition out of socialism in the late 1980s. One of the original estates commissioned in the 1830s to have access to the Lamaha Canal, the settlement is located on mostly swampland and abandoned plantations, with pockets of land suitable for rice cultivation. The first squatters remember being promised by Cheddi Jagan and the leaders of the transition-PNC government in 1986 that they would receive freehold titles. Recalling the early years of squatting in Sophia, a community council leader expressed to me how he has yet to experience the threat of seizure that many early illegal residents faced. He elaborated, "Now I got a title. That title guarantees I live here. It took time. But people [before me] worried about police raids." Under the ownership of GUYSUCO, the Sophia area was sold to private investors around the time the first squatters settled. The threat of eviction by the army and the police force was so prevalent that people took to hiding in trenches and submerging themselves under canals' weeds to avoid being arrested or having their homes permanently seized (Edwards 2006).

Sophia has thus come to function as a space that embodies citizens' putatively shared political sympathies for settlement at any cost alongside the distinct political insecurities of apaan jaat that characterized liberalization in the late 1980s and early 1990s. "The PPP, when they came into power, promised we get titles. The PNC wasn't happy. They [PNC] didn't want us there; that made them look bad, like the PPP gave us what they [PNC] promised but never could deliver," explained one longtime Sophia resident. But not everyone received titles as promised, and although it was public knowledge that titles sat in limbo, thousands of people continued to pour into Sophia, particularly from nearby divested housing cooperatives. Many of these people settled its north end, expanding Sophia's residential boundaries to the north side of the Environmental Protection Agency's headquarters and the PNC headquarters. The expansion of neighborhood boundaries, coupled with the sheer number of rural migrants who settled in such a short period of time, led many to speculate that Sophia was the largest squatter community in the Caribbean during the early 1990s.

At first glance, the story of Sophia's settlement seems to be about (dis) possession. During the socialist era, squatters were understood as a segment of the urban poor and figured as citizens in need of protection through cooperative housing. But by 1992, squatters had been identified by the state as the cause rather than the symptom of failed urban housing. Sophia continues today to supply land to Guyana's poor and migrant rural-urban populations. Whether many of these people intend to forever squat or to eventually purchase a land deed is unclear. Despite the consistent flow of people, there is no coherent national land-tenure policy or orders that stipulate the rights or privileges of squatters in transition to becoming landowners.[3]

As a haphazardly reclaimed abandoned rice estate, Sophia has become a neighborhood of a most vibrant sort. One-room, multifamily wooden shacks and two-story, single-family concrete homes; paved and mud roads; burgeoning small businesses and corner rum shops; communal pastures and elaborate kitchen gardens—all coexist. Sophia has attracted rural migrants from all over the country who have successfully integrated small-scale farming (e.g., mostly tubers), shepherding, and cowherding on vacant lands.

Unlike other working-class, poor neighborhoods in Georgetown, access to cultivatable land has contributed to Sophia's racial diversity. With over thirty thousand residents and seven thousand households, it has a majority Afro-Guyanese (60 percent) population but a significant number of people self-identifying as Indo-Guyanese (15 percent), Mixed Race (12 percent), Amerindian (10 percent), and other (3 percent) (Marks 2008, 5). The early 2000s publication of censuses and maps tentatively included the settlement within the boundaries of Georgetown, and it has since been officially incorporated.[4] But while Sophia is written into censuses and mapped as part of the city, at the time of writing, it has neither a community democratic council nor neighborhood democratic council members represented in parliament. As a consequence, Sophia has institutionalized an urban-rural dichotomy within its borders as a functioning greenbelt/housing settlement within the city.

For many Sophia residents, this heterogeneity informs more than just land tenure, apaan jaat, and electoral representation. As a neighborhood still overwhelmingly viewed by the public and state officials as a squatter settlement, Sophia has been on the receiving end of state policy to improve and regularize housing, roads, garbage services, and water (Ministry of the Presidency 2017). In many respects, Sophia residents have reaped the benefits of national urban housing policy geared toward affordable housing while bearing the brunt of social stigma and being labeled delinquent citizens. A Ministry of Housing antisquatting campaign in the years following the 2005 disaster, for instance, included billboards posted in Sophia and around city waterways that read "No Squatting Zones" and "No Littering." These campaigns have targeted squatters as "responsible for 80 percent of garbage found in city canals" (*Kaieteur News* 2010b), which many engineers and city officials argue is the root "cause" of flooding in Georgetown.

The threat of the delinquent citizen has been further traced by policy makers from the antidote to the statistic. Government reports estimate that the overuse of land plots has contributed to an increase of well over 60 percent in the number of flood events in and around Georgetown since the early 1970s (Pelling 1999). Public services, including garbage collection and canal dredging in Sophia, remain inconsistent, while many areas are drained by makeshift trenches that residents have planned and dug. To this extent, vulnerability in Sophia is contoured by poverty and insecure land tenure, but its flood hazards parallel those of greater Georgetown.

World Making

One afternoon in 2009, I sat with Louie on the balcony of the Sophia/Patterson Community Centre in Sophia's B Field District, looking at photographs. They were black and white and printed on typing paper. The reflected glare of the sun blurred the images of murky trench water and debris. One by one, he pulled photographs from his manila folder, exclaiming, "I just didn't have enough film to catch everything." A few weeks prior, he had ridden on his bicycle through B Field looking for eroded canal embankments. His pictures resembled the aerial photographs of the compromised EDWC taken by engineers during the 2005 disaster. Late to the scene, Louie and the engineers were witnesses who did not know when the disturbance began or would end. Louie boasted about how meticulous he was but admitted that his photographs depicted only part of the story. He reminded me, "I didn't get into people's yards. I don't know what they do to stop floods." Louie surmised that Sophia residents' yards and, by extension, their homes are much more complex sites for a range of intimacies with flooding and its containment (see figure 7.2).

I knew Louie because he helped spearhead a number of activities at the Sophia/Patterson Community Centre along with founding member and Sophia resident Colin Marks (pictured in figure 7.3). They first met as converts to Rastafari in the 1980s, attending services and community functions and playing in a band together. Despite their spiritual connection they took different career paths; Louie trained to become an electrician while Colin worked for his father's blueprinting business. Colin eventually left Rastafari, hoping to develop ways to channel his interest in social advocacy that did not confine him to what he called the "rigidity of a movement/religion." By the

FIGURE 7.2. Louie documenting burnt trash, a known pollutant and flood hazard in Sophia

FIGURE 7.3. Colin Marks sweeping the Sophia/Patterson Community Centre before a meeting

early 2000s, he was invested in a life of consultancy work, connecting with various state ministries and NGOs to facilitate community policing and HIV/AIDS awareness in Sophia. Louie used his free time to organize youth wood-carving lessons and art exhibitions, activities that created a gateway of sorts to develop community pride among younger residents.

During my time in Sophia, Colin and Louie became known for mobilizing residents to participate in the Red Cross project. Like Louie, Colin shared with me plenty of memories about the numerous floods and clogged canals he experienced. He named a road after his wife, where she often slipped because of the muddy pegasse. Walking these roads, I gathered, was Colin's testament to a self-effacing belief in luck and care. And so, seemingly everybody in Sophia—from itinerant livestock to multitasking engineers to bored youth to overworked community organizers—was implicated in floods. There is no easy way to detach oneself from the irrigation and drainage grid. It is a partial achievement to live with floods year after year.

These achievements and intimacies were often the topic of discussion at VCA training. At the community center, Red Cross workers focused a number of meetings on teaching VCA trainees how to assemble and use do-it-yourself water filtration kits. The kits include towels, chlorine bleach, and bottles—items found in most Georgetown households. Trainees have to be careful not to contaminate the bottles and towels when collecting water to boil from vats, wells, buckets, and faucets. Likewise, the trainees have to be vigilant even after initial collection of water and monitor their bodies for exposure to dysentery, cholera, or leptospirosis. Puddles in yards increase the possibility of exposure, even after floods. Red Cross workers suggested that not only should each household in Sophia have a water filtration kit but that VCA trainees should agree to hold periodic tutorials at the community center. A routinized procedure, the water filtration kits provide guidelines for how to respond to health risks whatever the conditions of a particular household (Redfield 2013).

What is significant here is not that VCA training is tied to ideals about acts of volunteerism. These ideals are shot through with a mix of cynicism and aspiration, sentiments that informed many VCA trainees' interest in the Red Cross in the first place. Instead, the importance of the training reflects what Kathleen Stewart (2005, 1015) calls "cultural poesis" or an intense attention to the generativity and endurance of things in daily life—a kind of attention that "arises in the effort to know what is happening or to be part of it, [and] the exciting presence of traces, remainders, and excesses." While the water filtration kits provide a routinized procedure, they also cull VCA trainees' attention to moments of impact between bodies and floods that are far from straightforward or causal.

A cultural poesis of flood hazards, while a complex relation of things, also depends on how trainees are hailed by others who might experience flood-related loss, damage, or injury in different ways. The trainees struggled to talk about these experiences when they developed household vulnerability surveys. They brainstormed a number of questions for the survey: Does your family have a water filtration kit? How high were the last floodwaters in your home? Do you have an evacuation route? They also developed an appendix for the surveys that included a space for each respondent to list the responsibilities of family members, neighbors, and local state agencies in the event of a flood. As VCA trainees brainstormed, a Red Cross worker interjected to help, explaining, "This is bottom up. . . . We never know exactly what to expect, but you can come together to help bring out the best in each other."

With a successful track record managing other community-based environmental programs, this Red Cross worker was well rehearsed in making participatory decision-making appear self-evident. He encouraged VCA trainees to share testimonials about floods and their use of water filtration kits. As a trainee noted, "We don't want to have to keep each other company [at meetings]. . . . And I say we deal with this [kit] now and get this over so that when something really big happens again we need everyone to understand that we need to be *sufficient*. I don't have all the information. . . . This is why we need training. We all need to know where flooding happens . . . to know that even if we take care of everything, some water will still come in your yard." This VCA trainee recognizes that he has some understanding about drainage on his property but a very minimal understanding of its dynamics throughout greater Sophia. In these terms, he does not know in advance of a flood how the water filtration kit will help him. He can only guess. His testimonial dramatizes the plural uses of the kits while creating a metanarrative about the common occurrence of flood hazards in Sophia.

Testimonials served multiple purposes for training in water filtration. On the one hand, they facilitated discussion about the kind of material evidence trainees can find and gather in their daily lives to monitor water supplies. On the other, testimonials triggered conversations about the rather open-ended dynamics of caring for things and bodies that climate change demands. As an activity, testimonials remind us that "crisis ordinariness" depends on people withholding judgment about the future (Berlant 2011a, 51–96). In referring to this future, a number of VCA trainees talked about leptospirosis to emphasize the deep sense of nervousness they have come to attribute to water contamination. Livestock owners in Sophia used their bottom flats as spaces to herd mostly sheep and cattle during the 2005 disaster. The tense mix of human and more-than-human bodies registered in exchange.

Some passed on health officials' warnings to not handle livestock carcasses and to keep them as far away from the interior of the house as possible to limit the spread of infection. Others started a relief system whereby people volunteered to go to a shelter or a hospital in Georgetown to retrieve drugs (prophylaxis or doxycycline) to pass along to family, neighbors, and friends. Trainees admitted that, based on their 2005 disaster experience, they had not developed a good sense for infection and often attributed their nausea, headaches, or fever to other diseases—just about every bodily ailment they have come to associate with leptospirosis. They discovered that concentrating on how much rain saturates the ground is their best chance at diagnosis.

Colin emphasized this point about diagnosis when he suggested during a meeting that intense flooding challenges reason:

> I'm trying to provoke a thought about what to do with different levels of water. Say it's like two feet of water. Right away you gotta think of health, the latrine, you know. . . . Say you begin with five or three feet [of water], but again, what's the difference? You have to now move because it's

beyond, you know, bearable. But wherever you go, you are still exposed to a health risk. That's the thing; we know that 90 percent of our septic tanks aren't constructed the way they need for safety. But with the flood it compromises both, the person and the infrastructure. The kits are helpful, to a point I guess. But I still *feel* that with a septic tank I am safer than without.

Even as one who helped organize with the Red Cross to get Sophia's VCA, Colin has become less confident in the area's drainage and therefore even more reliant on water filtration kits.

He references the three- and five-foot water levels experienced during the 2005 disaster as his new norm for living comfortably with floods. Yet Colin also notes that flood hazards related to leptospirosis and faulty septic tanks are difficult to discern, no matter a flood's water level. As a knowledge practice, testimonials shape the powerful tension between what can be known and what remains unspeakable about the impacts of a changing climate on the ordinary.

Mark Carey and colleagues (2016) have described parallel concerns about glaciology knowledge and climate change. Shaped by an ontic-epistemic framework embedded in daily life of not only science but also humble forms of water management equipment, glaciology knowledge represents "ice itself as an element of change and . . . as a thing that is part of society" (1). Given the prominent place of glaciers in the global discourse about climate change, Carey suggests that the idiom *cryoscapes* is one way to describe the relations between people and ice. A similar dynamic is at play in Guyana, as I have demonstrated throughout this book, and here as well for VCA trainees, where *floodscapes* mediate ethical decisions about what counts as a water filtration kit and the kinds of knowledge it shapes about the unpredictability of daily life affected by climate change. The testimonials reinforce the idea that crisis ordinariness cannot be contained through rigid training or, for that matter, witnessing. At times the reality of this mundane fact can cease to be significant, or it can burst into VCA trainees' lives and demand that it not be ignored.

Accommodating Experts

A few weeks into their efforts, VCA trainees completed pilot surveys of households in an area of Sophia known as North Field. Deemed to be on the fringes of Sophia's fertile lands, North Field postdates Sophia's era of informal squatting (circa 1999). More homes are built on surveyed plots, but it is located in a catchment near the outfalls of the Atlantic. Despite the lack of census data, it is rumored to be a high-income, Indo-Guyanese and Mixed Race area, albeit with numerous female-headed households. My interlocutors were intrigued about the data they would collect. The mere presence of these households complicated their collective awareness of vulnerability. These households are economically secure but inhabit a space that is more flood prone than the rest of Sophia. The trainees recognized that floods do not care who lives where but that it was their responsibility to create alliances between vulnerable bodies and spaces.

Data collection for the surveys was not easy. For the survey, Sophia's VCA trainees were joined by staff from other Caribbean Red Cross branches looking to complete their volunteer certification. The irony was not lost on VCA trainees, given that Guyana's Red Cross staff suggested that they act as cultural ambassadors for the day. Many of the VCA trainees did not view these foreigners as intruders or as an affront to their work but as needed labor for the tall task of surveying. They surmised that the surveys would tell them something more general about how intense flooding might vary across space. The surveys circulated as a genre that became "delaminated from its location in someone's story or some locale's irreducibly local history" (Berlant 2011a, 12). This means that the surveys were not merely constituted by speech acts, such as brainstorming exercises and testimonials performed at prior meetings. The trainees' time surveying North Field and encounters with terrain and natures were also an embodied practice that created the terms for the surveys' circulation.

Take, for instance, the ditches, weeds, and fire ant hills that surrounded the entryways of many homes. Both harbingers and obstacles, they taught VCA trainees to slow their gait and brush insects off their bodies to avoid being injured. While most North Field residents ventured from their homes to their yards to greet VCA trainees, some shouted their answers from windows, and a few simply did not venture out to meet them on public roads. The obstacles VCA trainees faced dramatized that each survey made visible competing arrangements of vulnerability (see figure 7.4).

Data collection was not limited by the boundary between the home and the public road. It was performed within domestic spaces as well. Renee, a resident, spoke in extensive detail about cement blocks she used to protect her house's foundation from floodwaters. She insisted that while she felt high above the water, she often relied on her dog's movements and barking

FIGURE 7.4. A house the Red Cross team visited during the VCA survey. Upon entering the yard, Louie noted, "This is what vulnerability looks like."

to warn her of heavy rainfall. Her children moved furniture away from windows and put plastic tarps over holes in the tin roof when it rained. Renee's vulnerability emerged in discontinuity with things that crosscut human and more-than-human boundaries of the ordinary. Her testimonial convinced VCA trainees that Sophia's emergency contact list should include not only phone numbers and home addresses but also the number of pets in households.

But not all of North Field's residents were committed to an ethos that equated the VCA with testimonials about vulnerability. In one interview, a North Field resident interjected in the middle of questioning to suggest that the VCA matters only if engineers improve drainage. The VCA made him feel proud of Sophia but irritated by how he lives. He dramatized his point by making VCA trainees stand on top of an eroding canal embankment near his yard. Moved by their willingness to indulge him, he insisted that the VCA would only make North Field residents more accepting of floods.

At issue in his reprimand are concerns about the way private lives and flood hazards may often intersect but are processes that can conjure competing political imaginaries about daily life. The survey in North Field thus animates the genre of crisis in two ways. First, any evidence of a potential flood is made a case for collecting more testimonials to get a richer sample of probable scenarios of vulnerability. Second, Sophia residents use these testimonials to question the VCA trainees' authority and their conventional social identities as community advocates. Some, like Renee, claim to rise above water; others wear their vulnerability like a badge of honor, optimistic that with a bit more effort they can force other people and things to become (more) accountable. But is the VCA a tool to warn North Field residents of the vulnerabilities that might not have caught their attention, or is it intended to mobilize another kind of common world?

Trainees attempted to address this ambiguity, particularly if they wished to use the survey beyond Red Cross activities. Some planned to create a flood library and research station at the Sophia/Patterson Community Centre to have information on hand to improve future VCAs. Others intended to use the survey to lobby the Ministry of Agriculture to dredge canals and improve embankments. They debated how to present the survey to state officials. A PowerPoint, they surmised, was a distraction that would make them appear too well adapted to climate change. They agreed that an informal presentation was the best way to communicate. The conversation would be directed by no more than ten residents so as not to overwhelm state officials and remind them that Sophia is a cumbersome place. They desired to take on the persona of accommodating experts who, out of urgency and need, could work with state agencies' limited resources. Surviving the everyday requires a light touch and the ability to assimilate the possibilities and foreclosures that flood hazards incite.

Despite these plans, they never made it to the ministry and instead drafted a letter that outlined their grievances. The interplay of knowledge, self-presentation, ecobiological processes, and testimonials established through VCAs created a discernible communicative context for ethical commitments to participation. Yet, the VCA does not guarantee redress or even a better life. To say all this is not to dismiss outright VCAs and the moral economies in which they traffic as various kinds of antipolitics (cf. Ferguson 2006). They may be antipolitics, but they may be not only that. As with the Hope/Doch-four farmers, the VCA trainees' claims to expertise are a refutation of floods as simply moments to critique notions of developmentalism and apaan jaat. Instead, through their commitments to the VCA they position counter-racial thinking as the grounds for doing climate adaptation.

Such commitments are quite different from what Bruno Latour (2004) calls matters of concern or the defense of facts for the sake of ideological or political gain. This is because as long as they took the initiative, VCA trainees believed they were adapting and that their injuries due to intense flooding could be addressed on a case-by-case basis. Training began as a routinized effort to convey flood knowledges and a skill set in water filtration, but it shifted in the real time of data collection and unfolded into a scene of adaptation itself. The VCAs are not the result of the technical or political compulsions of a few people. Nor are they mere expressions of vulnerability that follow historically formalized understandings of apaan jaat through socialism, neoliberal development, or even state abandonment. Yet, for that reason, they are not solely dependent on the local particularities of a hazardous place. The trainees understand that climate adaptation entails the constant adjustment of expectations about expertise, inclusion, and counter-racial thinking. They build up the capacity to identify flood hazards and learn to live with them. A case in point is the stockpile of water filtration kits, which is not only a method of preparedness but also a hope for the resurrection of biovalue in new and more secure terms (Keck 2017).

Participatory climate adaptation decenters apaan jaat from its determinative scope in Guyana's coastal settlement. Through VCA participation, Sophia residents have come to treat apaan jaat for what it is: another obstacle in the way of climate adaptation. This sort of ecological realism can be stifling, just as much as it can be a foundation for change beyond pragmatism and an insistence on a new materialism. Between VCA trainees' testimonials and Louie's photography lies a difference not in textual interpretation, translation, or citation but in making ethical demands on each other about what kinds of practices should entail ways of knowing disturbance.

The combined efforts of Sophia residents suggest that one of the more pernicious effects of climate change has been the erosion of the status of the expert. By this I do not mean that the expert has been alienated, delegitimized, or marginalized in favor of populist narratives of redemption or apocalyptic climatic futures, though there is some truth to these claims. There is nothing unique about the order of social cost paid for the benefit of empoldering, large-scale damming, or apaan jaat that has brought about coastal settlement in Guyana. Similar stories have been told by scholars the world over from India to South Africa and from Egypt to China. Rather, I am referring to a more radical and less visible process whereby the broad social canvas in which the expert (both as category and as social fact) has been thinned out in favor of a more general description of the contemporary interval of human activity destroying the planet. Many scientists and social theorists have described this interval as the Anthropocene.

I have, however, taken a different approach throughout this book to describe human activity. The interval of ordinary life or, more specifically, the day-to-day knowledge production and exchange across social groups offers us a nuanced understanding of what is required to imagine life beyond mass extinction. Ordinary life is something perhaps like the geostrata from which the expert emerges, the precursor and precondition of thinking relations of accountability in the midst of a warming planet. My proposition that an ordinary life requires one learning to become accountable squares the circle of climate adaptation as a practice that reduces expertise not to questions of the biopolitical but to the art of pursuit. Far from a definitive appraisal of state discipline or even racism that has contributed to climate change, climate adaptation illuminates ways of knowing that inform desires for the continued settlement of a place. It recognizes the hubris involved in such a task. At the same time, climate adaptation gestures to the limits of human knowledge, while leaving open the possibility of finding models other than those of race for future life on a warming planet.

CONCLUSION. Materializing Race and Climate Change

"They don't care about us," Colin explained as we sat on the Sophia/Patterson Community Centre balcony in 2014, five years after we first met. I had come back to wrap up what I thought were loose ends of research. The Red Cross participatory climate adaptation project had concluded, and Colin's focus in community organizing had shifted to job development. I was not surprised. I remember once having a conversation with him about policing in Sophia taking away the life chances of some and not others. He worried that Afro-Guyanese teenage boys were becoming the targets of crime and perpetrators of it. But he explained that the idea of Sophia being a dangerous place was overblown. The real criminals, he noted, come from elsewhere. Sophia was simply a scapegoat for a society under siege. "Everyone," he argued, knew this to be true, yet the image of Sophia as an unsafe, urban, and Black settlement persisted.

I asked him why this was the case. Sophia's population is racially heterogenous compared to other neighborhoods in Georgetown. And well over thirty years after its founding, Sophia could boast of upward mobility among lower- to middle-class households, like his own. He insisted that, with a bit more outside help, the myths of danger and crime could be easily transformed into stories about prosperity and employment. I did not press him about who could help, but after knowing him for so long I assumed he meant state officials.

Colin spent much of his time organizing meetings to encourage teenagers, no longer attending school, to enter trade/vocational programs (e.g., information technology, electrical engineering, masonry, and entrepreneurship) sponsored by NGOs and local employment centers. His determination was palpable, but so was his resignation. These programs reinvigorated his commitment to Sophia. Afterall, the area had not experienced a disaster since 2005. Their fortune, perhaps, could be attributed to Colin and others regularly canvassing the area for derelict minibridges, clogged trenches, and crumbling dirt roads. What's more, the residents who completed the trade/vocational programs could aid the climate adaptation of Sophia's roads, electrical grids, and bridges. The possibilities seemed endless.

Colin's uneven experience changing public attitudes about Black, urban settlement demonstrates that Sophia was more similar than not to other locales in coastal Guyana. What connected Sophia to the rest of the coast were not racial, crime, or employment statistics but residents' desires for climate adaptation. The 2005 disaster was one event that made these desires palpable. The event forced those living in Sophia to ask, "Is this the last flood I'll remember?" And those living elsewhere on longer stilts and with more rations, "Are we the next to go?" Irrigation and drainage infrastructures are evidence of what Colin describes as the state's indifference and of his efforts to think otherwise to apaan jaat. More than a mere assessment of vulnerability, Colin uses climate adaptation to transport him to a better, or at least different, space-time.

What I gathered from my ongoing conversations with Colin and others is that the impetus for climate adaptation is the fear of small numbers. Guyana's situation seems to parallel that of many other nation-states. A post–Cold War global agenda for democratic liberalism and free trade has only intensified forms of racial inequalities and in some instances has exacerbated ethnic conflict and violence. At the same time, this social uncertainty has animated new types of social alliances that challenge a conventional understanding of nation-state identity as dependent on sovereignty, territorial boundaries, and especially the binarism between racial majority/minority. Climate adaptation is a prime example of how these new social alliances play out within and across national borders. And as varying governing bodies and global treaties commit to climate adaptation, the fear of small numbers has surfaced as a complex articulation of rage, doubt, hope, and indifference.

The catch, however, is that not only are racial minority groups vulnerable to climate change but so are racial majority groups. In the case of coastal Guyana's intense flooding, experts and ordinary citizens alike have struggled to make sense of the fissures in biopower *while* enacting new modes of solidarity that challenge apaan jaat. Put another way, representations of racial groups in Guyana are now being organized around electoral patterns, uncertain climate change projections, and dissenting opinions on the procedural matters of climate adaptation. From this perspective, climate adaptation is a technological feat invested not only in calculating and representing the future but also in an ethics of (re)distribution.

For his part, Colin suggests that overcoming the fear of small numbers may require not only empathetic souls but a reserve of measuring apparatuses that speak to the needs of people's varied experiences of settlement. In short, the fear of small numbers has a prehistory. During the Dutch and British colonial era and Guyana's postcolonial era, settler colonialism has stood in as a governing framework for flood management. Along the way, the engineering sciences morphed into a practice that gained political authority through its struggle to both recognize forms of racism and address them through dam design. Internal to this struggle are questions about who counts as expert and whether coastal settlement ought to continue at the expense of settlement and infrastructural development in other regions of the country, including the interior.

Thus, the idea that in postcolonial Guyana most people appreciate irrigation and drainage infrastructures but remain suspicious of their racializing operations is not a contradiction. Rather, this ethical stance defines the interests of the individual settler in relation to the values of a national collective at a particular moment in history. The theoretical variants of historical materialism and political economy that informed mid- to late twentieth-century ethnography and historiography of Guyana and the Caribbean make this ethical stance clear. This literature tends to have an understanding of history that is linear and treats an analysis of settlement as unfolding in a coherent narrative form, starting with colonial contact, moving to slavery-emancipation, indentureship, decolonization, and transitioning through (post)socialism. But climate adaptation unsettles this narrative form in ways that turn people's attention to the historical contingencies of floodscapes and, more generally, vulnerability.

The EDWC's enhancements, for instance, suggest that the act of permanently settling a place is without guarantees. And the basic assumptions people
in Guyana carry about the coast—its terrain, nature, politics, infrastructure, and
sensibility—are becoming less and less familiar, perhaps even uncanny, as they
confront climate change. This is a delicate situation. Many offer critical reflections on racial political orders, such as slavery and apaan jaat, to tell
stories about surviving intense flooding, erratic weather, failing infrastructure, and unresponsive institutions. Within these stories, second-order
questions emerge. What does it mean to belong? Who has the capacity (and
responsibility) to become hospitable to others? When do claims to racial solidarity morph into ethnocentrism or racism? What are the ethical, affective,
and political registers that lend themselves to settlement? Such questions
account for people's racialized experiences of inequality and climate change
alongside their aspirations for new kinds of sociality that are not dictated
by race. Counter-racial thinking, in other words, is central to climate adaptation activities. It challenges universalizing concepts of the human, nature, the
nation-state, and modernity while commenting on the fact that forms of racial domination make living with climate change unbearable. Thus the
effects of counter-racial thinking are never simply local. Counter-racial
thinking makes explicit that the knowledge practices of so-called peripheral locales have never been separate or isolated from so-called cosmopolitan centers.

More than this, counter-racial thinking explores what the best possible
forms of sociopolitical and ecological existence might be. By this I mean
that race is a relational category that shapes descriptors—of, say, Blackness,
Whiteness, and Indianness as well as who or what constitutes a collectiv-
ity of experts (see also Rusert 2017). In this respect, I treat counter-racial
thinking as also shaping varied subject-positions, values, beliefs, and attitudes toward the more-than-human. Following the insights of Black studies
scholars, the turn to posthumanist claims and theory in the social sciences
and humanities entails a deconstruction of the parasitical forms of White,
liberal thought that have historically contributed to racial inequalities and
death (see King 2017; and Weheliye 2014).

At the same time, this book demonstrates that processes of knowledge
exchange between non-Whites and Whites are essential to our understanding of how the Anthropocene came to be. Climate adaptation is a crucial
practice for acknowledging uneven and sometimes violent forms of knowledge exchange and thereby the story of the universal realization of vulnerability to climate change. Theory and reality of race converge in the moments

people make decisions about climate adaptation. Or, to put it in posthumanist terms, climate adaptation challenges an anthropocentric view of history while making visible human activities that are entangled with racism and the destruction of environments. But telling this story may not only depend on scholars offering variations of the term *Anthropocene* that incorporate racialized perspectives on capitalism, technology, natures, and so on. Rather, scholars need to unpack canonical formulations of historicity in environmental philosophy or the ways people write and think about an ethics of the environment.

Take, for instance, that discussions about race in environmental studies are overwhelmingly framed around the concept of environmental justice: the inclusion of all people in the development of governance systems and laws that protect natures and that enact the fair distribution of environmental resources. Adopting liberal principles of equality and personhood, environmental justice positions the issue of race within the time frame of human (in)action to manage the environment. A similar preoccupation undergirds climate justice, which focuses on identifying the institutions and people responsible for emitting carbon emissions. Both of these iterations of justice are laudable in that they help explain the sociopolitical processes that produce racialized identities and investments in the environment. But environmental justice also assumes that liberal governmentality manages race only as a source of conflict, thereby conditioning the aspiration for a type of scholarship that can locate or identify an authentic racialized *and* vulnerable subject. Throughout this book, I have pushed against this aspiration by examining ethics as more than the question of justice. Specifically, I have foregrounded the forms of expertise, activities, and conditions of possibility that make accountability imaginable in the first place.

In the context of climate adaptation, accountability requires a critical reassessment of the relationship between race, causality, and vulnerability. Demands for accountability often materialize through people's use of measuring apparatuses. As the efforts of Hope-Dochfour farmers, Sophia VCA trainees, CDC staff, and engineers demonstrate, measuring apparatuses do not assemble a racially disinterested view from nowhere; they gain uneven traction across power-saturated institutions. An analysis of measuring apparatuses asks if and when climate adaptation needs to take a racializing form as people seek to establish relations of accountability. Climate adaptation never completely escapes the calculus of race, even in moments of direct challenge wherein counter-racial thinking becomes the most feasible mode of survival for people.

The more interesting question still may be: What sustains people's efforts at counter-racial thinking in climate adaptation? An ethnography of climate adaptation gives attention to the ways measuring apparatuses produce what Karen Barad (2007) calls agential cuts or the contours/boundaries that linger in matter over time. In Guyana's case, where and how people empolder and dig large-scale dams has always been dependent on the composition of pegasse and its geological record. Pegasse creates relations between the past, present, and future of forests cut or desired to be protected, people enslaved and freed, rebellion, sabotage, migration, love made and lost, people gone missing, violence, agriculture reigning king, science made concrete, and disaster. Pegasse reminds us that desires for climate adaptation may come from a variety of sources that do not have their origins in race, even as people struggle to respond to climate adaptation's racializing effects in the present.

And yet, even as people advocate and develop new epistemologies for climate adaptation, they may also encounter numerous forces that block its uptake across national borders. Here I am thinking of the broad appeal and belief in climate skepticism. If the 1992 Rio Earth Summit and the Kyoto Protocol of 1997 were intended to solidify global action on climate change, the hacked emails of scientists at the Climate Research Unit in 2009 ("climategate") solidified global inaction. From the view of the Global North, inaction has been informed by debates about the accuracy of hockey stick–shaped graphs and climate models, which have in turn helped incite doubt among people about the scientific consensus on climate change (Hulme 2009). This doubt has fed into, and in some cases reconstituted, broader processes of extractive capitalism, migrations, and democracy (Connolly 2017). Kari Marie Norgaard (2011), for instance, suggests that climate skepticism is more than a condition of ignorance or nonknowledge. As a worldview, it makes it possible for the individual to deny the vulnerability not only of the self but of humanity as a whole.

Perhaps one of the more dramatic embodiments of this worldview is the populism narrated by former US president Donald Trump as the "deconstruction of the administrative state." The Trump administration's formal withdrawal of the United States from the Paris climate accord and reversal of carbon emissions regulations for the American fossil fuel industry are but two examples. These decisions were supposedly intended to improve GDP alongside bettering the life chances of working-class White Americans, who, in his understanding, have been more disenfranchised by global markets and financial capital than other Americans. The problem, of course, is that deconstructing the administrative state requires more than a focus on the economy. As a challenge to Trump's populism, technocrats from across federal environmental agencies continued to make investments in research related to climate change and conservation for legislation such as the farm bill.

Meanwhile, NGOs, including the National Audubon Society, that have long regarded themselves as proponents of such legislation, find themselves being held accountable by broader publics. They now communicate issues about climate change as a way to expand their membership base and its diversity across culture, ethnicity, and race while paying less attention to populations that do not believe in climate change (Colman 2020). Here, once again, climate adaptation has room for particular kinds of diverse natures and human populations as long as they help contribute to settlement, in this case for the sake of bird conservation. Climate skepticism, in short, has accelerated the ruin of the planet, but it still produces a heterogeneous array of racialized exclusions, as well as efforts that push back, to create modes of sociality that are understood as antiracist.

Similar dynamics of climate skepticism have been expressed in Guyana. In recent years, the government and its citizenry have been working toward a new, fantastic vision of coastal settlement. The country's 2015 national election ushered in for the first time a government that explicitly ran on a platform of bridging the Afro-Guyanese leadership of David Granger, a member of the PNC-R, with the multiracial leadership of the Partnership for National Unity party in the name of doing what the PPP did not focus on: linking climate change to the creation of jobs in not only the interior region (e.g., sustainable logging and mining) but also the coastal region (oil exploration). Partnerships of Exxon Mobil with the Ministry of the Environment have since brought fantasies of extractivism that may ring anachronistic but follow the moves of its Venezuelan, Surinamese, and Trinidadian neighbors in the midst of becoming so-called low-carbon petrostates.

Guyana's turn to becoming a petrostate is in seeming dissonance with its now nearly fifteen years of climate adaptation and centuries-old plantation-based economy. This is a wicked outcome of climate adaptation: at the same time that it can breathe life into new models for settlement, it can suck the life out of others. Climate adaptation requires that people learn to stay vigilant. Features in international media, such as the *New York Times* proclaiming that these oil deposits will make Guyana the richest country in the Southern Hemisphere in due time, fuel these fantasies. Dailies in Guyana include columns that explain to people how to become oil-minded citizens and to be wary of Venezuelan provocations and claims to oil finds in the Atlantic frontier. In the meantime, engineering bids are still plenty, as the Ministry of Agriculture and the Ministry of Public Infrastructure continue to invest in the climate adaptation of the EDWC and sea defense.

The dual economies of carbon markets and oil alongside the climate adaptation of irrigation and drainage and sea defense infrastructures only make Guyana's coastal settlement a seemingly spectacular and magical reinvention of vulnerability. For instance, a 2018 no-confidence vote in Guyana's parliament of the Granger administration only put more pressure on the new PPP administration to use oil as a means to transform the coast for the better. But again, this confidence in oil may be a fleeting form of optimism or at least one that is contingent on a very particular set of conditions. There have been, of course, less anticipated and less obvious obstacles to Guyana's coastal settlement than extractivism. Global pandemics such as COVID-19 are just one example, whereby travel bans and quarantines have delayed Guyana's oil production, slashed local revenues, and dashed hopes about the country's not-yet-realized prosperity (*Stabroek News* 2020). This is not to say, however, that those nation-states already moving away from oil as a main energy source have been spared. The coronavirus pandemic has only further laid bare the global conditions—overexploited food-supply chains, deforestation, and mass biodiversity loss—that accelerate vulnerability to climate change. Climate adaptation, in other words, is a precondition for the future.

So if climate skepticism originates from a Western liberal zeitgeist of carbon-dependent capitalism, climate skepticism gains global traction because places on its margins, such as Guyana, have for centuries been indebted to its economic rationalities. But methods for eradicating this debt may not only make themselves legible through language or sentiments about race. And it is by way of holding tight to a critical analysis of climate change that posits race/racism as the key to understanding human survival in the Anthropocene that scholars often lose sight of the heterogeneous knowledge practices that seek to eradicate carbon dependencies the world over. The title of this book, *Engineering Vulnerability*, alludes to such blind spots and has sought to create a space to begin to think otherwise. This book has grounded thinking about climate adaptation and its possible political alignments and misalignments. It points to what we learn by pausing to consider the locales where knowledge of race and climate change are already being reconfigured (and challenged) through practice. With this in mind, we might begin to treat ethnography not only as a skill set invested in diagnosis and critique but as one of many human encounters with a warming planet Earth.

INTRODUCTION

1 In the months prior to the 1997 election, several independent forums were established to develop a model for power sharing that departed from the Westminster system, which was inherited from the British colonial period (Thakur 2019).

2 This is not to say that rural areas of the coast were racially homogenous (Beaie 2007). Afro-Guyanese households were equally distributed across urban and rural areas, while Indo-Guyanese households were heavily concentrated in rural areas. Overall, 52 percent of Afro-Guyanese lived in rural areas compared to 73 percent of Indo-Guyanese (Gampat 2002). This racial and geographic distribution remains more or less the same today. Even within Georgetown, and especially within coastal rural villages, communities are heavily segregated along racial-ethnic and class lines. This is a divide that dates back to the racial political violence of the preindependence period. Before these riots, many people attest that coastal villages and Georgetown neighborhoods were relatively integrated among Afro-Guyanese and Indo-Guyanese.

3 Those with means took refuge in the handful of hotels located in Georgetown, and those without means moved to shelters, while countless others, like Margaret, opted to stay in their homes.

4 The exception are villages located adjacent to the EDWC and within the catchment of the Mahaica River (see chapters 4 and 5).

5 See Schipper 2006 for a brief history of climate adaptation as a term and strategy and its place in UN governmental protocol. For a brief history of the UNFCCC, see Agrawala 1998a and 1998b.

6 Monies for the EDWC-related projects did not come from LCDS. They were earmarked through World Bank loans and the country's PetroCaribe Rice Compensation Scheme with Venezuela. The EDWC's climate adaptation projects started before LCDS was finalized; nevertheless, the government used related project reports as references and models for future LCDS funding schemes for coastal climate adaptation engineering activities. Other engineering activities include mangrove restoration co-organized by engineers, agronomists, geoscientists, and ecologists to enhance sea defense (Vaughn 2017).

7 The small-island-state coalition is a reaction to the indifference high-emitting Global South and Global North states have shown low-emitting Global

South states throughout history. Copenhagen marks a turning point in IPPC agreements because unlike the 2001 Marrakesh Accords, there was explicit dialogue about what climate adaptation entails and not simply who funds it or how (Schipper 2006). Other regional identities in the name of climate adaptation have emerged in recent years, such as the Caribbean's "1.5 to Stay Alive" campaign. Such commitments to rethinking regionality through vulnerability suggest that there is "no shared common future" for the planet but rather multiple and ongoing climate crises that have inspired various frameworks of calculation, intervention, and diplomacy (Latour 2018).

8   While beyond the scope of this book, the question of how different technosciences become associated with race in climate adaptation projects also plays into the way states imagine the rights and liberties of its citizens. As Nikolas Rose and many others have argued, technosciences have a critical role in shaping racial conceptions of the vital human being and the racial characteristics of the actual and desirable citizen.

9   Guyana's low-lying coastal strip depends on three other large-scale embankment dams: the Boeraserie Conservancy, the Tapakuma Conservancy, and the Abary Conservancy. Given that the EDWC was the sole site of dam overtopping during the 2005 disaster, this book does not focus on the operations of the other three.

10 Climate adaptation is animated by the idea that nature is a form of infrastructure, as Ashley Carse (2014) notes when describing the operations of the Panama Canal. He and others have shown that the rapid growth of public and private sector investments in environmental engineering exposes the speculative operations of governance and its collective social agencies (Ballestero 2019; Disco 2002; Helmreich forthcoming).

11 This emphasis distinguishes recent work in anthropology on climate change from the political ecology approaches in geography on risks and hazards and the social constructivist approaches in the field of science and technology studies on the vulnerability of sociotechnological systems. Rather than a discrete condition, "ways of knowing disturbance" gesture to relations of dependency not only between humans (Butler, Gambetti, and Sabsay 2016) but also between human and more-than-human forms. From this perspective, vulnerability constitutes a range of ethical-affective processes that underscore what counts as adaptation to climate change.

12 These writings have two diverging concerns. On the one hand, they remind us that vulnerability provides an alternative vantage point from which people can begin to act against political and economic systems that support excessive carbon consumption, species extinction, inequality, and the like. On the other, they track the relations of capital that accelerate climate change and its pernicious arrangements of abandonment that privilege some life forms over others.

13 When referring to apaan jaat and its capacity to label human bodies and divide groups into singular entities, I prefer to use the term *individual*. I use the term

while recognizing the ways that race can never be disentangled from claims of personhood that are historically informed by the Enlightenment's emphasis on reason (e.g., mathematics), modern descriptions of the human (e.g., census categories), and liberalism's ethico-political claims to the body (e.g., citizenship). With that said, I find that the term *individual* helps delineate the various forms of address—as much as recognition, at stake in racial political orders. On race and personhood, see Comaroff and Comaroff 2001; on enumeration, theories of race, and categories of the individual, see Winant 2000.

14 My reading of boundary making and agential cuts is primarily based on Barad's *Meeting the Universe Halfway* (2007) and "Posthumanist Performativity: Toward an Understanding of How Matter Comes to Matter" (2003). In these texts she is concerned with explaining what counts as representationalism and the ethical relations that emerge from knowledge-making practices and their material reconfiguration. The concept of agential cuts is part of a broader analytic approach called posthumanist performativity, which treats human and more-than-human agencies as shaping the conditions of possibility for ethical action. Barad's emphasis on the distribution of agency and the practices that enact responsibility for different actors distinguishes her work from other scholars taking a new materialist approach to examine agency, who tend to deploy the concepts of force (Bennett 2010) and assemblage (DeLanda 2019). Barad's reading of agential cuts is worthwhile to the extent that it treats ethics as an issue that emerges from the way people perceive boundaries/difference rather than as a given or assumed category of subjectivity or even identity. For a sharp critique of Barad's notions of subject formation, nonduality, and responsibility, see Braunmühl 2018.

15 The terms *intense flooding* and *big flood* were repeated by many of my informants to describe above-average rainfall that contributed to floods. When they spoke of intense flooding, the actual watermarks did not always meet or exceed the three seven-foot watermarks of 2005; nevertheless, the watermarks reminded them of this possibility.

16 Measuring apparatuses dramatize the moments when people decide whether or not to interpret their place in the world as structured by race. Here I part with scholars, especially within the disciplines of security studies and geography, who assume that climate adaptation activities necessarily advance arrangements of biopower (see Evans and Reid 2014). They often critique climate adaptation activities as doing three things: conflating social values with the biological capacities of infrastructural systems; privileging emergent modes of self-organization instead of those that persist over time; and reinforcing structures of political power through lifestyle choices and modes of sustainable consumption. In such accounts, measuring apparatuses are often described primarily as preserving liberal ideologies about the management of life (e.g., development or the welfare state) (see Oels 2005). But conflating measuring apparatuses with the management of life leaves unanswered how and why life becomes a problem of concern in the first place for some people

and not others. Throughout this book, my focus on race looks to ask how and why this flattening occurs while simultaneously asking what other political forms race takes beyond questions of life and death.

17 Although many political commentators and historians mark the 1957 election as inaugurating apaan jaat, there is still a debate about what caused the internal PPP party split between Jagan and Burnham in the first place. I attribute this debate to issues of historiography and power-knowledge. On the one hand, in the early 2000s files on the preindependence state of emergency, constitutional crisis, and labor disputes were declassified in the British and American archives. (For a fascinating analysis of British archival policy and decolonization in British Guiana, see Cobain 2017.) Since then, there has been a renaissance of sorts in Guyanese studies and Caribbean historiography that reconsiders the significance of preindependence British Guiana and early Guyana in the Cold War and the British Empire. Much of this literature corroborates the memoirs and personal accounts of political figures of the period. On the other hand, there are discussions about whether an individual political figure or the collective body politic should be held accountable for apaan jaat (see, for example, Kissoon 2012). Did Jagan first invoke the term to rally support from Indo-Guianese, or was it Burnham, in an effort to further marginalize Jagan within the ranks of the PPP? How does the phrase index the reproduction of gendered political relations and opportunities? Given these concerns, I characterize apaan jaat as situated within what Lee Drummond (1980) calls a "cultural continuum," or the *uneven* processes of communicative exchange that shape power relations. Specifically, one could argue that in its initial use, during the 1957 electoral campaign, apaan jaat was informed by metadiscourses about imperialism, colonialism, sovereignty, and political legitimacy. Further elaboration on the origins of apaan jaat is beyond the main concerns and scope of this book, but for a discussion on sentiment, race, and language, see McElhinny 2010.

18 I recognize that the word *racism*, similar to the terms *racial bias* and *discrimination*, takes on varied meaning and value given the context of its use. This being said, I follow Mullings's (2005, 668) point that *racism* is a relatively new term that came into popular use (at least within Western English-speaking contexts) during World War II. Mullings's periodization would fall in line with broader readings of raciology and biological sciences used as tools for the reproduction of nationalism and bare life. Nonetheless, other processes of racism more broadly conceived as racial bias or racial discrimination have similar origins and effects. This point is made in Cedric Robinson's (2000, 2) interpretation of the term *racialism*, which he argues has had a longer historical presence within discourses of state formation: "Racialism is the legitimatization and corroboration of social organization as natural by reference to the 'racial' components of its elements. Though hardly unique to European peoples, its appearance and codification, during the feudal period, into Western conceptions of society was to have important and enduring consequences." Finally,

I also take seriously David T. Goldberg's (2015) point that racism should be theorized as a tension between stand-alone events and long-term historical structures (longue durée) through which people learn to articulate claims to dignity, rights, and social possibility because of one's perceived race.

19   For instance, given that Guyana's national census counts people of Mixed descent as a distinct race, the national census challenges the national motto "the land of six peoples" (inclusive of African, Amerindian, Chinese, Indian, Portuguese, and European). Taking into account this distinction between the national census and the national motto, the Guyanese state enacts a form of liberal multicultural governance that is distinctive to the Caribbean. Specifically, the state acknowledges the various historical moments of migration that brought about the displacement of Amerindians from the coast for the labor of enslaved Africans. It highlights the role of indentured labor on racial identity formation, particularly the identity of Mixed Race, which in recent decades most often refers to someone of Afro- or Indo- descent (see chapter 4; for other examples, see Crosson 2020; Munasinghe 2001 on Trinidad). In addition, the Portuguese census category is not counted as inclusive of the census category *European* because of the historical role of Portuguese indentured laborers, alongside those of Indian and Chinese descent, in settlement after slave emancipation.

20   Apaan jaat is either uttered or invoked in everyday discourse to reference one's *indifference* or *dissatisfaction* with a politician, an election outcome, or state activity. In most instances, people go out of their way to avoid invoking the phrase by abruptly ending a conversation or staying silent when "politics" or "parties" are mentioned (see also Rickford 2019).

21   I do not dispute, for instance, the cross-cutting ways in which concepts such as "Black geographies," "Indigenous geographies," and "Black ecologies" highlight the plural modalities of race that characterize environmental and climate change awareness. Collectively, these concepts challenge White subjectivity as the norm of environmental action and thought. Moreover, I would interpret these concepts as in line with the democratic ideals of the New Left and intellectual traditions such as Black radical thought, intersectionality, and queer theory. At the same time, I worry about these concepts' modes of disciplinary and epistemic address, particularly in their reference to literary and environmental humanities as emancipatory fields, at the expense of considering the sciences' emancipatory potential. Instead, I look to problematize the modernist underpinnings of race concepts by treating the humanities and the sciences as always already co-constituted domains of knowledge. In doing so, I highlight the geohistorical contingencies of their formations and susceptibility to being co-opted by both racist and antiracist projects.

22   For a broader discussion on the investments of the social sciences and the humanities in varied theories of new materialism and specifically debates about posthuman epistemologies, see Braidotti 2019.

23   I draw on a long tradition in the subfield of historical anthropology that centers the relation between ethnography and history in the conditions of

fieldwork as much as a critical stance toward philosophical traditions of historicism. For an elaboration of this point, see Axel 2002; Gordillo 2014; Stewart 2016.

CHAPTER 1: DISASTER EVIDENCE

1 Of critical importance to this scholarship is Ulrich Beck's (1992) *Risk Society: Towards a New Modernity*. Beck shows that risks are uncertainties about the future that stem from industrial modernity's undesired side effects. The great contribution of risk society theorists has been to historicize the sociomaterial construction of risks alongside the modern entanglement of bureaucratic, scientific, infrastructural, and technological systems. But the limits of risk society as an analytic framework become evident around social uncertainties related to the status of who gets counted as vulnerable and who does not. Early versions of the risk society thesis could not explain, for instance, the uneven national occurrence of jihad-inspired terrorism and the differential exposure of nation-states to climate change. Instead of "societies" at risk, Beck (2008) revised the thesis to also account for a "world" at risk. From this point of view, the risk society thesis defines disaster as the result of the failure of nation-states to see themselves as part of a global system of economy, knowledge, affect, and politics. But historically, some people and places—particularly in the Global South and postcolonial nation-states—were, by design, never fully integrated into this global system (Oliver-Smith 2004). There has always been a stark dichotomy between the knowledge of global risk and the lived experience of global risk in national life. Anthropologists have offered concepts to address this spatial-political tension and elision in Beck's work. The point is that coastal Guyana, similar to other Global South locales across the planet, has past disasters it has to account for in its efforts at climate adaptation. Ethnographically grounded concepts for understanding global risk society from "beyond" America and Western Europe include "enunciatory communities" (Fortun 2001, 12–14); see also Samimian-Darash 2013.

2 Here, I do not claim to offer an account of all activities that informed the day-to-day unfolding of Guyana's 2005 disaster; there are a growing number of accounts that do this (Liverpool 2009; Sutherland 2020). Rather, I offer a preliminary sketch of the way disaster evidence can create the conditions of possibility for climate adaptation.

3 Most of the agricultural lands flooded out for months were rice paddies. The rice sector, the most robust in the agricultural sector with a mix of state- and privately owned estates, lost well over 80 percent of its annual gross domestic product (GDP) that year (Blommestein et al. 2005). The majority of land under sugar cultivation is owned and operated by the private-state–owned firm GUYSUCO, which has drainage operations separate from those used for the rest of the coast. Many argue that this was

the reason why GUYSUCO did not experience such dramatic financial losses compared to the rice sector.

4 State media and health reports count only leptospirosis deaths toward the final number of flood-related mortalities; however, local media counted drowning for the other known deaths.

5 Events surrounding Hurricane Maria in Puerto Rico in 2017 also speak to the significance of nationals who live in the diaspora and perceive their duty as citizens is to give back disaster relief aid and provide technical support to their Caribbean homelands. In the case of Puerto Rico, a territory that is not sovereign, the critical importance of the spatial concept of diaspora to the idea of how nation-states become empowered to act and do climate adaptation is only more pronounced.

6 I am not suggesting that one practice is exclusive of the other or that disaster preparedness/management activities need occur before people, institutions, or nation-states recognize the need for climate adaptation activities. They are related activities, but climate adaptation takes on a longer duration and can shift its focus or aim given the changing intensity of a climate-related risk, threat, or danger over time.

CHAPTER 2: THE RACIAL POLITICS OF SETTLERS

1 On the one hand, European settlers sought to eliminate Indigenous peoples in order to appropriate their lands; on the other, they exploited the remaining Indigenous peoples and imported enslaved Africans to work these lands. The settler appropriation of land rationalized how and which peoples were obligated to labor and who was entitled to prosper because of that labor. Settler colonialism relies on a whole range of institutional policies that grant people access to land according to both their racial and their native versus nonnative status. The explicit goal of these institutional policies "[has not been] just to rupture in the name of enforced labor, but to chart the direct transit from life to death for certain peoples and not for others" (Byrd 2011, 83).

2 I use the phrase *settler identity* to describe and situate Guyanese within a broader scholarship that privileges land tenure as central to understanding White domination in both the legal system and daily life after slavery (Cooper, Holt, and Scott 2014). For instance, the racial category *White* is not used in everyday language in Guyana to describe Guyanese, in the sense that less than 1 percent of the population today identifies with the racial-ethnic census category *European*. However, *White* as a racial category does persist in the way Guyanese talk about the colonial past and in knowing the difference in race relations throughout the circum-Caribbean as well as within geographies of the Guyanese diaspora, particularly in the United States, England, and Canada. In this respect, I look to detail and make conceptual space for "non-White settler identity," which is often ignored in the scholarship on the legacies of postemancipation.

3 Indeed, this is an argument made by economists and political scientists deploying a cost-benefit analysis to explain the intersection of voting patterns with underdevelopment in Guyana (see Khemraj 2019). Also, on the limits of labor as a way to conceptualize Black and Indigenous settler colonialism, see Jackson 2014.

4 This is not to say that the recommendations of the water boards in the Netherlands were always equitable or acquiesced to the demands of well-connected landowners or those with technically sound construction materials (see Bijker 1996).

5 The stakes of Dutch hydraulic engineering, and specifically empoldering, were different in Southeast Asia, where indigenous methods of damming were self-evident and integral to conquest (see Ravesteijn and Kop 2008).

6 Da Costa (1997, 315) argues that the use of a fiscal was inherited from Spanish colonial administrators and had a "function similar to those of the Protector of Indians in the Spanish colonies." The Dutch also used fiscals in the Cape Colony in Africa.

7 Historians argue that the village movement was the most aggressive land settlement by freedmen in the British Caribbean and, some historians argue, by a peasantry in modern history (see Adamson 1973; Farley 1954; Rodney 1981).

8 Because lands were purchased collectively, many of the villages developed a communal or cooperative style of land tenure. In practice, this system was called "joint possession or ownership," with one or two people signing a transport title on behalf of others (Smith 1955, 65). All shareholders enjoyed freehold rights to the land, but there was no registered subdivision. They divided the land as rectangular plots in both the farming and housing areas. All burial sites, forests, and other resources, along with canals, were the property and responsibility of the shareholders. The drainage costs and taxes on lands were often prohibitive. In some cases, shareholders abandoned lands altogether or ascribed to a complicated mix of farming and working for cash wages outside of the village. Nonetheless, as some scholars have argued, cooperative land tenure became the model for peasant land settlement not only among freedmen but for indentured laborers as well (see Seecharan 2000).

9 For an analysis of the relationship between Dutch and British slavery systems and their impacts on coastal land tenure and property, see Ramsahoye 1966.

10 Moreover, Rodney offers a Marxist reading of capitalism that emphasizes technological progress (and machinery) as central features of wealth accumulation (Marx 2004, esp. chaps. 15–17; Roth 2010). At the same time, Rodney treats technological progress as a historically contingent process and suggests that in order to facilitate it the colonial state needs to redistribute capital to non-White landowners. To this end, I view Rodney not as offering a critical reading of technology but instead offering one on labor in colonial state formation. Rather than ask whether technology exists for multiple cultural or social purposes, Rodney follows Marx closely to treat it as solely a tool for capital

accumulation. Contemporaneous scholars of Caribbean development, including Norman Girvan (1979), offer a different perspective on technology to suggest that the ways in which it becomes embodied take on forms beyond those of market exchange to include political thought, sensibilities, and, organizations. On this point, I follow Girvan to ask how engineers and other social figures, including farmers and squatters, differently imagined technology as shaped by race.

11 For an analysis and discussion of Burnham's strategy of socialism as a mode for national development in comparison to the trajectory of socialist-communist projects and ideology across the Caribbean, see Eckstein 2003; Prescod 1976; Rose 2002; Scott 2014.

12 Pelling (1998) argues that the manner in which different local government bodies distributed flood relief resources and employment granted to them from the city council became highly contentious political and moral disputes. A number of government jobs, for instance, slashed under structural adjustment policies were held by Georgetown residents, most of whom were Afro-Guyanese. Unemployment left many people with more time and thus the opportunity to become more acutely aware of flood hazards in their neighborhoods. Also, the lack of flood relief resources stood as an uncomfortable reminder of the technical drift that their unemployment created for municipal and national agencies.

CHAPTER 3: ENGINEERING, ARCHIVES, AND EXPERTS

1 My use of the phrase *absence of ruins* is in the spirit of Orlando Patterson and of Richard Price's (1985) subsequent call for anthropologists to be more lyrical with the use of memory in narrating the past. But I also use the phrase to suggest that the relationship between technoscience and lay knowledge is not a static one. It is a relationship that in ethnographies of technoscience is overwhelmingly interpreted in binary terms, domination and resistance, as if the introduction of Western technosciences to any context necessarily leads to strife or the cannibalization of lay knowledge/non-Western epistemic practices. I emphasize that claims to memory are more than a reference to modern hybrids and are implicated in the production of expertise writ large.

2 In *Timehri*, this point was demonstrated by the section "Report of Meetings of the Society," which offered brief summaries of current events affecting the colony. Many of these notes detailed findings from soil surveys that compared soil compositions across the colony's administrative districts and their utility not only for agriculture but also for mining and construction.

3 Unsurprisingly, engineers have historically emphasized the interaction between rivers and dams. Earlier arguments made by seventeenth-century French geographer Pierre Perrault emphasized that "rainfall alone is sufficient to supply springs and rivers" (Molle 2009, 485).

4 To offer an extensive case, the multinational firm Booker Brothers, McConnell and Co. had a prominent presence in British Guiana and the wider British

West Indies as well as in India, Belgium, Nigeria, and East Africa. In British Guiana, it held influence over the sugar industry and shaped the governor's reformist vision for improving flood management on estate laborers' land settlements (Smith 1962). Yet, as some political elites observed, "with every ship which landed from the UK, came between ten and thirty people to fill vacancies at Booker, thus augmenting the European elite at the expense of Guyanese [Guianese]. . . . These people soon get themselves integrated into the autocratic social class . . . while hundreds of local men and women . . . languish in the streets unemployed" (quoted in Seecharan 2005, 142). Prominent labor organizers, including Lionel Lukhoo and Cheddi Jagan of the Political Affairs Committee, responded to the unemployment and racial discrimination by sitting as expert witnesses for the 1934 Flood Commission and the 1949 Venn Commission, respectively. Across class, race, and occupational status, their observations helped shape the outcomes of social reforms as well as the technical planning for the EDWC.

5 By the time of Giglioli's research, four of his colleagues had completed surveys that suggested a handful of other species had already migrated as a result of "human interference" on the coast (Giglioli 1948, 37). *A. darlingi* was the species that multiplied, venturing out from the comfortable confines of the forested interior rivers to canals.

6 For an extended discussion on TVA-style damming in the United States and across the world, see McCully 2001.

7 Burnham tended to focus his science and technological development policies around Cuba's world-renowned public health and medical training initiatives. During his administration, 77 percent of Guyana's medical personnel were either Cuban or Guyanese trained in Cuba (Brotherson 1991, 11; Feinsilver 1989).

CHAPTER 4: COMPENSATION AND RESETTLEMENT

Parts of chapter 4 appear in "Inundated with Facts: Flooding and the Knowledge Economies of Climate Adaptation in Guyana," in *Unmasking the State: Politics, Society, and Economy in Guyana, 1992–2015*, ed. Arif Bulkan and D. Alissa Trotz (Kingston, Jamaica: Ian Randle, 2019), 479–500.

1 Indeed, in many climate adaptation ethnographies, compensation is symbolic of a socioracial life reinforced by the violence of inequitable or culturally insensitive nation-states (Adger et al. 2005; Lipset 2013). But if race is a social category through which people imagine or critique compensation for climate adaptation, it may not always be politically expedient or necessary for people to express their racial attitudes in the register of victimization; they might instead embrace the limitation of racial discourses to explain the scope of the law and redress, as the Hope Canal case suggests.

2 The 2012 census does not have a publicly available report of demographics tabulated at the village level.

3 For an extended perspective on clientelism and racial-gendered exclusions from both domestic and informal economies, see Trotz and Peake 2001.

4 I am not suggesting that the small man is the opposite of or antithetical to the Big Man, for whom, in the Anglophone Caribbean, performances of masculinity, (control over) violence, and clientelism are important. On categories of the Big Man, see Brown 1990. The small man can take on such roles, but small men also recognize their performances as integral to a broader knowledge economy vis-à-vis the state.

5 Since the socialist period, local government ministries such as Neighbourhood Democratic Councils (NDCs) have also played a crucial role in irrigation and drainage. NDCs are the equivalent of local governing bodies with the constitutional authority to represent the interests of people within a given "neighborhood" to national institutional bodies. The system includes four branches: community democratic councils (CDCs) report to NDCs; NDCs report to Regional Democratic Councils (RDCs); and RDCs to the Office of the Prime Minister/President. Although the intent of NDCs and RDCs is to offer a way to efficiently decentralize the allocation and distribution of state resources and power across Guyana, in practice the system does not often work this way. Critics of the system suggest that the formation of these different levels of "central" governing bodies reporting back to the Office of the Prime Minister allowed Burnham to further secure unconstitutional powers, diminishing what was already viewed by many to be a dubious process of electorate voting. Even still, Burnham's administration did not completely dismantle but "built on" the models of local democratic governance already in place from the colonial era. For a historical overview of local government as a concept in British Guianese and preindependence government, see Young 1958.

6 For an analysis of political debates about coastal land tenure in relation to Amerindian collective land titling and the idea of land inheritance in Guyana, see Lemel 2001.

7 This is not to say that the Grow More Food campaign was altogether new. Many claim that it mirrored the socialist era's Feed, Clothe, and House the Nation campaign.

8 Other scholars have used the concept *mati* to analyze egalitarian politics under Black slavery as well. For instance, Gloria Wekker (2006) argues that the concept is widely used by Black Surinamese, particularly women, to describe same-sex intimacies and partnerships that date back to slavery. Regardless of origins, *mati* is associated with modes of empowerment and egalitarianism within plantation communities writ large. For a counterexample of solidarity through an analysis of class, dependency theory, and Indo-Guianese/Indo-Guyanese identity, see Silverman 1979.

9 The Indo-Guyanese farmers I know used jhandis as an opportunity to display to family members, as well as to village residents, their wealth and fortune from a seasonal crop. They made a clear distinction about the value of jhandis as a celebration and a way to keep up social obligations rather than as an

activity for flood management. Indeed, when I asked if they make *pujas* (offerings) to stop floods, they responded with a sharp comment about the improvements or shortcomings of engineers' work on their land. The same attitude is true of Indo-Guyanese farmers I worked with in less racially and culturally heterogeneous villages in Mahaica near the EDWC. They stressed that their jhandis were a rare chance to invite people from outside their families—particularly Muslims and Amerindians—for a *lime* (party).

10 I am not suggesting that the Guyanese state since the 2005 disaster has always been benevolent with regard to providing its citizenry compensation or basic resources for dealing with climate adaptation. Some, including residents of the former urban squatter town Sophia, which is majority Afro-Guyanese, have struggled to receive from state agencies financial support and rights to land. But these residents, similar to the Hope/Dochfour farmers, have found that by engaging the state about their grievances, they are also repositioning the ways they engage with engineers or decide to create an alternative arrangement of care for the EDWC.

11 For a broader discussion on the limits of "race war" as a concept, see Gilroy 2002; Goldberg 2001; and Mamdani 2020.

CHAPTER 5: LOVE STORIES

1 Many scholars invested in Guyanese studies point to practices of censorship during the socialist regimes as the first instances of resentment between the intellectual class and state bureaucrats (see Chung 2012; Lewis 1998). Others have suggested that state investments in extractive industries (e.g., forestry, mining, and oil) have closed off potential research frameworks in Guyanese studies, particularly those related to the social aspects of ecology (see Bulkan and Palmer 2016).

2 Verran (2001, 42) uses the Yoruba metaphor of a child's "corpse" cited in praise poetry (*oriki*) about indigo dying rituals to expand on this idea about a hauntology of numbers: "My guess is that 'the corpse that was put a stop to' featured in an authoritative interpretation of the disturbing event by the knowledge authorities. I guess also that this credited the (non)corpse with a meaning that worked to distribute praise and blame. . . . The incorporation of the (non)corpse in oriki serves to unsettle that past legislation. In a similar way, everting the figure of *founded number* unsettles as a decomposing moment" (emphasis added).

3 My point is quite simple: mathematical equations describe numerical relations in modeling operations. For this reason, many scholars have made relentless critiques about the pitfalls of using mathematics to draw "philosophical conclusions," such as Alain Badiou's appropriation of set theory to analyze such concepts as political freedom (Nirenberg and Nirenberg 2011; Rotman 1993).

4 For debates about the extent to which these environmental changes created the conditions for Amazonian mound cultures and therefore the first human adaptation to flooding in the region, see Meggers 1994.
5 While the idea of humans as geological agents has been tied to the techno-scientific theorization of human carbon consumption and emissions, human geological agency can manifest in incommensurable ways, especially for those activities devoted to a particular technoscience (see Chakrabarty 2009).
6 Arjun Appadurai's (1988) ideas about methodological fetishism and the social biographies of things remain important here. In climate adaptation, the social biographies of experts are tied to the circulation of models. However, the extent to which these social biographies matter is dependent on both the culture of scientific institutions/epistemic communities and the actual occurrence of disaster. This means that models in climate adaptation have a generic quality that sets them apart from experts' everyday encounters with at-risk places and things. Thus, one of the possibilities provided by climate adaptation activities other than modeling is to placate public fears about disaster.

CHAPTER 6: ACCOUNTABILITY AND
THE MILITARIZATION OF TECHNOSCIENCE

Parts of chapter 6 appear in "Gridlock: Vigilance and Early Warning in the Shadow of Climate Change," *Hau: Journal of Ethnographic Theory* 11 (2) (2021).
1 My use of the terms *data* and *data sets* emphasizes the importance of the national flood plan as an effort to collect statistics for an analysis of flood hazards and relevant decision-making. In this respect, this chapter's conversation about the militarization of technoscience, and of data more broadly, is distinct from recent scholarship in critical data studies that directs attention to how society, government, and business convert information into quantifiable data sets useful for the valuation of goods and services. The term *datafication* is an expression of this process, which acknowledges that data sets have a history predating digitization, and is dependent on data sourced from records that were previously considered of little to no value (Mayer-Schönberger and Cukier 2013). Datafication is distinct from but related to the phenomenon of big data or data sets characterized by high volume, velocity, and variety (Kitchin 2014a). Not only is the scalar function of big versus small data an effect of computation; it is shaped by the way experts within policy groups perceive some markets (and not others) as equipped for exchanging profit-laden data sets (Thatcher, O'Sullivan, and Mahmoudi 2016).
2 Military training in the interior was a pillar of Burnham's national security strategy well before the emergence of a police state in the 1980s. For instance, in 1969 the police force and Guyana National Defence quelled an insurrection in a savannah/interior administrative district colloquially known as the Rupununi. A separatist movement headed by members of Guyana's Amerindian

Party defended the protection of Amerindians' constitutional rights and their further integration into Guyanese society. Burnham did not concede to their demands and accused the Venezuelan government of supporting the insurrection. Ultimately, the uprising killed over one hundred civilians and drove many Amerindians to flee into neighboring Brazil and Venezuela. For an extended discussion of the insurrection and its impact on the constitution of Amerindian-centered identity in the (trans)national politics of postindependence Guyana, see Bulkan 2013 and Jackson 2012.

3 The project was eventually halted in 1983 when Guyana lost support from the World Bank (Colchester 1997).

4 Many Guyanese I know remember the incident as a folly of foreigners who had ambitions to make multiracial socialism in a land and with political figures they did not know how to tame. While only a few Guyanese, all children, died in the mass suicide, many suspected that Jones had weapons and ammunition smuggled in with the help of Guyanese state officials (Vidal 1978).

5 Some of these reforms revolved around monitoring military and state officials' commercial banking, postal, and travel immigration activities. Such surveillance was intended to align with American efforts in the region to curb the growth of so-called Islamic terrorism cells and their financing through the drug trade.

6 Perhaps one of the better-known examples of these impacts is Texas's Hurricane Harvey in 2017, which has been described by engineers as a five-hundred-year storm. While engineers and atmospheric scientists had numerous models that could predict the path of hurricanes, few could provide details of their intensity (Vossen 2017). Harvey was the worst storm engineers could imagine for Houston because, as in the Guyana case, water overtopped dams. The concern engineers have about Houston's floodplain is that the existing system of dams, levees, dikes, and canals was not designed for five-hundred-year storms and is insufficient for the city's urban sprawl. Beyond the issue of hydraulic modeling, dam overtopping problematizes whether a true base time can be planned for different kinds of flood early warning management protocols.

7 I do not read Mbembe's category of the Black Man as being in tension with Sylvia Wynter's writings on what it means to be human and the category of Man. I interpret both scholars as pointing to the ways in which the human capacity to witness history slips easily in some cases and not others into a problem of racism. As Mbembe (2017) elaborates, the act of witnessing involves people assuming that some places in the world and the people who inhabit them are more important than others. His main claim here is that Africa and Black peoples' contributions to the history of humanity have been either denigrated or ignored in the theorization of history, temporality, and narration. He writes, "It is the living witness, certainly the most worrying, of the violence of our world and the iniquity that is its mainspring. As we ponder the world and its future, the scandal of humanity confronts us with the most urgent of demands, beginning with responsibility and justice. For the word

'Africa' stands as a fundamental negation of these very terms" (53). In the case of the national flood plan, human witnessing is shaped by the overlapping ways CDC staff struggle to overcome both the category of the Black Man and the category of Man through collaboration with engineers to prove to themselves and Others that they are experts. In other words, recentering questions around technoscience, universalism, and race are essential to a critical theory of climate adaptation.

8   For instance, they recognized that using racial discourses to justify disaster management interventions has its risks. On the one hand, it slips into further reinforcing the humanitarian appeal to the unspoken selfishness of so-called White countries, presumably those in Euro-America. On the other, the CDC staff's desire to identify with Haiti leaves unchallenged the intraracial hierarchies of Black countries that make it feasible to know about, say, the 2010 Haitian earthquake as a well-known event in global history and in the history of the Black diaspora but not Guyana's 2005 disaster.

9   The Ministry of Agriculture, the main state agency that worked with private firms to implement the flood early warning system, is more racially integrated than the CDC. I knew of only one female engineer who consistently worked on EDWC-related adaptation projects.

CHAPTER 7: THE ORDINARY

A modified version of chapter 7 appears in "Imagining the Ordinary in Participatory Climate Adaptation," *Weather, Climate, and Society* 9 (3) (2017): 533–43. © American Meteorological Society. Used and adapted with permission.

1   For a discussion about the role of the case study form and method in anthropological analyses of vulnerability, see Biehl 2005.

2   However, within the past five years, investments have been made in mid-tier and economy hotels to accommodate tourism, day laborers traveling from the hinterland for short stays, and a rise in the number of consultancy and contract skill-laborers for state-sponsored projects, particularly in offshore oil speculation. Many of these investments have been made by Guyanese in the diaspora or operated by their kin in Georgetown. This geography of real estate raises a number of questions about not only new settlement patterns within Georgetown but also shifting ideas of urbanism across coastal Guyana more broadly.

3   By 1999, the Central Housing and Planning Authority counted a backlog of over twenty thousand claims for land titles dating back to 1993.

4   The 2002 national census (the last village-level census completed) has detailed the racial-ethnic breakdown of Sophia as encompassing nearby suburbs Pattersen and Turkeyen.

Abell, W. P. 1897. "Index of Inventions: Furnace for Burning Bagasse, Sawdust, Etc. No. 578,531: Patented March 1897." *Scientific American: A Weekly Journal of Practical Information, Art, Science, Mechanics, Chemistry, and Manufactures* 76 (13): 205.

Abu El-Haj, Nadia. 2002. *Facts on the Ground: Archaeological Practice and Territorial Self-Fashioning in Israeli Society.* Chicago: University of Chicago Press.

Aceituno, Patricio, María del Rosario Prieto, María Eugenia Solari, Alejandra Martinez, Germán Poveda, and Mark Falvey. 2009. "The 1877–1878 El Niño Episode: Associated Impacts in South America." *Climatic Change* 92 (3–4): 389–416.

Adams, Vincanne. 2013. *Markets of Sorrow, Labors of Faith: New Orleans in the Wake of Katrina.* Durham, NC: Duke University Press.

Adamson, Alan. 1973. *Sugar without Slaves: The Political Economy of British Guiana, 1838–1904.* New Haven, CT: Yale University Press.

Adger, W. Neil, Jouni Paavola, Saleemul Huq, and M. J. Mace, eds. 2005. *Fairness in Adaptation to Climate Change.* Cambridge, MA: MIT Press.

Agrawal, Arun. 2005. *Environmentality: Technologies of Government and the Making of Subjects.* Durham, NC: Duke University Press.

Agrawala, Shardul. 1998a. "Context and Early Origins of the Intergovernmental Panel on Climate Change." *Climatic Change* 39 (4): 605–20.

Agrawala, Shardul. 1998b. "Structural and Process History of the Intergovernmental Panel on Climate Change." *Climatic Change* 39 (4): 621–42.

Anand, Nikhil. 2017. *Hydraulic City: Water and the Infrastructures of Citizenship in Mumbai.* Durham, NC: Duke University Press.

Anderson, Casper. 2011. "Colonial Connections and Consulting Engineers 1850–1914." *Engineering History and Heritage* 164 (4): 201–9.

Andreas, Joel. 2009. *Rise of the Red Engineers: The Cultural Revolution and the Origins of China's New Class.* Stanford, CA: Stanford University Press.

A Partnership for National Unity (APNU). 2011. *APNU Manifesto 2011: A Good Life for All Guyanese.* Georgetown, Guyana: APNU.

Appadurai, Arjun. 1988. *The Social Life of Things: Commodities in Cultural Perspective.* Cambridge: Cambridge University Press.

Appadurai, Arjun. 2006. *The Fear of Small Numbers: An Essay on the Geography of Anger.* Durham, NC: Duke University Press.

Appiah, Kwame Anthony. 2019. *The Lies That Bind: Rethinking Identity*. New York: Liveright.

Arndt, R., P. Roberts, and T. Wahl. 2000. *Hydraulic Modeling: Concepts and Practice*. Reston, VA: American Society of Civil Engineers.

Asaka, Ikuko. 2017. *Tropical Freedom: Climate, Settler Colonialism, and Black Exclusion in the Age of Emancipation*. Durham, NC: Duke University Press.

Austin-Boos, Diane J. 1997. *Jamaica Genesis: Religion and the Politics of Moral Order*. Chicago: University of Chicago Press.

Axel, Brian Keith, ed. 2002. *From the Margins: Historical Anthropology and Its Futures*. Durham, NC: Duke University Press.

Bache, Alfred, compiler (secretary). 1889. "Memoirs: William A. Russell." *Institution of Mechanical Engineers: Proceedings* 40 (1): 338–39.

Baker, Lee D. 1998. *From Savage to Negro: Anthropology and the Construction of Race, 1896–1954*. Berkeley: University of California Press.

Baldwin, Andrew. 2013. "Racialisation and the Figure of the Climate-Change Migrant." *Environment and Planning A: Economy and Space* 45 (6): 1474–90.

Ballestero, Andrea. 2019. *A Future History of Water*. Durham, NC: Duke University Press.

Barad, Karen. 2003. "Posthumanist Performativity: Toward an Understanding of How Matter Comes to Matter." *Signs* 28 (3): 801–31.

Barad, Karen. 2007. *Meeting the Universe Halfway: Quantum Physics and the Entanglement of Matter and Meaning*. Durham, NC: Duke University Press.

Barad, Karen. 2011. "Nature's Queer Performativity." *Qui Parle: Critical Humanities and Social Sciences* 19 (2): 121–58.

Barad, Karen. 2012. *What Is the Measure of Nothingness? Infinity, Virtuality, Justice? / Was ist das Maß des Nichts? Unendlichkeit, Virtualität, Gerechitgkeit*. Munich: Erschienen im Hatje Cantz Verlag.

Barnes, Jessica. 2014. *Cultivating the Nile: The Everyday Politics of Water in Egypt*. Durham, NC: Duke University Press.

Barnes, Jessica, and Michael R. Dove, eds. 2015. *Climate Cultures: Anthropological Perspectives on Climate Change*. New Haven, CT: Yale University Press.

Barton, Neil. 2020. "Absence Perception and the Philosophy of Zero." *Synthese* 197 (9): 3823–50.

Baviskar, Amita. 2005. *In the Belly of the River: Tribal Conflicts over Development in the Narmada Valley*. Oxford: Oxford University Press.

Beaie, Sonkarley Tiatun, ed. 2007. *The Co-operative Republic of Guyana Population and Housing Census 2002*. Georgetown, Guyana: Government of Guyana.

Beatty, John. 2001. "Scientific Collaboration, Internationalism, and Diplomacy: The Case of the Atomic Bomb Casualty Commission." In *Science, Technology and Research and Development in Japan*, edited by Morris Low, 83–107. London: Routledge.

Beck, Ulrich. 1992. *Risk Society: Towards a New Modernity*. London: Sage.

Beck, Ulrich. 2008. *World at Risk*. London: Polity.

Beck, Ulrich. 2015. "Emancipatory Catastrophism: What Does It Mean to Climate Change and Risk Society?" *Current Sociology* 63 (1): 75–88.

Beckford, George, and Kari Levitt. 2012. *The George Beckford Papers*. Bridgetown, Barbados: Canoe.

Bellairs, Seaforth M. 1892. "Twenty Years' Improvements in Demerara Sugar Production, Part II." *Timehri: The Journal of the Royal Agricultural and Commercial Society of British Guiana* 4: 1–21.

Benjamin, Anna. 1992. "A Preliminary Look at the Free Amerindians and the Dutch Plantation System in Guyana during the Seventeenth and Eighteenth Centuries." *Guyana Historical Journal* 4–5: 1–21.

Bennett, Jane. 2010. *Vibrant Matter: A Political Ecology of Things*. Durham, NC: Duke University Press.

Berlant, Lauren. 2011a. *Cruel Optimism*. Durham, NC: Duke University Press.

Berlant, Lauren. 2011b. "A Properly Political Concept of Love: Three Approaches in Ten Pages." *Cultural Anthropology* 24 (4): 683–91.

Biehl, João. 2005. *Vita: Life in a Zone of Social Abandonment*. Berkeley: University of California Press.

Bijker, Eco W. 1996. "History and Heritage in Coastal Engineering in the Netherlands." In *History and Heritage of Coastal Engineering*, edited by Nicholas C. Kraus, 390–412. New York: American Society of Civil Engineers.

Bijker, Wiebe E. 2007. "American and Dutch Coastal Engineering: Differences in Risk Conception and Differences in Technological Culture." *Social Studies of Science* 37 (1): 143–51.

Birbalsingh, Frank, ed. 2007. *The People's Progressive Party of Guyana, 1950–1992: An Oral History*. London: Hansib.

Bjornerud, Marcia. 2006. *Reading the Rocks: The Autobiography of the Earth*. Cambridge, MA: Basic.

Blanchot, Maurice. 1995. *The Writing of the Disaster*. Translated by Ann Smock. Omaha: University of Nebraska Press.

Bleackley, David. 1956. *British Guiana Geological Survey: The Geology of the Superficial Deposits and Coastal Sediments of British Guiana*. Georgetown, Guyana: Daily Chronicle.

Blommestein, Erik, Radcliffe Dookie, Michael Henrickson, Asha Kambon, Hossein Kalali, Vincent Little, Esteban Perez, and David Smith. 2005. *Guyana: Socio-Economic Assessment of the Damages and Losses Caused by the January–February 2005 Flooding*. Georgetown, Guyana: Economic Commission for Latin America and the Caribbean (ECLAC) and the United Nations Development Program (UNDP).

Bolland, O. Nigel. 1981. "Systems of Domination after Slavery: The Control of Land and Labor in the British West Indies after 1838." *Society for Comparative Studies in Society and History* 23 (4): 591–619.

Bovolo, Isabella. 2014. *Managing Flood Risk in Guyana: The Conservancy Adaptation Project, 2008–2013*. Washington, DC: International Bank for Reconstruction and Development/World Bank.

Bowker, Geoffrey C. 2005. *Memory Practices in the Sciences*. Cambridge, MA: MIT Press.

Boyer, Dominic. 2008. "Thinking through the Anthropology of Experts." *Anthropology in Action* 15 (2): 38–46.

Braidotti, Rosi. 2019. *Posthuman Knowledge*. Cambridge: Polity.

Braun, Bruce P. 2014. "A New Urban Dispositif? Governing Life in the Age of Climate Change." *Environment and Planning D: Society and Space* 32 (1): 49–64.

Braunmühl, Caroline. 2018. "Beyond Hierarchical Oppositions: A Feminist Critique of Karen Barad's Agential Realism." *Feminist Theory* 19 (2): 223–40.

British Guiana Constitutional Commission. 1954. *Report of the British Guiana Constitutional Commission 1954*. London: Her Majesty's Stationery Office.

Broich, John. 2007. "Engineering the Empire: British Water Supply Systems and Colonial Societies, 1850–1900." *Journal of British Studies* 46 (2): 346–65.

Brotherson, Festus. 1991. "Cuba and the Anglophone Caribbean in the 1990s." Paper presented as part of the panel "Caribbean Foreign Relations in the 1990s" at the Sixteenth Annual Conference of the Caribbean Studies Association, May 21, Havana.

Brown, Paula. 1990. "Big Man, Past and Present: Model, Person, Hero, Legend." *Ethnology* 29 (2): 97–115.

Brown, Wendy. 2003. "Neo-Liberalism and the End of Liberal Democracy." *Theory and Event* 7 (1): 1–19.

Brzoska, Michael. 2012. "Climate Change and the Military in China, Russia, the United Kingdom, and the United States." *Bulletin of the Atomic Scientists* 68 (2): 43–54.

Buchanan, R. A. 1986. "The Diaspora of British Engineering." *Technology and Culture* 27 (3): 501–24.

Buck-Morss, Susan. 2009. *Hegel, Haiti, and Universal History*. Pittsburgh: University of Pittsburgh Press.

Buck-Morss, Susan. 2020. "Translations in Time." *October*, no. 172: 147–58.

Bulkan, Arif, and D. Alissa Trotz. 2019. "Introduction." In *Politics, Society and Economy in Guyana 1002–2015*, edited by Arif Bulkan and D. Alissa Trotz, xv–xl. Kingston, Jamaica: Ian Randle.

Bulkan, Janette. 2013. "The Struggle for Recognition of the Indigenous Voice: Amerindians in Guyanese Politics; The Round Table." *Commonwealth Journal of International Affairs* 102 (4): 367–80.

Bulkan, Janette. 2016. "Hegemony in Guyana: REDD-Plus and State Control over Indigenous Peoples and Resources." In *The Caribbean: Aesthetics, World-Ecology, Politics*, edited by Chris Campbell and Michael Niblett, 118–44. Liverpool: Liverpool University Press.

Bulkan, Janette, and John Palmer. 2016. "Rentier Nation: Landlordism, Patronage and Power in Guyana's Gold Mining Sector." *Extractive Industries and Society* 3 (3): 676–89.

Bullard, Robert D. 2000. *Dumping in Dixie: Race, Class, and Environmental Quality*. 3rd ed. Boulder, CO: Westview.

Bullard, Robert D., and Beverly Wright, eds. 2009. *Race, Place, and Environmental Justice after Hurricane Katrina: Struggles to Reclaim, Rebuild, and Revitalize New Orleans and the Gulf Coast.* New York: Routledge.

Bump, Phillip. 2017. "We'll Probably Never Know Exactly How Many People Died in the Aftermath of Hurricane Maria." *Washington Post,* October 12. https://www.washingtonpost.com/news/politics/wp/2017/10/12/well-probably-never-know-exactly-how-many-people-died-in-the-aftermath-of-hurricane-maria/.

Burnett, Graham. 2000. *Masters of All They Surveyed: Exploration, Geography, and a British El Dorado.* Chicago: University of Chicago Press.

Burton, Eric. 2020. "Engineering Socialism: The Faculty of Engineering at the University of Dar es Salaam (Tanzania) in the 1970s and 1980s." In *Education and Development in Colonial and Postcolonial Africa: Policies, Paradigms, and Entanglements, 1890s–1980s,* edited by Damiano Matasci, Miguel Bandeira Jerónimo, and Hugo Gonçalves Dores, 205–30. Cham, Switzerland: Palgrave Macmillan.

Bush, Barbara. 2013. "Colonial Research and the Social Sciences at the End of Empire: The West Indian Social Survey, 1944–1957." *Journal of Imperial and Commonwealth History* 41 (3): 451–74.

Butler, Judith, Zeynep Gambetti, and Leticia Sabsay, eds. 2016. *Vulnerability in Resistance.* Durham, NC: Duke University Press.

Byrd, Jodi A. 2011. *The Transit of Empire: Indigenous Critiques of Colonialism.* Minneapolis: University of Minnesota Press.

Callison, Candis. 2014. *How Climate Change Comes to Matter: The Communal Life of Facts.* Durham, NC: Duke University Press.

Callon, Michel. 2010. "Performativity, Misfires, and Politics." *Journal of Cultural Economy* 3 (2): 163–69.

Camacho, R. F. 1961. *The Mahaica-Mahaicony-Abary Water Control Project: Report on Stage 1, The Control of the Abary.* Georgetown, Guyana: British Guiana Lithographic Co. Lt. Irrigation and Drainage Box, National Archives of Guyana, Georgetown.

Carey, Mark, M. Jackson, Alessandro Antonello, and Jaclyn Rushing. 2016. "Glaciers, Gender, and Science: A Feminist Glaciology Framework for Global Environmental Change Research." *Progress in Human Geography* 40 (6): 770–93.

Carney, Jane. 2002. *Black Rice: The African Origins of Rice Cultivation in the Americas.* Cambridge, MA: Harvard University Press.

Carr, E. Summerson. 2006. "'Secrets Keep You Sick': Metalinguistic Labor in a Drug Treatment Program for Homeless Women." *Language in Society* 35 (5): 631–53.

Carruthers, Ian, Mark W. Rosegrant, and David Seckler. 1997. "Irrigation and Food Security in the 21st Century." *Irrigation and Drainage Systems* 11 (2): 83–101.

Carse, Ashley. 2014. *Beyond the Big Ditch: Politics, Ecology, and Infrastructure at the Panama Canal.* Cambridge, MA: MIT Press.

Carto, Abyssinian. 2012. "Abyssinian Carto." In *Walter Rodney: A Promise of Revolution,* edited by Clairmont Chung, 35–58. New York: Monthly Review Press.

Cavell, Stanley. 1994. *Quest of the Ordinary: Lines of Skepticism and Romanticism.* Chicago: University of Chicago Press.

Chabrol, Denis. 2020. "Prospect of Guyanese Citizenship Revocation Now a PPP Campaign Issue." *Demerara Waves*, February 9. https://demerarawaves .com/2020/02/09/prospect-of-guyanese-citizenship-revocation-now-a-ppp -campaign-issue/.

Chakrabarty, Dipesh. 2009. "The Climate of History: Four Theses." *Critical Inquiry* 35 (2): 197–222.

Chakrabarty, Dipesh. 2021. *The Climate of History in a Planetary Age.* Chicago: University of Chicago Press.

Chandarpal, Navin, ed. n.d. *President Cheddi Jagan Speaks on Environment and Development*, edited by Navin Chandarpal, i–iii. Georgetown, Guyana: Guyana Agricultural and General Workers Union.

Chandisingh, Rajendra. 1982. "Guyana's New Constitution and the Elections of 1980: A Case of People's Power?" *Verfassung und Recht in Ubersee / Law and Politics in Africa, Asia and Latin America* 15 (2): 145–61.

Chandler, David. 2019. "Digital Governance in the Anthropocene: The Rise of the Correlational Machine." In *Digital Objects, Digital Subjects: Interdisciplinary Perspectives on Capitalism, Labour, and Politics in the Age of Big Data*, edited by David Chandler and Christian Fuchs, 23–42. London: University of Westminster Press.

Chase, Ashton. 1964. *A History of Trade Unionism in Guyana: 1900 to 1961.* Georgetown, Guyana: New Guyana Company.

Chung, Clairmont, ed. 2012. *Walter Rodney: A Promise of Revolution.* New York: Monthly Review Press.

Church, Christopher M. 2017. *Paradise Destroyed: Catastrophe and Citizenship in the French Caribbean.* Lincoln: University of Nebraska Press.

Civil Defence Commission (CDC). 2010. "Draft: Guyana Flood Preparedness and Response Plan." Unpublished report.

Clark, Harrison, ed. 1953. *The Economic Development of British Guiana: Report of a Mission Organized by the International Bank for Reconstruction and Development.* Baltimore: Johns Hopkins University Press.

Clarke, Kamari M. 2019. *Affective Justice: The International Criminal and the Pan-Africanist Pushback.* Durham, NC: Duke University Press.

Cobain, Ian. 2017. *The History Thieves: Secrets, Lies and the Shaping of a Modern Nation.* London: Portobello.

Colchester, Marcus. 1997. *Guyana, Fragile Frontier: Loggers, Miners and Forest Peoples.* London: Latin American Bureau.

Collier, Stephen J., and Andrew Lakoff. 2014. "Vital Systems Security: Reflexive Biopolitics and the Government of Emergency." *Theory, Culture and Society* 32 (2): 19–51.

Collins, John. 2015. *Revolt of the Saints: Memory and Redemption in the Twilight of Brazilian Racial Democracy.* Durham, NC: Duke University Press.

Colman, Zack. 2020. "Audubon Society Hit by Claims of 'Intimidation and Threats.'" *Politico*, November 12. https://www.politico.com/news/2020/11/12 /audubon-society-claims-intimidation-threats-436215.

Comaroff, John L., and Jean Comaroff. 2001. "On Personhood: An Anthropological Perspective from Africa." *Social Identities* 7 (2): 267–83.

Connolly, William E. 2017. *Facing the Planetary: Entangled Humanism and the Politics of Swarming*. Durham, NC: Duke University Press.

Cons, Jason. 2018. "Staging Climate Security: Resilience and Heterodystopia in the Bangladesh Borderlands." *Cultural Anthropology* 33 (2): 266–94.

Cooper, Frederick, Thomas C. Holt, and Rebecca J. Scott, eds. 2014. *Beyond Slavery: Explorations of Race, Labor, and Citizenship in Postemancipation Societies*. Chapel Hill: University of North Carolina Press.

Corbin, Hisakhana Pahoona, and Luis Eduardo Aragon. 2014. "Fluxos e usos das remessas da diáspora pelos domicílios receptores na Guiana." *Novos Cadernos NAEA* 17 (2): 325–47.

Corren, François. 2010. *Action and Agency in Dialogue: Passion, Incarnation, and Ventriloquism*. Amsterdam: John Benjamins.

Crate, Susan. 2011. "Climate and Culture: Anthropology in the Era of Contemporary Climate Change." *Annual Review of Anthropology* 40: 175–94.

Crichlow, Michaeline A. 2005. *Negotiating Caribbean Freedom: Peasants and the State in Development*. Lanham, MD: Lexington.

Crosson, Brent. 2020. *Experiments with Power: Obeah and the Remaking of Religion in Trinidad*. Chicago: University of Chicago Press.

Da Costa, Emilia Viotti. 1997. *Crowns of Glory, Tears of Blood: The Demerara Slave Rebellion of 1823*. New York: Oxford University Press.

Davis, Mike. 2002. *Late Victorian Holocausts: El Niño Famines and the Making of the Third World*. London: Verso.

De Barros, Juanita. 2003. *Order and Place in a Colonial City: Patterns of Struggle and Resistance in Georgetown, British Guiana, 1889–1924*. Montreal: McGill University Press.

De Boer, Reint. 2005. *The Engineer and the Scandal: A Piece of Science History*. Berlin: Springer.

Dechet, Amy M., Michele Parsons, Madan Rambaran, Pheona Mohamed-Rambaran, Anita Florendo-Cumbermack, Shamdeo Persaud, Shirematee Baboolal, et al. 2012. "Leptospirosis Outbreak Following Severe Flooding: A Rapid Assessment and Mass Prophylaxis Campaign; Guyana, January 2005–February 2005." *PLoS One* 7 (7): e39672.

de la Cadena, Marisol. 2015. *Earth Beings: Ecologies of Practice across Andean Worlds*. Durham, NC: Duke University Press.

DeLanda, Manuel. 2019. *A New Philosophy of Society: Assemblage Theory and Social Complexity*. New York: Continuum.

Delbourgo, James. 2012. "The Newtonian Slave Body: Racial Enlightenment in the Atlantic World." *Atlantic Studies: Literary, Cultural, and Historical Perspectives* 9 (2): 185–207.

Derrida, Jacques. 2006. *Specters of Marx: The State of Debt, the Work of Mourning, and the New International*. Translated by Peggy Kamuf. New York: Routledge.

Disco, Cornelis. 2002. "Remaking 'Nature': The Ecological Turn in Dutch Water Management." *Science, Technology and Human Values* 27 (2): 206–35.

Drayton, Richard. 2000. *Nature's Government: Science, Imperial Britain, and the "Improvement" of the World*. Telangana, India: Orient Longman.

Drummond, Lee. 1980. "The Cultural Continuum: A Theory of Intersystems." *Man* 15 (2): 352–72.

D'Souza, Rohan. 2006. *Drowned and Dammed: Colonial Capitalism and Flood Control in Eastern India (1803–1946)*. New Delhi: Oxford University Press.

Du Bois, W. E. B. 2007. *The Souls of Black Folk*. Oxford: Oxford University Press.

Dumm, Thomas L. 1999. *A Politics of the Ordinary*. New York: New York University Press.

Eckstein, Susan Eva. 2003. *Back from the Futures: Cuba under Castro*. New York: Routledge.

Edwards, Paul N. 2010. *A Vast Machine: Computer Models, Climate Data, and the Politics of Global Warming*. Cambridge, MA: MIT Press.

Edwards, Paul N., Matthew S. Mayernik, Archer L. Batcheller, Geoffrey C. Bowker, and Christine L. Borgman. 2011. "Science Friction: Data, Metadata, and Collaboration." *Social Studies of Science* 41 (5): 667–90.

Edwards, Rene. 2006. "Exploring the Effects of Upgrading and Land Tenure Regularisation on the Flood Vulnerability and Coping Strategies of Squatters/Residents: A Case Study of Sophia Located in Georgetown, Guyana." Master's thesis, Institute of Social Studies, The Hague.

Edwards, Rene, S. C. Wu, and J. Mensah. 2005. "Georgetown, Guyana." *Cities: International Journal of Urban Policy and Planning* 22 (6): 446–54.

Edwards, W., and K. Gibson. 1979. "An Ethnohistory of Amerindians in Guyana." *Ethnohistory* 26 (2): 161–75.

Ekbladh, David. 2002. "'Mr. TVA': Grass-Roots Development, David Lilienthal, and the Rise and Fall of the Tennessee Valley Authority as a Symbol for U.S. Overseas Development, 1933–1973." *Diplomatic History* 26 (3): 335–74.

Evans, Brad, and Julian Reid. 2014. *Resilient Life: The Art of Living Dangerously*. Malden, MA: Polity.

Evans, Clifford, and Betty J. Meggers. 1960. *Archeological Investigations in British Guiana*. Smithsonian Institution Bureau of American Ethnology Bulletin 177. Washington, DC: United States Government Printing Office.

Farbotko, Carol, and Heather Lazrus. 2012. "The First Climate Refugees? Contesting Global Narratives of Climate Change in Tuvalu." *Global Environmental Change* 22 (2): 382–90.

Farley, Rawle. 1954. "The Rise of the Peasantry in British Guiana." *Social and Economic Studies* 2 (4): 87–103.

Farley, Rawle. 1955. "The Shadow and the Substance: A Study of the Economic and Social Structure and the Change of Social Relations between Whites and Coloured Free in Slave Society in British Guiana." *Caribbean Quarterly* 4 (2): 132–53.

Feinsilver, Julie M. 1989. "Cuba as a 'World Medical Power': The Politics of Symbolism." *Latin American Research Review* 24 (2): 1–34.

Ferguson, James. 2006. *Global Shadows: Africa in the Neoliberal Order*. Durham, NC: Duke University Press.

Ford, J. R. Deep, V. Lallbachan, and P. Ramnarine. 1985. *Small Farmer Development in Guyana*. Georgetown, Guyana: Inter-American Institute for Cooperation on Agriculture.

Forde, Mr., and Residents. 2009. Letter to Mr. Rampersad. Guyana Human Rights Association Archive, Georgetown.

Fortun, Kim. 2001. *Advocacy after Bhopal: Environmentalism, Disaster, New Global Orders*. Chicago: University of Chicago Press.

Foucault, Michel. 1990. *The Birth of Biopolitics: Lectures at the Collège de France, 1978–1979*. Translated by Robert Hurley. New York: Vintage.

Foucault, Michel. 2003. *Society Must Be Defended: Lectures at the Collège de France, 1975–1976*. Translated by Graham Burchell. New York: Picador.

France, Hollis. 2005. "Continuity or Change? Structural Adjustment Decision-Making in Guyana (1988–1997): The Hoyte and Jagan Years." *Social and Economic Studies* 54 (1): 83–128.

Fraser, Carey. 1996. "The Twilight of Colonial Rule in the British West Indies: Nationalist Assertion vs. Imperial Hubris in the 1930s." *Journal of Caribbean History* 30 (1): 1–27.

Fraser, Carey. 2004. "The PPP on Trial: British Guiana in 1953." *Small Axe: A Caribbean Journal of Criticism* 8 (1): 21–42.

Fraser, Carey. 2007. Foreword to *The People's Progressive Party of Guyana, 1950–1992: An Oral History*, edited by Frank Birbalsingh, 9–17. London: Hansib.

Freeman, Carla. 2014. *Entrepreneurial Selves: Neoliberal Respectability and the Making of a Caribbean Middle Class*. Durham, NC: Duke University Press.

Fullwiley, Duana. 2011. *The Encultured Gene: Sickle Cell Health Politics and Biological Difference in West Africa*. Princeton, NJ: Princeton University Press.

Galison, Peter. 2001. "War against the Center." *Grey Room*, no. 4: 5–33.

Gampat, Ramesh. 2002. "Guyana: Population, Poverty, and Ethnicity." *Journal of Indo-Caribbean Research* 5 (1): 1–40.

Ghosh, Amitav. 2016. *The Great Derangement: Climate Change and the Unthinkable.* Chicago: University of Chicago Press.

Giglioli, George. 1946. "Malaria and Agriculture in British Guiana." *Timehri: The Journal of the Royal Agricultural and Commercial Society of British Guiana* 27: 46–52.

Giglioli, George. 1948. *Malaria, Filariasis and Yellow Fever in British Guiana: Methods with Special Reference to Progress Made in Eradicating* A. darlingi *and* Aedes aegypti *from the Settled Coastlands*. Georgetown, Guyana: British Guiana Mosquito Control Service.

Gilroy, Paul. 2000. "The Sugar You Stir . . ." In *Without Guarantees: In Honour of Stuart Hall*, edited by Paul Gilroy, Lawrence Grossberg, and Angela McRobbie, 126–33. London: Verso.

Gilroy, Paul. 2002. *Against Race: Imagining Political Culture beyond the Color Line*. Cambridge, MA: Belknap Press at Harvard University Press.

Giroud, J. P. 2006. "Geosynthetics Engineering: Successes, Failures, and Lessons Learned." Paper presented at the Vienna Terzaghi Lecture, Japanese chapter of the International Geosynthetics Society, Yokohama, Japan, September 18.

Girvan, Norman. 1979. "The Approach to Technology Policy Studies." *Social and Economic Studies* 28 (1): 1–53.

Glennie, P. R. A. 1966. "Fuels and Furnaces." *Proceedings of the South African Sugar Technologists' Association*, March, 64–68.

Goldberg, David Theo. 2001. *The Racial State*. Oxford: Wiley-Blackwell.

Goldberg, David Theo. 2015. *Are We All Postracial Yet?* Cambridge: Polity.

Gordillo, Gastón R. 2014. *Rubble: The Afterlife of Destruction*. Durham, NC: Duke University Press.

Government of Guyana. 2010. *Transforming Guyana's Economy While Combating Climate Change: A Low Carbon Development Strategy*. Georgetown, Guyana: Office of the President.

Grove, Kevin. 2014. "Biopolitics and Adaptation: Governing Socio-Ecological Contingency through Climate Change and Disaster Studies." *Geography Compass* 8 (3): 198–210.

Guerre, John L. A. 1971. "The Moyne Commission and the West Indian Intelligentsia, 1938–39." *Journal of Commonwealth Political Studies* 9 (2): 134–57.

Gunaratnam, Yasmin, and Nigel Clark. 2012. "Pre-Race Post-Race: Climate Change and Planetary Humanism." *Darkmatter* 9 (1). http://www.darkmatter101.org/site /2012/07/02/pre-race-post-race-climate-change-and-planetary-humanism/.

Günel, Gökçe. 2019. *Spaceship in the Desert: Energy, Climate Change and Urban Design in Abu Dhabi*. Durham, NC: Duke University Press.

Gupta, Akhil. 2018. "The Future in Ruins: Thoughts on the Temporality of Infrastructure." In *The Promise of Infrastructure*, edited by Nikhil Anand, Akhil Gupta, and Hannah Appel, 62–79. Durham, NC: Duke University Press.

Guyana Chronicle. 2012. "Head of State Inspects EDWC Hope Canal Project." March 28. https://guyanachronicle.com/2012/03/28/head-of-state-inspects -edwc-hope-canal-project.

Guyana Chronicle. 2015. "Guyana's First Climate Change Refugees." October 11. http://guyanachronicle.com/2015/10/11/guyanas-first-climate-change-refugees.

Guyana Defence Force Strategic Review Working Group. 2009. *Organizational Analysis of Guyana Defence Force*. Georgetown, Guyana: Guyana Defence Force.

Guyana Times. 2016. "Hope Canal Project Costs over $4B—Forensic Audit." July 12. http://guyanatimesgy.com/hope-canal-project-costs-over-4b-forensic-audit/.

Haff, Peter K. 2013. "Prediction in Geology versus Prediction in Engineering." *Geological Society of America Special Paper*, no. 502: 127–34.

Halpern, Orit. 2015. *Beautiful Data: A History of Vision and Reason since 1945*. Durham, NC: Duke University Press.

Hartigan, John. 2017. *Care of the Species: Cultivating Biodiversity in Mexico and Spain*. Durham, NC: Duke University Press.

Hartman, Saidiya V. 1997. *Scenes of Subjection: Terror, Slavery, and Self-Making in Nineteenth-Century America*. New York: Oxford University Press.

Haynes, Tonya. 2016. "Sylvia Wynter's Theory of the Human and the Crisis School of Caribbean Heteromasculinity Studies." *Small Axe: A Caribbean Journal of Criticism* 20 (1): 92–112.

Hecht, Gabrielle. 2012. *Being Nuclear: Africans and the Global Uranium Trade.* Cambridge, MA: MIT Press.

Helmreich, Stefan. 2009. *Alien Ocean: Anthropological Voyages in Microbial Seas.* Berkeley: University of California Press.

Helmreich, Stefan. 2011. "Nature/Culture/Seawater." *American Anthropologist* 113 (1): 132–44.

Helmreich, Stefan. Forthcoming. *A Book of Waves.* Durham, NC: Duke University Press.

Hill, Sheridon M., and Patrice K. Morris. 2018. "Drug Trafficking and Gang Violence in the Caribbean." In *Crime, Violence and Security in the Caribbean,* edited by Raymond Izarali and Ramesh Deosaran, 52–76. New York: Routledge.

Hintzen, Percy C. 1989. *The Costs of Regime Survival: Racial Mobilization, Elite Domination and Control of the State in Guyana and Trinidad.* Cambridge: Cambridge University Press.

Hintzen, Percy C. 2019. "Race, Ideology, and International Relations: Sovereignty and the Disciplining of Guyana's Working Class." In *Unmasking the State: Politics, Society, and Economy in Guyana 1992–2015,* edited by Arif Bulkan and D. Alissa Trotz, 178–208. Kingston, Jamaica: Ian Randle.

Hoeksema, Robert J. 2007. "Three Stages in the History of Land Reclamation in the Netherlands." *Irrigation and Drainage* 56 (1): S113–26.

Hoeppe, Götz. 2014. "Working Data Together: The Accountability and Reflexivity of Digital Astronomical Practice." *Social Studies of Science* 44 (2): 243–70.

Hogg, Dominic. 1993. *The SAP in the Forest: The Environmental and Social Impacts of Structural Adjustment Programmes in the Philippines, Ghana and Guyana.* London: Friends of the Earth.

Holdridge, Desmond. 1939. "An Investigation of the Prospect for White Settlement in British Guiana." *Geographical Review* 29 (4): 622–42.

Hossein, Caroline Shenaz. 2014. "The Exclusion of Afro-Guyanese Hucksters in Micro-Banking." *European Review of Latin American and Caribbean Studies* 96: 75–98.

Hulme, Mike. 2009. *Why We Disagree about Climate Change: Understanding Controversy, Inaction and Opportunity.* Cambridge: Cambridge University Press.

Hutchinson, F. H. 1950. *Report on the Mahaica Dam and Lamaha Conservancy Project.* Georgetown, Guyana: British Guiana Lithographic Co. CO 111/817/4; former reference, 60466/22, folio. National Archives Digital Collection, Kew (London).

International Commission of Jurists (ICJ). 1965. *Report of the British Guiana Commission of Inquiry: Racial Problems in the Public Service.* Geneva: International Commission of Jurists.

International Federation of Red Cross and Red Cross Societies (IFRC). 2009. "Independent Evaluation of the Second Phase of the Preparedness for Climate Change Programme ('PfCC2')." In *International Federation of Red Cross and Red Cross Societies,* 1–20. Geneva: IFRC.

Jackson, Shona N. 2012. *Creole Indigeneity: Between Myth and Nation in the Caribbean.* Minneapolis: University of Minnesota Press.

Jackson, Shona N. 2014. "Humanity beyond the Regime of Labor: Antiblackness, Indigeneity, and the Legacies of Colonialism in the Caribbean." *Decolonization: Indigeneity, Education, and Society* (blog). June 6. https://decolonization.wordpress.com/2014/06/06/humanity-beyond-the-regime-of-labor-antiblackness-indigeneity-and-the-legacies-of-colonialism-in-the-caribbean/.

Jagan, Cheddi. 1997. *The West on Trial: My Fight for Guyana's Freedom*. Hertford, UK: Hansib.

James, C. L. R. 2001. *Mariners, Renegades, and Castaways: The Story of Herman Melville and the World We Live In*. Dartmouth, NH: Dartmouth University Press.

Jasanoff, Sheila. 2003. "Technologies of Humility: Citizen Participation in Governing Science." *Minerva* 41: 223–44.

Jayawardena, Chandra. 1968. "Ideology and Conflict in Lower Class Communities." *Comparative Studies in Society and History* 10 (4): 413–46.

Jewish Telegraph Agency. 1938. "British Guiana Seen Willing and Able to Absorb 500,000 Jews." December 11, 1–6. https://www.jta.org/1938/12/11/archive/british-guiana-seen-willing-and-able-to-absorb-500000-jews.

Johnson, Merrill L. 2006. "Geographical Reflections on the 'New' New Orleans in the Post-Hurricane Katrina Era." *Geographical Review* 96 (1): 139–56.

Joint United Nations Environment Program and the UN Office for the Coordination of Humanitarian Affairs (UNEP/OCHA). 2005. *Guyana Floods: UNDAC Geotechnical and Hydraulic Assessment of the East Demerara Water Conservancy Dam*. Geneva: Joint UNEP/OCHA Environment Unit.

Josiah, Barbara. 2011. *Migration, Mining, and the African Diaspora: Guyana in the Nineteenth and Twentieth Centuries*. New York: Palgrave Macmillan.

Kaieteur News. 2010a. "Amerindian Community Slams LCDS Consultation." May 10. https://www.kaieteurnewsonline.com/2010/03/10/amerindian-community-slams-lcds-consultation/.

Kaieteur News. 2010b. "Squatting Remains Major Bugbear in G/town—King." September 20. https://www.kaieteurnewsonline.com/2010/09/10/squatting-remains-major-bugbear-in-gtown-king/.

Kaieteur News. 2014. "Striving to Build a United Country." January 1. https://www.kaieteurnewsonline.com/2014/01/01/striving-to-build-a-united-country/.

Kaieteur News. 2016. "St. Cuthbert's Mission Hosts APA General Assembly." May 6. https://www.kaieteurnewsonline.com/2016/05/06/st-cuthberts-mission-hosts-apa-general-assembly/.

Keck, Frédéric. 2017. "Stockpiling as a Technique of Preparedness: Conserving the Past for an Unpredictable Future." In *Cryopolitics: Frozen Life in a Melting World*, edited by Joanna Radin and Emma Kowal, 117–41. Cambridge, MA: MIT Press.

Kelsey, Chris. 2014. "A Brief History of Geotextiles: A 40-Year Update." *Land and Water* (blog), March/April. https://docplayer.net/50741230-A-brief-history-of-geotextiles.html.

Khan, Naveeda. 2014. "Dogs and Humans and What the Earth Can Be: Filaments of Muslim Ecological Thought." *Hau: Journal of Ethnographic Theory* 4 (3): 245–64.

Khemraj, Tarron. 2019. "Politics and Underdevelopment: The Case of Guyana." In *Unmasking the State: Politics, Society, and Economy in Guyana 1992–2015*, edited by Arif Bulkan and D. Alissa Trotz, 91–119. Kingston, Jamaica: Ian Randle.

King, Tiffany Lethabo. 2017. "Humans Involved: Lurking in the Lines of Posthumanist Flight." *Critical Ethnic Studies* 3 (1): 162–85.

Kirke, Henry. 1893. "The Early Years of the Lamaha Canal." *Timehri: The Journal of the Royal Agricultural and Commercial Society of British Guiana* 7: 284–99.

Kissoon, Freddie. 2012. "Apaan Jaat: Then and Now." *Kaieteur News*, July 18. https://www.kaieteurnewsonline.com/2012/07/18/apaan-jaat-then-and-now/.

Kitchin, Rob. 2014a. "Big Data, New Epistemologies and Paradigm Shifts." *Big Data and Society* 1 (1): 1–12.

Kitchin, Rob. 2014b. *The Data Revolution: Big Data, Open Data, Data Infrastructures and Their Consequences*. London: Sage.

Klooster, Wim. 2016. *The Dutch Moment: War, Trade, and Settlement in the Seventeenth-Century Atlantic World*. Ithaca, NY: Cornell University Press.

Knox, Hannah, and Penny Harvey. 2015. *Roads: An Anthropology of Infrastructure*. Ithaca, NY: Cornell University Press.

Kwayana, Eusi. 1999. *Buxton Friendship in Print and Memory*. Georgetown, Guyana: Red Thread Women's Press.

Kwayana, Eusi. 2019. *A New Look at Jonestown*. Los Angeles: Carib House.

Lakhan, V. Chris. 1994. "Planning and Development Experiences in the Coastal Zone of Guyana." *Ocean and Coastal Management* 22 (3): 169–86.

Lakoff, Andrew. 2017. *Unprepared: Global Health in a Time of Emergency*. Berkeley: University of California Press.

Latour, Bruno. 1988. *Science in Action: How to Follow Scientists and Engineers through Society*. Cambridge, MA: Harvard University Press.

Latour, Bruno. 2004. *Politics of Nature: How to Bring the Sciences into Democracy*. Translated by Catherine Porter. Cambridge, MA: Harvard University Press.

Latour, Bruno. 2018. *Down to Earth: Politics in the New Climatic Regime*. Translated by Catherine Porter. Cambridge: Polity.

Lemel, Harold. 2001. *Patterns of Property Insecurity in Guyana*. Madison: Land Tenure Center, University of Wisconsin.

Lewis, Rupert. 1998. *Walter Rodney's Intellectual and Political Thought*. Kingston, Jamaica: University of the West Indies Press.

Li, Tania Murray. 2019. "Politics, Interrupted." *Anthropological Theory* 19 (1): 29–53.

Lilienthal, David. 1944. *TVA: Democracy on the March*. New York: Harpers.

Lipset, David. 2013. "The New State of Nature: Rising Sea Levels, Climate Justice, and Community-Based Adaptation in Papua New Guinea (2003–2011)." *Conservation and Society* 11 (2): 144–58.

Liverpool, Charles E. 2009. *Tropical Palms, Portraits and Rain: The Guyana Flood of 2005*. Baltimore: PublishAmerica.

MacKenzie, Donald. 2008. *An Engine, Not a Camera: How Financial Models Shape Markets*. Cambridge, MA: MIT Press.

Macnamara, C. E. 1894. "Reflections on the Increase of Town Populations." *Timehri: The Journal of the Royal Agricultural and Commercial Society of British Guiana* 8: 78–86.

Mamdani, Mahmood. 2020. *When Victims Become Killers: Colonialism, Genocide, and Nativism in Rwanda*. Princeton, NJ: Princeton University Press.

Mandle, Jay R. 1972. "The Plantation Economy: An Essay in Definition." *Science and Society* 36 (1): 49–62.

Mangru, Basdeo. 2012. *Benevolent Neutrality: Indian Government Policy and Labour Migration to British Guiana 1854–1884*. Hertford, UK: Hansib.

Marco, Guy. 2013. "'Water People' not 'Land of Many Waters.'" *Stabroek News*, September 13. https://www.stabroeknews.com/2013/09/07/opinion/letters/water-people-not-land-of-many-waters/.

Marcus, George. 2000. *Para-Sites: A Casebook against Cynical Reason*. Chicago: University of Chicago Press.

Marks, Colin. 2008. "Sophia Catchment Area, Fact Sheet and Info: The Background and History." Unpublished document.

Marks, Marvin Guion, and Leighton A. Ellis. 2013. "Delays in Major Agricultural Infrastructure Projects in Guyana: Causes and Proposed Solutions." *West Indian Journal of Engineering* 36 (1): 79–85.

Mars, Joan. 2009. "Postcolonial Policing and the Subculture of Violence in Guyana." In *Anthropologies of Guayana: Cultural Spaces in Northeastern Amazonia*, edited by Neil L. Whitehead and Stephanie W. Alemán, 167–84. Tucson: University of Arizona Press.

Mars, Perry. 2009. "The Guyana Diaspora and Homeland Conflict Resolution." In *The New African Diaspora*, edited by Isidore Okpewho and Nkiru Nzegwu, 483–99. Bloomington: Indiana University Press.

Marx, Karl. 2004. *Capital*. Vol. 1, *A Critique of Political Economy*. New ed. New York: Penguin Classics.

Mathews, Andrew. 2017. "Ghostly Forms and Forest Histories." In *Arts of Living on a Damaged Planet: Ghosts and Monsters of the Anthropocene*, edited by Anna Lowenhaupt Tsing, Elaine Gan, and Heather Anne Swanson, 145–56. Minneapolis: University of Minnesota Press.

Mayer-Schönberger, Viktor, and Kenneth Cukier. 2013. *Big Data: A Revolution That Will Transform How We Live, Work, and Think*. Boston: Houghton Mifflin Harcourt.

Mbembe, Achille. 2017. *Critique of Black Reason*. Translated by Laurent Dubois. Durham, NC: Duke University Press.

Mbembe, Achille. 2019. *Necropolitics*. Durham, NC: Duke University Press.

McCully, Patrick. 2001. *Silenced Rivers: The Ecology and Politics of Large Dams*. London: Zed.

McElhinny, Bonnie. 2010. "The Audacity of Affect: Gender, Race, and History in Linguistic Accounts of Legitimacy and Belonging." *Annual Review of Anthropology* 39: 309–28.

McLean, Stuart. 2011. "Black Goo: Forceful Encounters with Matter in Europe's Muddy Margins." *Cultural Anthropology* 26 (4): 589–619.

McWatt, Clive. 2010. "History . . . Timehri: Life History of the Journal of the Royal Agricultural and Commercial Society of British Guiana, Part II." *Stabroek News*, April 29. https://www.stabroeknews.com/2010/04/29/guyana-review/history -timehri-life-history-of-the-journal-of-the-royal-agricultural-commercial -society-of-british-guiana-2/.

Meggers, Betty. 1994. "Archeological Evidence for the Impact of Mega-Niño Events on Amazonia during the Past Two Millennia." *Climatic Change* 28: 321–38.

Menezes, Mary Noel. 2011. *British Policy towards the Amerindians in British Guiana 1803–1873*. Georgetown, Guyana: Caribbean.

Mentore, Laura H. 2011. "Waiwai Fractality and the Arboreal Bias of PES Schemes in Guyana: What to Make of the Multiplicity of Amazonian Cosmographies?" *Journal of Cultural Geography* 28 (1): 21–43.

Ministry of the Presidency. 2017. " 'Government Won't Leave Sophia Behind'—President at Commissioning Ceremony for New Road, Water Distribution System." Guyana Department of Public Information (website), February 25. https://dpi.gov.gy/government-wont-leave-sophia-behind-president-at -commissioning-ceremony-for-new-road-water-distribution-system/.

Mintz, Sidney. 1974. "The Caribbean Region." *Daedalus* 103 (2): 45–71.

Mitchell, Timothy. 2002. *Rule of Experts: Egypt, Techno-Politics, Modernity*. Berkeley: University of California Press.

Molle, Francois. 2009. "River-Basin Planning and Management: The Social Life of a Concept." *Geoforum* 40 (3): 484–94.

Mooney, Chris. 2021. "An Enormous Missing Contribution to Global Warming May Have Been Right under Our Feet." *Washington Post*, June 4. https://www .washingtonpost.com/climate-environment/2021/06/04/an-enormous-missing -contribution-global-warming-may-have-been-right-under-our-feet/.

Moore, Amelia. 2019. *Destination Anthropocene: Science and Tourism in the Bahamas*. Berkeley: University of California Press.

Morgan, Arthur. 1971. *Dams and Other Disasters: A Century of the Army Corps of Engineers in Civil Works*. Westford, NY: Porter Sargent.

Morgan, Lewis Henry. 1886. *The American Beaver and His Works*. Peribo, Australia: Dover.

Morton, John, and Armando Guzmán. 2014. *Implementation Complementation and Results Report for a Conservancy Adaptation*. Georgetown, Guyana: World Bank.

Mott MacDonald. 2005. *East Demerara and Boereserie Conservancy Dams Condition Assessment by Dams Specialist*. Georgetown, Guyana: Mott MacDonald.

Mrázek, Rudolf. 2002. *Engineers of a Happy Land: Technology and Nationalism in a Colony*. Princeton, NJ: Princeton University Press.

Mukerji, Chandra. 2015. *Impossible Engineering: Technology and Territoriality on the Canal du Midi*. Princeton, NJ: Princeton University Press.

Mullenite, Joshua. 2020. "History, Colonialism, and Archival Methods in Socio-Hydrological Scholarship: A Case Study of the Boerasirie Conservancy in British Guiana." *World* 1 (3): 205–15.

Mullings, Leith. 2005. "Interrogating Racism: Toward an Antiracist Anthropology." *Annual Review of Anthropology* 34: 667–93.

Munasinghe, Viranjini. 2001. *Callaloo or Tossed Salad? East Indians and the Cultural Politics of Identity in Trinidad*. Ithaca, NY: Cornell University Press.

Munro, Carol Ann. 2016. "A Description of Horror and Evil by a Freed Treason Accused." *Kaieteur News*, January 31. https://www.kaieteurnewsonline.com/2016/01/31/a-description-of-horror-and-evil-by-a-freed-treason-accused/.

Naipaul, V. S. 2003. *The Writer and the World: Essays*. New York: Vintage.

Narayan, Kailas. 2006. "Climate Change Impacts on Water Resources in Guyana." In *Climate Variability and Change: Hydrological Impacts*, edited by Siegfried Demuth, 413–18. Wallingford, UK: International Association of Hydrological Sciences.

Nelson, Alondra. 2002. "Introduction: Future Texts." *Social Text* 20 (2): 1–16.

Nigel Hinds Financial Services. 2015. "National Drainage and Irrigation Authority: Forensic Audit Report for the Period November 1, 2011 to May 31, 2015." Unpublished document.

Nirenberg, Ricardo L., and David Nirenberg. 2011. "Badiou's Number: A Critique of Mathematics as Ontology." *Critical Inquiry* 37 (4): 583–614.

Nixon, Rob. 2013. *Slow Violence and the Environmentalism of the Poor*. Cambridge, MA: Harvard University Press.

Nordlinger, Eric A. 1976. *Soldiers in Politics: Military Coups and Governments*. Upper Saddle River, NJ: Prentice Hall.

Norgaard, Kari Marie. 2011. *Living in Denial: Climate Change, Emotions, and Everyday Life*. Cambridge, MA: MIT Press.

Oels, Angela. 2005. "Rendering Climate Change Governable: From Biopower to Advanced Liberal Government?" *Journal of Environmental Policy and Planning* 7 (3): 185–207.

Oliver-Smith, Anthony. 2004. "Theorizing Vulnerability in a Globalized World: A Political Ecological Perspective." In *Mapping Vulnerability: Disasters, Development and People*, edited by Greg Bankoff, Georg Frerks, and Dorothea Hilhorst, 10–24. New York: Earthscan.

O'Reilly, Jessica. 2017. *The Technocratic Arctic: An Ethnography of Scientific Expertise and Environmental Governance*. Ithaca, NY: Cornell University Press.

Oreskes, Naomi, and John Krige, eds. 2014. *Science and Technology in the Global Cold War*. Cambridge, MA: MIT Press.

Orlove, Benjamin. 2009. "The Past, the Present, and Some Possible Futures of Adaptation." In *Adaptation to Climate Change: Thresholds, Values, Governance*, edited by Neil Adger, Irene Lorenzoni, and Karen O'Brien, 131–63. New York: Cambridge University Press.

Palmer, Colin A. 2010. *Cheddi Jagan and the Politics of Power: British Guiana's Struggle for Independence*. Chapel Hill: University of North Carolina Press.

Pan American Health Organization (PAHO). 2003. *Regional Evaluation Municipal Solid Waste Management Services: Country Analytical Report Guyana/ Evaluation 2002*. Georgetown, Guyana: Regional Office of the World Health Organization.

Parenti, Christian. 2011. *Tropics of Chaos: Climate Change and the New Geography of Violence*. New York: Nation.

Parmar, Inderjeet. 2015. *Foundations of the American Century: The Ford, Carnegie, and Rockefeller Foundations in the Rise of American Power*. New York: Columbia University Press.

Pelling, Mark. 1998. "Participation, Social Capital and Vulnerability to Urban Flooding in Guyana." *Journal of International Development* 10 (4): 469–86.

Pelling, Mark. 1999. "The Political Ecology of Flood Hazards in Urban Guyana." *Geoforum* 30 (3): 249–61.

Pelling, Mark. 2010. *Adaptation to Climate Change: From Resilience to Transformation*. New York: Routledge.

People's National Congress (PNC). 1979. *Report on the Third Biennial Congress of the People's National Congress, August 22–26, 1979*. Vol. 2. Georgetown, Guyana: PNC.

Persaud, Joe. 2015. "Why Only Dutch Engineers?" *Stabroek News*, July 23. https://www.stabroeknews.com/2015/07/23/opinion/letters/why-only-dutch-engineers/.

Persram, Nalini. 2004. "The Importance of Being Cultural: Nationalist Thought and Jagan's Colonial World." *Small Axe: A Journal of Caribbean Criticism* 8 (1): 82–105.

Petryna, Adriana. 2015. "What Is a Horizon? Navigating Thresholds in Climate Change Uncertainty." In *Modes of Uncertainty: Anthropological Cases*, edited by Limor Samimian-Darash and Paul Rabinow, 147–64. Chicago: University of Chicago Press.

Plew, Mark. 2009. "Pleistocene—Early Holocene Environmental Change: Implications for Human Adaptive Responses in the Guianas." In *Anthropologies of Guayana: Cultural Spaces in Northeastern Amazonia*, edited by Neil L. Whitehead and Stephanie W. Alemán, 23–35. Tucson: University of Arizona Press.

Poovey, Mary. 1998. *A History of the Modern Fact: Problems of Knowledge in the Sciences of Wealth and Society*. Chicago: University of Chicago Press.

Povinelli, Elizabeth. 2016. *Geontologies: A Requiem to Late Liberalism*. Durham, NC: Duke University Press.

Premdas, Ralph R. 1982. "Guyana: Changes in Ideology and Foreign Policy." *World Affairs* 145 (2): 177–202.

Prescod, Colin. 1976. "Guyana's Socialism: An Interview with Walter Rodney." *Race and Class* 18 (2): 109–28.

Price, Richard. 1985. "An Absence of Ruins? Seeking Caribbean Historical Consciousness." *Caribbean Review* 14 (3): 24–29.

Puri, Shalini. 2014. *The Grenada Revolution in the Caribbean Present: Operation Urgent Memory*. New York: Palgrave.

Pyne, Steph. 2001. *Fire: A Brief History*. Seattle: University of Washington Press.

Quintero, Ricardo Smith, John de Beer, and Jerry Lochan. 1991. *Water Balance Study Report 1990*. Georgetown, Guyana: Ministry of Agriculture, Hydraulics Division, Government of Guyana (GoG).

Rabe, Stephen. 2005. *U.S. Intervention in British Guiana: A Cold War Story*. Chapel Hill: University of North Carolina Press.

Raffles, Hugh. 2002. *In Amazonia: A Natural History*. Princeton, NJ: Princeton University Press.

Raghunandan, Moolchand, and Balraj Kistow. 1998. "The Cooperative Movement in the Midst of Economic Chaos: The Guyanese Experience." *Journal of Small Business Management* 36 (2): 74–78.

Rahman, Shabna. 2016. "Beni Sankar Betting Big on Coconuts—Cold Press Oil, Flour, Cosmetics among Products." *Stabroek News*, May 30. http://www.stabroeknews.com/2016/news/stories/05/30/beni-sankar-betting-big-coconuts/.

Ramsahoye, Fenton H. W. 1966. *The Development of Land Law in British Guiana*. Dobbs Ferry, NY: Oceana.

Ranganathan, Malini. 2015. "Storm Drains as Assemblages: The Political Ecology of Flood Risk in Post-Colonial Bangalore." *Antipode* 47 (5): 1300–1320.

Rasmussen, Kim Su. 2011. "Foucault's Genealogy of Racism." *Theory, Culture and Society* 28 (5): 34–51.

Ravesteijn, Wim, and Jan Kop, eds. 2008. *For Profit and Prosperity: The Contribution Made by Dutch Engineers to Public Works in Indonesia, 1800–2000*. Zaltbommel, Netherlands: KITLV.

Reddock, Rhoda. 2012. *Interrogating Caribbean Masculinities: Theoretical and Empirical Analyses*. Mona, Jamaica: University of the West Indies Press.

Redfield, Peter. 2013. *Life in Crisis: The Ethical Journey of Doctors without Borders*. Berkeley: University of California Press.

Rickford, John R. 2019. *Variation, Versatility and Change in Sociolinguistics and Creole Studies*. Cambridge: Cambridge University Press.

Robertson, Henry. 1903. "The Storage of Water." *Transactions of the British Association of Waterworks Engineers* 1 (8): 180–98.

Robinson, Cedric. 2000. *Black Marxism: The Making of the Black Radical Tradition*. Chapel Hill: University of North Carolina Press.

Rodney, Walter. 1981. *A History of the Guyanese Working People, 1881–1905*. Baltimore: Johns Hopkins University Press.

Rodway, James. 1997. *The Story of Georgetown*. Georgetown, Guyana: Guyana Heritage Society.

Rodway, James. 2010. *History of British Guiana: From the Year 1668 to the Present Time (1893)*. Whitefish, MT: Kessinger.

Rogers, Adams. 2017. "With Harvey, Imperfect Engineering Meets a Perfect Storm." *Wired*, August 31. https://www.wired.com/story/houston-dams -probable-maximum-flood-vs-500-year-flood/.

Rose, Euclid A. 2002. *Dependency and Socialism in the Modern Caribbean: Superpower Intervention in Guyana, Jamaica, and Grenada, 1970–1985*. Lanham, MD: Lexington.

Roth, Regina. 2010. "Marx on Technical Change in the Critical Edition." *European Journal of the History of Economic Thought* 17 (5): 1223–51.

Rotman, Brian. 1993. *Ad Infinitum . . . The Ghost in Turing's Machine: Taking God Out of Mathematics and Putting the Body Back in*. Stanford, CA: Stanford University Press.

Roy, Ananya. 2005. "Urban Informality: Toward an Epistemology of Planning." *Journal of the American Planning Association* 71 (2): 141–58.

Rusert, Britt. 2017. *Fugitive Science: Empiricism and Freedom in Early African-American Culture*. New York: New York University Press.

Russell, William. 1882. "Farming and Irrigation." *Timehri: The Journal of the Royal Agricultural and Commercial Society of British Guiana* 1: 87–99.

Sabin, Paul. 2010. "'The Ultimate Environmental Dilemma': Making a Place for Historians in the Climate Change and Energy Debates." *Environmental History* 15 (1): 76–93.

Sagan, Scott D. 1996. "Why Do States Build Nuclear Weapons? Three Models in Search of a Bomb." *International Security* 21 (3): 5–68.

Samimian-Darash, Limor. 2013. "Governing Future Potential Biothreat: Toward an Anthropology of Uncertainty." *Current Anthropology* 54 (1): 1–22.

Sande Lie, Jon Harald. 2015. *Developmentality: An Ethnography of the World Bank–Uganda Partnership*. Oxford: Berghahn.

Sanders, Andrew. 1976. "American Indian or West Indian: The Case of the Coastal Amerindians of Guyana." *Caribbean Studies* 16 (2): 117–44.

Schipper, E. Lisa F. 2006. "Conceptual History of Adaptation in the UNFCCC Process." *Review of European, Comparative and International Environmental Law* 15 (1): 82–92.

Schomburgk, Richard. (1922) 2015. *Richard Schomburgk's Travels in British Guiana, 1840–1844*. Vol. 1. Emeryville, CA: Alibris.

Schwartz, Mattathias. 2017. "Maria's Bodies." *New York*, December 25. https:// nymag.com/intelligencer/2017/12/hurricane-maria-man-made-disaster .html.

Schwartz, Stuart. 2016. *Sea of Storms: A History of Hurricanes in the Caribbean from Columbus to Katrina*. Princeton, NJ: Princeton University Press.

Scott, David. 2004. "Counting Women's Work: An Interview with Andaiye." *Small Axe: A Caribbean Journal of Criticism* 8 (1): 123–217.

Scott, David. 2014. *Omens of Adversity: Tragedy, Time, Memory, Justice*. Durham, NC: Duke University Press.

Scott, James C. 1999. *Seeing like a State: How Certain Schemes to Improve the Human Condition Have Failed*. New Haven, CT: Yale University Press.

Sealey-Huggins, Leon. 2017. "'1.5 °C to Stay Alive': Climate Change, Imperialism, and Justice for the Caribbean." *Third World Quarterly* 38 (11): 2444–63.

Second Legislative Council. 1934. *Report by the Floods Investigation Committee, 1934*. Georgetown, Guyana: British Guiana Lithographic Co. CSO 1131/34:2, British Guiana Sessional Paper No. 6 of 1934. National Archives Digital Collection, Kew (London).

Seecharan, Clem. 2000. *Bechu: Bound Coolie Radical in British Guiana 1894–1901*. Mona, Jamaica: University of the West Indies Press.

Seecharan, Clem. 2005. *Jack Campbell: The Booker Reformer in British Guiana, 1934–1966*. Kingston, Jamaica: Ian Randle.

Sheller, Mimi. 2012. *Citizenship from Below: Erotic Agency and Caribbean Freedom*. Durham, NC: Duke University Press.

Sherman, A. J. 1994. *Island Refuge: Britain and Refugees from the Third Reich 1933–1939*. London: Routledge.

Silverman, Marilyn. 1979. "Dependency, Mediation, and Class Formation in Rural Guyana." *American Ethnologist* 6 (3): 466–90.

Silverstein, Paul A. 2005. "Immigrant Racialization and the New Savage Slot: Race, Migration, and Immigration in the New Europe." *Annual Review of Anthropology* 34: 363–84.

Singh, Chaitram. 1993. "Ethnic Guardians: The Role of the Military in Guyana's Politics." *Journal of Developing Societies* 9: 212–25.

Skempton, A. W. 1989. "Historical Development of British Embankment Dams to 1960." Keynote address to the Conference on Clay Barriers for Embankment Dams, organized by the Institution of Civil Engineers, London, October 18. https://www.icevirtuallibrary.com/.

Smith, Raymond T. 1955. "Land Tenure in Three Negro Villages in British Guiana." *Social and Economic Studies* 4 (1): 64–82.

Smith, Raymond T. 1962. *British Guiana*. London: Oxford University Press.

Smith, Raymond T. 1995. "'Living in the Gun Mouth': Race, Class, and Political Violence in Guyana." *New West Indian Guide / Nieuwe West-Indische Gids* 69 (3–4): 223–52.

Solomon, Susan, Dahe Qin, Martin Manning, Melinda Marquis, Kristen Averyt, Melinda M. B. Tignor, Henry LeRoy Miller Jr., and Zhenlin Chen, eds. 2007. *Climate Change 2007: The Physical Science Basis; Contribution of Working Group I to the Fourth Assessment Report of the Intergovernmental Panel on Climate Change*. Cambridge: Cambridge University Press.

Somers, Margaret. 2008. *Genealogies of Citizenship: Markets, Statelessness, and the Right to Have Rights*. Cambridge: Cambridge University Press.

Spencer, O. A. 1950. "Papers Relating to Development Planning. No. 2: 1950 Review and Revision of General Ten-Year Plan of Development and Welfare, 1947–1956. Legislative Council Paper No. 11/1948. Part 1: Memorandum by Economic Adviser and Development Commissioner." CO 111/818/11, former reference 60532/50 folio. National Archives Digital Collection, Kew (London).

Spivak, Gayatri Chakravorty. 2005. *Death of a Discipline*. New York: Columbia University Press.

St. Stanislaus College. 1968. "1968 News of Old Boys." *St. Stanislaus College of Guyana Alumni Magazine*. http://st-stanislaus-gy.com/Magazines/1968 /1968GradNews.pdf.

Stabroek News. 2007. "Bernard Kerik Closer to Facing New Federal Charges." October 14. http://www.stabroeknews.com/2007/archives/10/14/bernard-kerik -closer-to-facing-new-federal-charges/.

Stabroek News. 2010a. "Hope Canal: Compensation Payouts to Residents Under-way." March 18. https://www.stabroeknews.com/2010/03/18/news/guyana/hope -canalcompensation-payout-to-residents-underway/.

Stabroek News. 2010b. "Hope Canal . . . Dochfour Residents to Receive More Compensation after Budget." February 7. https://www.stabroeknews.com/2010/02 /07/news/guyana/hope-canal/.

Stabroek News. 2013. "No Environmental Assessment Was Recommended for Hope Canal: Ramsammy." April 18. https://www.stabroeknews.com/2013/04 /18/news/guyana/no-environmental-assessment-was-recommended-for-hope -canal-ramsammy/.

Stabroek News. 2019. "Number of Unaccounted for Cuba, Haitian Immigrants Alarming: PPP." August 4. https://www.stabroeknews.com/2019/08/04/news /guyana/number-of-unaccounted-for-cuban-haitian-immigrants-alarming -ppp/.

Stabroek News. 2020. "Guyoil to Reduce Fuel Prices." September 30. https://www .stabroeknews.com/2020/09/30/news/guyana/guyoil-to-reduce-fuel-prices/.

Stengers, Isabelle. 2000. *Invention of Modern Science*. Translated by Daniel W. Smith. Minneapolis: University of Minnesota Press.

Stengers, Isabelle. 2015. *In Catastrophic Times: Resisting the Coming Barbarism*. Translated by Andrew Goffey. Paris: Open Humanities.

Stewart, Charles. 2016. "Historicity and Anthropology." *Annual Review of Anthropology* 45: 79–94.

Stewart, Kathleen. 2005. "Cultural Poesis: The Generativity of Emergent Things." In *Handbook of Qualitative Research*, 3rd ed., edited by N. Denzin and Y. Lincoln, 1015–30. Thousand Oaks, CA: Sage.

Stoler, Ann Laura. 2010. *Along the Archival Grain: Epistemic Anxieties and Colonial Common Sense*. Princeton, NJ: Princeton University Press.

Strachan, A. J. 1983. "Return Migration to Guyana." *Social and Economic Studies* 32 (3): 121–42.

A Sufferer [pseud.]. "Letter to the Editor: Flood Conditions." 1934. *Argosy*, January 10. Lt. Irrigation and Drainage Box, National Archives of Guyana, Georgetown.

Subramanian, Ajantha. 2019. *The Caste of Merit: Engineering Education in India*. Cambridge, MA: Harvard University Press.

Sutherland, Laurel. 2020. "Remembering the 'Great Flood' 15 Years Later." *Stabroek News*, February 3. https://www.stabroeknews.com/2020/02/03/news/guyana /remembering-the-great-flood-15-years-later/.

Szerszynski, Bronislaw. 2019. "How the Earth Remembers and Forgets." In *Political Geology: Active Stratigraphies and the Making of Life*, edited by Adam Bobbette and Amy Donovon, 219–36. London: Palgrave Macmillan.

Taylor, Moe. 2015. "'One Hand Can't Clap': Guyana and North Korea, 1974–1985." *Journal of Cold War Studies* 17 (1): 41–63.

Terzaghi, Karl. 1943. *Theoretical Soil Mechanics*. New York: Wiley.

Thakur, Rishee S. 2019. "Crime, Ethnicity and the Political Impasse in Guyana." In *Politics, Society and Economy in Guyana 1992–2015*, edited by Arif Bulkan and D. Alissa Trotz, 120–153. Kingston, Jamaica: Ian Randle.

Thatcher, Jim, David O'Sullivan, and Dillon Mahmoudi. 2016. "Data Colonialism through Accumulation by Dispossession: New Metaphors for Daily Data." *Environment and Planning D: Society and Space* 34 (6): 990–1006.

Thomas, Clive Y. 1974. *Dependence and Transformation: The Economics of the Transition of Socialism*. New York: Monthly Review Press.

Thomas, Clive Y. 1984. *The Rise of the Authoritarian State in Peripheral Societies*. New York: Monthly Review Press.

Thomas, Deborah. 2011. *Exceptional Violence: Embodied Citizenship in Transnational Jamaica*. Durham, NC: Duke University Press.

Thorne, Carmichael. 2014. "Use of a Two-Dimensional Model to Analyse the Flood Response to a Reservoir and to Make Recommendation for Improvement of Reservoir Performance." Master's thesis, Newcastle University.

Thurn, E. F. Im. 1882. "Editorial Prologue." *Timehri: The Journal of the Royal Agricultural and Commercial Society of British Guiana* 1: 1–6.

Trotz, D. Alissa. 2010. "Shifting the Ground Beneath Us." *Interventions* 1 (12): 112–24.

Trotz, D. Alissa, and Linda Peake. 2001. "Family, Work, and Organizing: An Overview of the Contemporary Economic, Social, and Political Roles of Women in Guyana." *Social and Economic Studies* 50 (2): 67–101.

Trouillot, Michel-Rolph. 2002. "Culture on the Edges: Caribbean Creolization in Historical Context." In *From the Margins: Historical Anthropology and Its Futures*, edited by Brian Keith Axel, 189–210. Durham, NC: Duke University Press.

Trouillot, Michel-Rolph. 2004. *Global Transformations: Anthropology and the Modern World*. New York: Palgrave Macmillan.

Tsing, Anna Lowenhaupt. 2015. *The Mushroom at the End of the World: On the Possibility of Life in Capitalist Ruins*. Princeton, NJ: Princeton University Press.

Valencia, Cristina. 2020. "Venezuela's Refugee Crisis: Guyana." Draft. Georgetown, Guyana: Health Pioneers.

Vaughn, Sarah E. 2017. "Disappearing Mangroves: The Epistemic Politics of Climate Adaptation." *Cultural Anthropology* 32 (2): 242–68.

Vaughn, Sarah E. 2019. "Vulnerability." In *Anthropocene Unseen: A Lexicon*, edited by Cymene Howe and Anand Pandian, 517–22. New York: Punctum.

Velasco, Marco A. 2014. *Progress and Challenges in Disaster Risk Management in Guyana*. Georgetown, Guyana: United Nations Office for Disaster Risk Reduction.

Verill, A. Hyatt. 1918. "A Remarkable Mound Discovered in British Guiana." *Timehri: The Journal of the Royal Agricultural and Commercial Society of British Guiana* 5: 22–25.

Verran, Helen. 2001. *Science and an African Logic*. Chicago: University of Chicago Press.

Vezzoli, Simona. 2014. "The Effects of Independence, State Formation and Migration Policies on Guyanese Migration." International Migration Institute and University of Oxford Department of International Development Working Paper 94 (July). https://www.migrationinstitute.org/publications/wp-94-14.

Vidal, David. 1978. "Jonestown Was a Model; Now It's Embarrassment." *New York Times*, November 26. https://www.nytimes.com/1978/11/26/archives/jonestown-was-a-model-now-its-embarrassment-other-common-views-and.html.

Von Schnitzler, Anita. 2016. *Democracy's Infrastructure: Techno-Politics and Protest after Apartheid*. Princeton, NJ: Princeton University Press.

Vossen, Paul. 2017. "Hurricane Harvey Provides Lab for U.S. Forecast Experiments." *Science*, August 28. https://www.sciencemag.org/news/2017/08/hurricane-harvey-provides-lab-us-forecast-experiments.

Wagley, Charles. 1960. "Plantation America: A Culture Sphere." In *Caribbean Studies: A Symposium*, edited by Vera Rubin, 3–13. Seattle: University of Washington Press.

Walcott, Rinaldo. 2009. "Reconstructing Manhood; Or, the Drag of Black Masculinity." *Small Axe: A Caribbean Journal of Criticism* 28 (1): 75–89.

Walford, Antonia. 2015. "Double Standards: Examples and Exceptions in Scientific Metrological Practice in Brazil." *Journal of the Royal Anthropological Institution* 21 (1): 64–77.

Waters, Robert, and Gordon Daniels. 2005. "The World's Longest General Strike: The AFL-CIO, the CIA, and British Guiana." *Diplomatic History* 29 (2): 279–307.

Weart, Spencer R. 1997. "Global Warming, Cold War, and the Evolution of Research Plans." *Historical Studies in the Physical and Biological Sciences* 27 (2): 319–56.

Weber, Max. 1968. *Economy and Society: An Outline of Interpretive Sociology*. New York: Bedminster.

Weheliye, Alexander G. 2014. *Habeas Viscus: Racializing Assemblages, Biopolitics and Black Feminist Theories of the Human*. Durham, NC: Duke University Press.

Wekker, Gloria. 2006. *The Politics of Passion: Women's Sexual Culture in the Afro-Surinamese Diaspora*. New York: Columbia University Press.

West, Paige. 2016. "An Anthropology of the 'Assemblage of the Now.'" *Anthropological Forum: A Journal of Social Anthropology and Comparative Sociology* 26 (4): 438–45.

West Indies Royal Commission. 2011. *The Moyne Report*. Edited by Baron Walter Edward Guinness Moyne with an introduction by Denis Benn. Kingston, Jamaica: Ian Randle.

Whitaker, James A. 2016. "Amerindians in the Eighteenth Century Plantation System of the Guianas." *Tipití: Journal of the Society of Lowland South America* 14 (1): 30–43.

Whitehead, Neil L. 1998. "Indigenous Cartography in Lowland South America and the Caribbean." In *The History of Cartography*, vol. 1, book 3, *Cartography in Traditional African, American, Arctic, Australian, and Pacific Societies*, edited by David Woodward and Malcolm Lewis, 301–26. Chicago: University of Chicago Press.

Whitehead, Neil L. 2009. "Guayana as Anthropological Imaginary: Elements of a History." In *Anthropologies of Guayana*, edited by Neil L. Whitehead and Stephanie W. Alemán, 1–22. Tucson: University of Arizona Press.

Whitehead, Neil L., Michael Heckenberger, and George Simon. 2010. "Materializing the Past among the Lokono (Arawak) of the Berbice River, Guyana." *Anthropológica* 114: 87–127.

Whitington, Jerome. 2016. "What Does Climate Change Demand of Anthropology?" *PoLaR: Political and Legal Anthropology Review* 39 (1): 7–15.

Wilkinson, Bert. 2017. "Guyana Goes after Stolen Ancestral Lands." New York *Amsterdam News*, August 31. http://amsterdamnews.com/news/2017/aug/31/guyana-goes-after-stolen-ancestral-afro-land/.

Williams, Brackette. 1991. *Stains on My Name, War in My Veins: Guyana and the Politics of Cultural Struggle*. Durham, NC: Duke University Press.

Williams, Denis. 2003. *Prehistoric Guiana*. Kingston, Jamaica: Ian Randle.

Wilson, Peter J. 1969. "Reputation and Respectability: A Suggestion for Caribbean Ethnology." *Man* 4 (1): 70–84.

Winant, Howard. 2000. "Race and Race Theory." *Annual Review of Sociology* 26: 169–85.

Wishart, Jennifer. 2014. "Lokono (Arawak) Sites between the Corentyne and Demerara Rivers in Guyana Notes, Field Reports and Research 1984–1992." *Archeology and Anthropology* 18 (1): 19–39.

Wolfe, Patrick. 2006. "Settler Colonialism and the Elimination of the Native." *Journal of Genocide Research* 8 (4): 387–409.

Wolstenholme, G. L. 1953. "Jenman and the Georgetown Botanical Gardens." *Timehri: The Journal of the Royal Agricultural and Commercial Society of British Guiana* 32: 17–27.

World Bank. 2009. *International Development Association Country Assistance Strategy for Guyana, for the Period FY 2009–2012*. Georgetown, Guyana: Caribbean Country Management Unit Latin American and Caribbean Region.

World Bank Mission. 2005. *Guyana: Preliminary Damage and Needs Assessment Following the Intense Flooding of January 2005*. Georgetown, Guyana: World Bank.

Wynter, Sylvia. 1995. "1492: A New World View." In *Race, Discourse, and the Origin of the Americas: A New World View*, edited by Vera Lawrence Hyatt and Rex Nettleford, 5–57. Washington, DC: Smithsonian Institution Press.

Wynter, Sylvia. 2015. "The Ceremony Found: Towards the Autopoetic Turn/Over-turn, Its Autonomy of Human Agency and Extraterritoriality of (Self-)Cognition." In *Black Knowledges/Black Struggles: Essays in Critical Epistemology*, edited by Jason R. Amboise and Sabine Broeck, 184–252. Liverpool: Liverpool University Press.

Young, Allan. 1958. *The Approaches to Local Self-Governance in British Guiana*. London: Longmans, Green.

Yusoff, Kathryn. 2018. *A Billion Black Anthropocenes or None*. Minneapolis: University of Minnesota Press.

Zilberstein, Anya. 2016. *A Temperate Empire: Making Climate Change in Early America*. Oxford: Oxford University Press.

Znamenski, Andrei. 2021. *Socialism as a Secular Creed: A Modern Global History*. Baltimore: Lexington Press.

Page numbers in italics refer to figures and maps.

Booker Brothers, 16, 213n4
borders, 52; disputes, 146, 156
borehole drilling, 135, 137–38, 139, 142, 143, 173
Bovolo, Isabella, 144
Braun, Bruce, 183
British Empire, 56, 57, 73, 87, 88, 208n17; colonies, 54, 60, 63, 83
British engineers, 55, 76, 77–79, 91, 151, 152; mosquitoes and, 86–87; Mott MacDonlad, 130–31
British Guiana, 15–16, 59, 62, 208n17; embankment damming, 78–79, 87–88; flood management, 63, 84, 87, 199, 214n4; geological survey, 135; planters and laborers, 72–74
British settler colonialism, 26, 60, 63
British West Indies, 83–84, 213n4
Brown, Wendy, 67
Burnham, Forbes, 99, 155–57, 164–65, 214n7, 215n5; electoral campaigns, 16–18, 208n17; Make the Small Man a Real Man campaign, 103; on racial imbalance, 63–64; vision of socialism, 91–92, 164, 213n11

Callison, Candis, 23
Camacho, Robert F., 88–89
Campbellville, 24
canals, 7, 11, 37, 40, 110; clogged, 29, 43, 102, 133, 187; East Coast Demerara Road, 47; garbage in, 185; Georgetown, 180; Lamaha, 34, 72–76, 183; malaria and, 85–86; Sophia, 182, 185, 193; storm relief, 26, 82, 84–85, 97, 133, 160. See also Hope Canal
Canje pheasant, 143, 146
capitalism, 202, 204, 212n10; racial, 53, 201
carbon emissions, 9, 22, 201, 202
carbon markets, 1, 20, 204
Carey, Mark, 190
Caribbean Community (CARICOM), 168, 169
Caribbean ethnohistoriography, 112
Caribs, 52, 53
Carse, Ashley, 206n10
Carter, Bert, 134–35
cash crops, 33, 58, 104, 115, 116, 117
Church, Christopher, 61
citizenship, 124, 206n8; Black, 57
civic groups, 66–67; GHRA, 102, 104, 106

Civil Defence Commission (CDC): Black masculinity and, 166–67; collaboration with engineers, 128–29, 162, 172, 174, 219n7; coup conspiracy, 173; flood early warning system, 14, 27, 128, 146–50, 160–61; founding and jurisdiction, 155–57; Haitian earthquake (2010) and, 168–69, 219n8; headquarters, 158; love stories and, 151, 152; national flood plan, 151, 152, 157–59, 162–64, 166–68, 170–72; organization of shelters, 4, 35, 38–40, 100, 153; public engagement, 165–66, 169–70; staff history/diversity, 155, 158, 164; Volunteer Corps, 167–68
clientelism, 103, 215n4
climate adaptation, term usage, 8
climate change, 1–2, 123, 124, 175, 177; awareness, 5, 10, 209n21; Beck on, 43; EDWC and, 151, 153; experts, 194–95; glaciers and, 190; heavy rainfall and, 31, 33, 50, 105–6, 163; humanitarianism and, 182; impacts on Guyana, 8–9, 164; ordinary life and, 178, 180, 190, 195; race and, 20–21, 23, 25, 68, 199, 200, 204; skepticism, 201–2, 204; technoscience-military collaborations and, 154–55, 161, 169; vulnerability to, 12, 98, 113, 121, 142, 204, 206nn11–12; World Bank programs, 130
climate refugees, 20, 145, 165; Tuvaluan, 124
coastal settlement, 15, 20, 25, 124, 129, 194, 199; Black masculinity and, 165, 166, 167; empoldering practices and, 53–54; geological conditions, 135–36; postemancipation and, 58–61; temporality of, 49; vulnerability of, 204; Waraos and Arawaks, 51–52
coconut: estates, 98–100, 99; oil, 101; trees, 47, 114, 117, 119
Cold War, 154, 156, 162, 166, 208n17; militarization, 157, 170, 174
compensation: for climate adaptation, 110, 121–24, 216n10; Hope Canal construction and, 26, 97–98, 107–8, 113, 117, 214n1
compromises, engineers', 127
Conservation Adaptation Project (CAP), 43, 134, 143, 151; flood early warning system and, 149, 150; geotextiles and, 141–42; hydraulic modeling and, 130–31, 132; pegasse and, 138–39

engineering reports, 2, 25, 94, 153, 173
enslaved Africans, 111, 209n19, 211n1; in
   Barbados, 61; as canal diggers, 72–73;
   plantation labor and regulation of, 15,
   52–54, 55–57; population (in 1660s), 55
environmentalism, 65–66
environmental justice, 110, 201
Essequibo River, 63, 84, 102
ethical relations, 61, 181, 201; agential cuts
   and, 13, 207n14; vulnerability and, 12,
   206n11
ethnographic methods, 24–25; research
   clearance, 127–28
evacuation: bridges and, 6, 181, *182*; routes,
   12, 150, 173, 178, 188; state-mandated, 7, 81.
   See also shelters

farmers, 26, 54, 93; EDWC operations and,
   109–10, 121; Hope/Dochfour, 97–98, 100,
   107–9, 114–20, 129, *145*; knowledge of
   floodwaters, 150; LCDs and, 108, 121; marketing campaigns, 103–104; participation
   in WUAS, 104–5
fear of small numbers, 9–10, 15, 16, 20, 122,
   198–99
Feed, Clothe, and House the Nation campaign, 156, 215n7
field reports. *See* engineering reports
fires, 137–38
fiscals, 56, 57, 212n6
flood disaster (of 2005), 1–2, 11, 26, 108–9;
   conspiracy theories, 173; disease prevention, 36–37; event and damages, 4–7, 20;
   evidence of, 30, 44; information about,
   38; lingering disruption of, 29–30; rainfall and water levels, 31, 33–34, 41, 134,
   159; relief supplies and shelters, 35–36,
   38–41
flood early warning system, 14, 24, 27, 128,
   129, 153; anxiety about, 148; base time for,
   159–61, 162, 169, 170, 174, 218n6; divisions
   in expertise on, 151; interviews with state
   officials on, 146–47, 170; Japanese consultants for, 149; workshops for residents,
   149–50
flood knowledges, 50–51, 70, 102, 113, 194;
   Amerindian, 53, 55, 60; *apaan jaat* and,
   14, 27; climate adaptation and, 134, 168;

national development and, 64; racialized
   forms of, 26, 57–59, 68; women's, 168
flood management, 16, 66, 70, 78, 129;
   apaan jaat and, 13, 67, 68, 92; color-coded
   system for, 170–71, 174; river and dam
   interactions, 80, 89–90, 213n3; settler
   colonialism and, 26, 50, 55, 62, 199; slave
   emancipation and, 58–60; in Sophia,
   185–86, *186*, 191–92; stratified approach
   to, 90
flood relief supplies: food and shelter,
   35–36, 38–40, 100–101; Guyanese
   diaspora and, 41, 211n5; moral disputes,
   213n12; preparedness, 170, 171; relief
   checks, 6
floodwaters, 4, 6, 118, 177; contaminated,
   36–37, 180; drainage of, 11, 39, 82, 150;
   EDWC, 69, 70, 82, 109–10, 148, 160; Hope/
   Dochfour's proximity to, 101–2; in Sophia,
   191–92
foreign engineering firms, 91, 93, 130, 142,
   151–52
forests/forestry, 8, 15, 51, 54, 72, 107, 202
Fort Zeelandia, 52
Foucault, Michel, 122
freedmen, 16, 58–62, 78, 98, 124, 212nn7–8
freehold settlements, 58, 98, 212n8; titles,
   100, 183–84

Galison, Peter, 148
geology, 135–36, 217n5
Georgetown, 34, 185, 219n6; city council, 35,
   66, 213n12; farmers' markets, 115; population, 180, 184; racial-ethnic divide, 205n2;
   rainfall in, 29, 81; State House, 35; Thomas
   Lands, 158, 168; water supply, 33, 40, 59,
   72–73. *See also* Sophia
geotextiles, 106, 114, 129, 140–43, 151; photos
   of, *140–41*
Giglioli, Dr. George, 85–87, 214n5
Gilroy, Paul, 21
Giroud, J. P., 141
Girvan, Norman, 213n10
globalization, 9
Global South/North, 8, 25, 31, 162, 183,
   210n1; carbon emissions and, 9, 205n7
Goldberg, David T., 13, 209n18
good life, achieving a, 178, 179, 181

governance, 21, 27, 68, 180, 201, 206n10; environmental, 119; global, 8; liberal multicultural, 26, 209n19; local democratic, 215n5; participatory, 66–67

Granger, David, 203, 204

gross domestic product (GDP), 6, 109, 202, 210n3

Grow More Food, 108, 215n7

Guyana: administrative regions, 31, 32; coastal plain, 2, 24; constitution, 108, 109; geography and vegetation, 15, 21–22; map of, 3; national motto, 18, 209n19; petrostate future, 203; political parties and elections, 4, 16–19, 205n1; racial population, 6, 15, 19, 205n2, 211n3; as a small island state, 9. *See also* coastal settlement; interior region

Guyana Citizens' Initiative, 41

Guyana Defence Force, 155–57, 158, 165, 166, 168

Guyana Human Rights Association (GHRA), 102, 104, 106

Guyana Sugar Corporation (GUYSUCO), 104, 183, 210–11n3

Haitian earthquake (2010), 168–69, 219n8

Halpern, Orit, 81

health workers, 36–37, 214n7

Helmreich, Stefan, 138

Hogg, Quintin, 72

Hope Canal, 26, 48, *114*, 172, 173; civic action and, 102–3, 106; climate adaptation, 138; construction, 114–19, 123, 134–35; cost, 97; farmer skepticism of, 108–10; geotextile reinforcement, 140–43; *pegasse* and borehole drilling, 137–38; politics and power of, 119–20; resettlement and compensation packages, 97–98, 107–8, 113, 117, 145, 214n1

Hope/Dochfour villages: climate change and, 105–6, 145; farmers, 97, 102, 104, 107–10, 114–19, 129; flood disaster (of 2005) and, 100–101; history and population, 98–100; WUAS, 104–5

Hope Estate, *99*, 99–10

Hossein, Caroline Shenaz, 103

Houston (TX), 218n6

Hoyte, Desmond, 64–65

human equality, 110, 112

human rights, 102, 110, 173

hurricanes, 61–62; Gilbert (Jamaica), 163; Harvey (Texas), 218n6; Katrina (New Orleans), 7, 31, 182; Maria (Puerto Rico), 31, 211n5

Hutchinson, A. H., 84–85, 87–88

hydraulic models, 14, 37, 91, 106, 148, 149, 151; CAP negotiations and, 130; Caspian Sea, 133; climate adaptation and, 133–34, 138, 146; 'EDWC's, 70, 132, 173; Hope Canal construction and, 134–35, 173; for hurricanes, 218n6; skepticism and shortcomings of, 27, 142, 143–44, 152

Hydromet, 29, 33, 38, 160

identity: Amerindian, 218n2; Hindu caste, 111; nation-state, 198; racial, 12, 53, 68, 92, 201, 209n19; religious, 118; settler, 26, 50, 59, 61, 62, 68, 123, 211n2; small-man, 104; women's, 168. *See also* Black masculinity

immigrants, 19, 121

indentured laborers, 15–16, 50, 112; malaria outbreaks among, 73–74; settlements of, 58–61, 82

Indigenous peoples, 24, 53, 211n1. *See also* Amerindians

Indo-Guyanese/Indo-Guianese, 4, 16, 83, 103, 104; CDC staff, 158, 172; engineers, 94, 172; in Hope/Dochfour, 97–98, 100, 106, 107; Jagan supporters, 17, 208n17; *jhandis*, 215n9; laborers, 85, 87, 91, 111; landowners, 62, 79; military recruitment, 156; rural/urban population, 205n2; in Sophia, 184, 191

infant mortality rates, 87

intense flooding, 44–45, 110, 144, 146, 199, 200; attitudes toward, 101–2; climate change and, 105–6; losses from, 115; networks of communication and, 153; small men and, 103–4; term usage, 14, 207n15; VCA trainees and, 191, 194

Intergovernmental Panel on Climate Change (IPCC), 8, 122, 164, 182

interior region, 24, 53, 54, 107, 123, 203; Amerindian resettlement, 19, 50, 60, 209n19; European resettlement, 63; gold mining, 106; military training in, 156, 217n5; sustainable development, 65

international aid, 36, 41, 48, 63, 67, 91, 169
inverted vision, 148
irrigation infrastructure: *apaan jaat* and, 121, 198; contract bids, 42–43; data collection, 74; enhancement of, 1–2, 10; enslaved Africans and, 15, 50, 55–57, 72–73; government neglect of, 40; maintenance, 11, 66, 92–93; makeshift, 39; public and private responsibility for, 182; racial stereotyping and, 91, 92; slave emancipation and, 61, 62; state investment, 1, 41, 67; village-level, 78. *See also* canals

Jackson, Shona, 53
Jagan, Cheddi, 19, 33, 63, 183, 208n17, 214n4; environmental action plan, 65–66; ideology and elections, 16–17, 208n17
Jagdeo, Bharrat, 33, 35, 41, 43, 66, 173; plea for the LCDS, 8–9, 20
Jasanoff, Sheila, 44
Jayawardena, Chandra, 110–11, 112
jhandis, 25, 119, 215n9
Jones, Jim, 156, 218n4

Kirke, Henry, 72–73, 75
knowledge exchange, 57–58, 119, 162, 179, 195; climate adaptation and, 21, 50, 149, 200; engineers and, 86, 94, 117
knowledge networks, 39, 179
Kofi Canal, 109
Kwayana, Eusi, 99

labor, division of, 56, 135, 219n9; race and, 53, 63–64, 94
Lamaha Creek, 72–73, 75–76, 81–82
land appropriation, 124, 211n1. *See also* resettlement
landmarks, 75
land rights, 26, 50, 60, 98, 107, 109, 216n10; disputes and claims, 124, 165, 183, 219n3; village movement and, 58, 212n8. *See also* squatters
large-scale damming, 15, 26, 63–64, 68, 110, 202
Latour, Bruno, 194
leptospirosis, 4, 36–37, 40, 44, 81, 189–90, 211n4
levees, 7, 90, 106, 218n6

liberalization, 66–67, 157, 184, 198; market, 4, 18
life, management of, 207n16
logies, 58, 99, 100
love stories, 26, 128–29, 151–52
Low Carbon Development Strategy (LCDS), 20, 121, 205n6; Amerindian communities and, 107–8, 123, 167; description, 8–9
Lukhoo, E. A., 82–83

Mahaica-Mahaicony-Abary (MMA) Scheme, 85, 87, 88–90, 91, 104–5, 130
Mahaica River, 76, 110, 133, 153, 159, 173, 205n4; as a drainage channel, 33–34, 75, 131, 145; residents' interpersonal connections to, 149–51
malaria, 73, 74, 85–87
Man, category of, 20, 218n7
marine clays, 51
Marks, Colin, 186–87, *187*, 189–90, 197–99
Maroons, 54, 55
Marx, Karl, 212n10
mati, 111–13, 215n8
Mazaruni River basin, 156
Mbembe, Achille, 20, 166, 218n7
McLean, Stuart, 22
McWatt, Clive, 90
measuring apparatuses, 13, 14–15, 154, 182, 199, 207n16; bookkeeping, 115, 117; climate adaptation and, 201–2; EDWC files as, 161, 169; engineers' love stories and, 151–52; mathematical equations and, 216n3. *See also* hydraulic models; surveys
megasse, 56, 62
memory, 21, 80, 213n1; engineering, 75–76, 82, 86; mosquito, 87
meteorologists, 33, 147, 175
migration, 18, 19, 39, 64, 73, 124, 209n19; Maroon recruitment, 54; military and, 158–59; remittances, 180; Waraos and Arawaks, 51–52
military, 52, 112, 146, 175; Afro-Guyanese in, 158, 164, 168; Burnham's transformation of, 155–56; CDC staff and, 155, 158–59, 166–67; conflicts, 154–55, 169; disaster management and, 14, 35; earth sciences and, 162; growing diversity of,

Povinelli, Elizabeth, 124
presents policy, 55, 60
private engineering firms, 42, 48, 65, 130, 152
public awareness campaigns, 85–86, 143–44
pumps, 34, 35, 91

race: Burnham's views, 63–64; categories,
50, 121, 200, 211n2, 214n1; CDC and,
168–69; climate change and, 20–21, 23,
199, 200, 204; compensation and, 110, 113,
121, 123; concepts, 24, 209n21; division of
labor and, 53, 63–64; engineering profession and, 26, 70–71, 91–95; environmental
studies and, 201; flood knowledges and,
57–59; inequalities, 9–10, 88, 110, 122,
198, 200; materiality and, 23, 26–27; *mati*
norms, 111–13, 215n8; personhood and, 83,
207n13; political campaigns and, 17–19;
state and, 12–13; war, 122, 166
racial groups, 12, 19, 58, 111, 112; *apaan jaat*
and, 18; census categories, 6, 209n19;
climate adaptation and, 15, 123, 199;
geographic distribution, 6, 66, 205n2; in
Sophia, 184, 219n4
racialism, meaning, 208n18
racism, 18, 94, 123, 199, 201, 218n7; climate
change and, 23, 195, 204; environmental,
20; solidarity and, 111, 200; technological
progress and, 68; term usage, 208n18
rainfall: above-average, 207n15; climate
change and, 8, 105–6; data, 41, 80–82,
88–90, 161; flood disaster (of 2005),
31, 33–34, 133, 160; in Georgetown, 29;
hydraulic models and, 132; overtopping of
EDWC, 7–8, 69, 160–61
Raleigh, Sir Walter, 52
Red Cross, 5, 11, 24, 177–78; flood relief
supplies, 100–101; PAHO partnership, 36;
vulnerability capacity assessment (VCA)
training, 179–82, 187–94, 199
Regional Democratic Councils (RDCs),
215n5
regionality, 24, 206n7
religion, 118–19, 156, 186
resettlement: Amerindians, 19, 50, 60, 109,
209n19; displacement and, 121, 125; European, 63; Hope Canal construction and,
97–98, 100, 107–9, 117, 145

retired engineers, 43, 94, 109, 134
rice sector, 58, 65, 81, 104, 109; estates, 33, 85,
105, 184; financial losses, 210n3
riots: labor, 63, 84; race, 17, 112, 205n2
risk: climatic, 123, 162, 175, 182; health, 188,
190; investment, 79; modernity and, 30,
43; society, 44–45, 210n1
river-basin damming, 85, 89–90
river defense project, 93
Robinson, Cedric, 53, 208n18
Rockefeller Foundation, 85, 87
Rodney, Walter, 58, 111, 212n10
Roth, Vincent, 90
Royal Agricultural and Commercial Society
of British Guiana, 71
Rule on the Treatment of Servants and
Slaves (1772), 56
Russell, William, 77, 129; EDWC design
approach, 77–79; surveys and data collection, 74–76, 81, 86

savage, figure of the, 121–22
scalability, 132–34, 144, 151
Schomburgk, Robert, 48, 71, 75
Schwartz, Stuart, 61
sea defense projects, 42, 64, 90, 91–92, 111,
174, 204
sea-level rise, 124, 132, 133, 135–36, 149;
climate change and, 7, 9, 37, 51, 164
Seecharan, Clem, 87
settler colonialism, 50, 68, 199, 211n1, 212n3;
British, 26, 60, 63. *See also* Dutch settler
colonialism
Sheller, Mimi, 104
shelters, 4, 35–36, 38–40, 100, 205n3
Silverstein, Paul, 121–22
Simon, George, 128
slave emancipation, 15, 56–58, 61–62, 73, 110,
124. *See also* freedmen
slave trade. *See* enslaved Africans
sluices, 33, 48, 90, 91, 148
small man, figure of the, 103–4, 105, 215n4;
Indian, 26, 98, 113, 117, 120, 121, 124
social biographies, 217n6
socialism, 4, 17, 64, 103, 158, 213n11; Black
masculinity and, 164–65; end of state,
18, 19, 183; multicultural, 156–57, 218n4;
ujamma, 92, 164

Waraos, 51, 53

water boards, 53, 105, 212n4

water conservation, 75

water filtration, 177–78; kits, 14, 180, 187–90, 194

water levels: EDWC, 38, 41, 105, 147, 159, 161, 170; flood disaster (of 2005) and, 34, 159, 190; health risks and, 189–90; hydraulic models and, 11, 132; measuring, 33; readings at Flagstaff, 134, 148

water management equipment, 179, 180, 181, 190

watermarks, 29, 150, 207n15

water supply, 61, 72, 74, 76, 157, 189; Georgetown's, 33, 40, 59, 72–73; rainfall and, 80–81, 213n3; schedules, 105

Water User Associations (WUAS), 104–5, 113

wealth, 6, 215n9

Weber, Max, 169

Wekker, Gloria, 215n8

West Indian Federation, 16

West Indies Royal Commission, 83–84

White, as a racial category, 50, 211n2

Williams, Brackette, 18, 111–12

witnesses, 166, 218n6; accomplice, 161

World Bank, 130, 205n6; engineering consultants, 37–38, 43; Global Environment Facility, 1, 37; International Bank for Reconstruction and Development, 87; structural adjustment policies, 18–19; Upper Mazaruni hydro-electric project, 156, 218n3

Wynter, Sylvia, 218n7

zero, concept of, 122